Women in Accra:
Options for Autonomy

WOMEN IN ACCRA
Options for Autonomy

Deborah Pellow

REFERENCE PUBLICATIONS INC.

Published November 1977

Printed in the United States of America

Library of Congress Cataloging in Publication Data

Pellow, Deborah, 1945-
  Women in Accra.

  Based on the author's thesis, Northwestern University, 1974.
  Bibliography: p.
  Includes index.
  1. Women—Ghana—Accra—Social conditions.
  2. Women—Psychology. 3. Sex role. 4. Urbanization—Ghana.
  5. Social surveys—Ghana—Accra. I. Title.
HQ1816.Z8A276   301.41'2'09667   77-78740
ISBN 0-917256-03-4

Library of Congress Catalog Card Number: 77-78740
International Standard Book Number: 0-917256-03-4

Reference Publications Inc.
218 St. Clair River Drive
Algonac, Michigan 48001

Contents

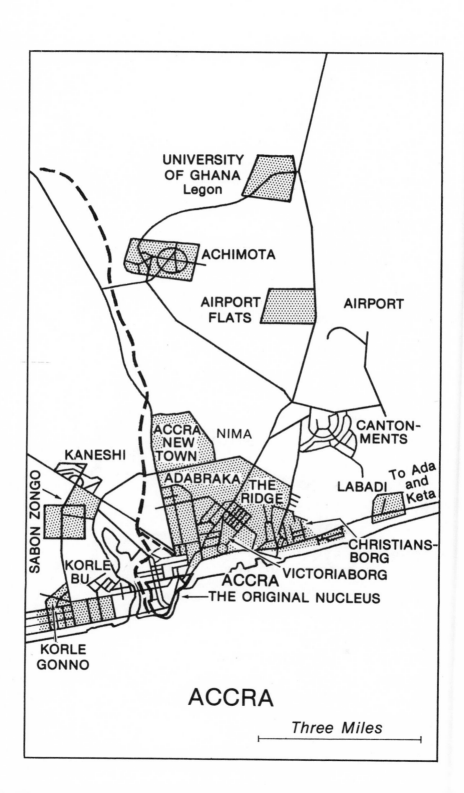

UNIVERSITY
OF GHANA
Legon

ACHIMOTA

AIRPORT
FLATS

AIRPORT

KANESHI

ACCRA
NEW
TOWN

NIMA

CANTON-
MENTS

SABON ZONGO

ADABRAKA

THE
RIDGE

LABADI

To Ada
and
Keta

KORLE
BU

CHRISTIANS-
BORG

ACCRA
THE ORIGINAL NUCLEUS

VICTORIABORG

KORLE
GONNO

ACCRA

Three Miles

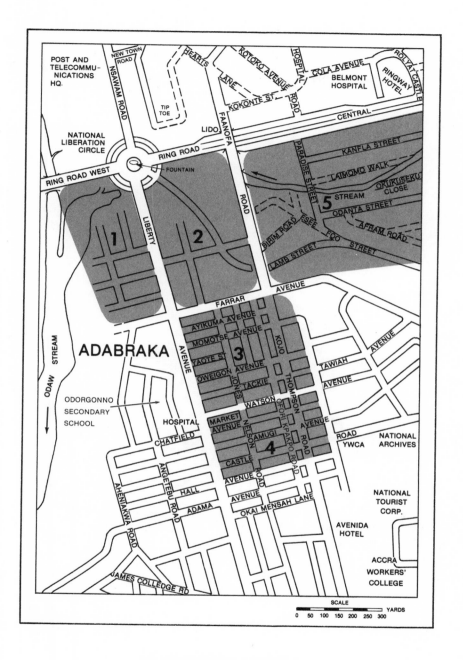

Street Map of Adabraka

1. Obuadan Terrace
2. Liberation Circle
4. Adabraka Market
4. Tuxedo Junction
5. Asylum Down

Introduction

More than half the world's population are women but their role in society has received scant attention until recently. Even now it remains common to analyze societies, particularly in developing countries, without adequate regard for the impact on women of the spread of urbanization. Despite the "success stories" of the national and international roles played by a few women in West Africa, the overwhelming majority suffer backwardness and inferiority. Modernization, the Mecca of modern Africa, has had dubious advantages for most of its women folk.

Change always exacts its own cost but it is paid most heavily by the women within West Africa who find themselves in transit between the traditional ties of village life and an insecure foothold in its burgeoning towns. By and large, traditional West African society accorded women both social position and responsibilities. In myth and religion, the earth mother was revered as the indispensable link between the past and the future. The life force flowing through women was the key to the perpetuity of the village.

In the towns, however, there are new standards and values. Achievement, measured in material terms, replaces the prestige paid to time-honored roles. Relationships change with new living

9

conditions. Instead of the familiar surroundings and routines of small, stable communities, there are strange neighbors, incessant movement, and a pervading sense of impermanence. Everywhere, there is competition for ways to earn the small extras that spell the difference between want and a modicum of comfort and, no less important, between utter dependence on husband, mother, or family, and the threshold of self-reliance.

In Adabraka, a popular low rent neighborhood of Accra, the capital of Ghana, Deborah Pellow spent months learning at first hand of the strains of transition suffered by women newly come from their villages and adjusting painfully to urban ways. Most women continued to maintain their links with their traditional villages and kin. As an anthropologist, Dr. Pellow's primary interest was originally to study the emerging society in Adabraka. The longer she remained, and even more after her return, she felt impelled to concentrate on the special problems faced by women in that neighborhood and their reactions to them. The result, so ably presented in this book, is a vivid account of the life of the women in Adabraka, all of them torn between the ties of the past and the needs imposed by daily living. Her work is also a social document of wide relevance to most developing societies.

It might be thought that women's continuing relationship to traditional society would provide them with a sense of stability that would insulate them from many of the vagaries of urban life. Pellow finds the opposite. Women, she says, become more, not less, dependent on men in the new urban setting both for status and for subsistence; they are further limited, not liberated, by the continuation of traditional bonds and accepted mores. The latter act to restrain the emergence of new associations based on propinquity rather than ethnicity, unless the two happen to coincide. Thus the village solidarity that reinforces the traditional respect for women common throughout West Africa fails to emerge within the new setting.

In a traditional Muslim society, a woman gains status first from her father, and then from her husband. Committed to obey him at all times, and without redress should he decide unilaterally to divorce her, her primary role is to produce children, especially male offspring. At the turn of the century, the French colonial administrators, especially in Algeria, sought to change these mores, forbidding child marriage and polygamy, and providing schools for

Gwendolen M. Carter was, from 1964-74, Melville J. Herskovits Professor of African Affairs and Director of the Program of African Studies at Northwestern University. She is presently Professor of Political Science and African Studies at Indiana University. Earlier, during her 20-year span at Smith College, she was Sophia Smith Professor from 1961-64.

Her many publications include **The Politics of Inequality: South Africa Since 1948** *(1958/59);* **South Africa's Transkei: The Politics of Domestic Colonialism** *(with Thomas Karis and Newell Stultz, 1967); and* **Government and Politics in the Twentieth Century** *(with John Herz, 3rd edition, 1972). She is the academic editor for the series "Africa in the Modern World" for Cornell University Press, and is a frequent contributor to journals dealing with Africa.*

---

girls. Paradoxically, as Algerian nationalism grew, these breaks with tradition became targets for opposition along with other evidences of Europeanization. Though women fought beside men during the Algerian revolution, and received the vote after independence, traditional arrangements for divorce and inheritance remained in force. Only gradually are Algerian women expanding their economic opportunities beyond those linked to their traditional domestic roles.

West African women have not suffered the kind of nationalist backlash that affected Algerian women, but European influences, in particular what Dr. Pellow calls the Victorian "lady" stereotype, have had their impact on shaping urban mores for women. "The British," she writes, "carried with them a mentality which emphasized the propriety and public invisibility of women." West African society, though less rigid in this respect than Muslim society, also has a double standard. A married woman owes obedience to her husband and is expected to be faithful to him.

Men, in contrast, can not only have several wives (if they can afford them), but in urban society can acceptably have "girlfriends" with whom they appear in public, rather than with a wife.

The role of the "girlfriend" is intriguing. She expects and receives presents in return for her favors but the relationship is an impermanent and shifting one on both sides. Whatever may seem its advantages, marriage remains a woman's goal for it, and it alone, provides status both for her and for her children. In contrast to the Western ideal of romantic love, both formal and informal sexual relations are looked on as two-sided bargains: marriage means the woman accepts all responsibilities for the household and in return the man becomes responsible for the support of his wife and children.

Transplanted British mores also affect women's chances for advancement in urban society, in both education and politics. Education for women, particularly of a technical or an applied character, came late in England itself; no wonder that this possibility did not cross the minds of colonial administrators. Even males were trained mainly for the clerical positions that they were most likely to find open to them. The suspicion long continued, moreover, that technical training was for inferiors and that traditional classical education such as Europeans received in Great Britain and France was the gateway to equality. Largely reserved for males at home, even primary, let alone advanced education, was only slowly extended to women abroad. Hence the jobs the latter can acquire in Adabraka are almost exclusively those related to their common domestic tasks.

Women have long been petty traders throughout West Africa so this role, so visible to any visitor, was not difficult to expand. But the products sold by the women of Adabraka, like those in other urban areas of West Africa, are largely food or small household necessities. Interestingly enough, there are also kinds of trading that only women do, either because it is unpleasant, or dirty, or is considered unsuitable for a male. Selling fried plantain is a woman's occupation "because of the pepper and fire" needed for its preparation. "Men don't like fire," says an 18-year-old girl. "They are afraid of fire." And she adds: "People will say 'Look at that man selling *kelewele* (fried plantain).' " Selling oil is similarly typed as a woman's occupation—"Because you will make dirty and is difficult for men" [sic].

In addition to lack of expectation that West African women would, or indeed could, assume economic roles other than those described, was the colonialist view that they lacked influence in the traditional political process and therefore should and would continue to do so in urban life. When Eastern Nigerian women demonstrated against unpopular regulations imposed by the colonial administrators, the latter could only conclude from their own home experience that they must be acting under the direction of men! Yet in traditional society there were, and are, queen mothers as well as kings. Moreover, the powerful male secret society of Poro in West Africa shared decision-making at the highest levels with its female counterpart, Sande. Wrenched out of their familiar settings, however, women were slow to demand or, indeed, to request educational facilities, economic opportunities, or political roles. It was to take new generations, new examples from abroad, and the growth of new images not only of the possible but also of the acceptable, before women in West Africa were to be touched by the fever of "women's lib."

In entitling her book *Options for Autonomy*, Deborah Pellow focuses on an issue that puzzles her. Why do the women of Adabraka not do more to seize the possibilities for change? Why do they remain tied to the domestic scene, and prisoners of traditional sexually-defined roles? She disagrees with Professor Kenneth Little's judgement that African urban women share the desire for independence. "They want to be able to decide their destiny," he has written, "and if they feel like it, to be independent of men altogether." Her judgement is based on the logic that to be independent, the individual must not only have options for alternatives, but must be aware of them. And her experience in Adabraka leads her in general to doubt that the latter is the case.

The reasons why Dr. Pellow comes to such conclusions are spelled out in abundant detail throughout this book. The setting is West Africa, and Adabraka is within the capital of the country that was the first sub-Saharan state to achieve independence from colonial rule. Yet along with the distinctive characteristics of the experiences she portrays are also some universals that keep tantalizing the reader. It is rare that one has the chance to delve so deeply into the lives of human beings as through these pages. One learns to know Auntie Rose and Georgina and Akosua far better than one's own next door neighbor. And in the end, one realizes the affinity of every woman or every man to oneself.

Indiana University   **GWENDOLEN M. CARTER**
Bloomington
May 1977

Acknowledgements

From September 1970 through November 1971, I carried out doctoral fieldwork in Adabraka, a sub-neighborhood of Accra, Ghana. During most of that period, I lived in one of its sub-areas, Liberation Circle. This book is based upon the resulting dissertation, which I submitted to Northwestern University, for the degree of Ph.D. in Anthropology. Vast revisions have resulted in a change of theoretical emphasis from West African urbanization to women's studies.

My research was made possible by a Fulbright-Hays Research Grant, for which I shall ever be grateful. I also thank the Program of African Studies, at Northwestern, for awarding me supplementary funding; this enabled me to extend my stay in Ghana and subsist when I first started writing upon my return to the United States. The generous financial assistance was undeniably important; but the conceptualization, execution, and analysis of the project would have been impossible, were it not for the fine intellectual guidance I received. My greatest debt is to my advisor, Professor Ronald Cohen. He has always encouraged intellectual contentiousness, supervising but never dictating my course of study. He read my material carefully and gave crucial editorial comments.

15

Professors John Paden and Rémi Clignet also provided critical both at the conceptual stage before I embarked upon my study, and during the solitary period of analysis. Dolores Koenig and Judith Wittner read drafts of the rewritten material, providing me with new and valuable perspectives.

My intellectual debt is also tied to an emotional debt. Professors Cohen and Paden, along with others in the Program of African Studies, shared with me their love of West Africa, its life-styles and people. The women in Adabraka, with whom I worked and played, allowed me to experience this first-hand. It is to them that I owe the particular character of the study. They allowed me entry into their homes, giving up precious amounts of free time to answer my never-ending questions. They also kept an eye on me; they made loneliness an empty category for me. At holidays, I was included in the celebrations; during my numerous bouts with malaria, I was nursed. Without their words and thoughts and kindnesses, there would have been no book to write. I have changed all of their names, in order to protect their privacy.

I also gratefully acknowledge the help of the many individuals I met in the course of my fieldwork who took me in and made me feel at home. These include the Rev. Gabriel Adom and his family; Elizabeth Addae and her family; the women of *Zumunchi*; Nana Atakorah Amaniampong II; and a host of others. During my fieldwork, I was affiliated with the Department of Sociology at the University of Ghana, Legon. University personnel were very helpful, simplifying much of the bureaucratic red tape associated with gaining visas and residence permits, and otherwise helping in the preliminaries to my work. A short visit from my mother increased my credibility—showing that I too had kin attachments.

Upon my return to the United States, I found it to be very different from when I had left. The Women's Movement was at its peak and greatly influenced me. My feminist activities made me deal with many of the philosophical issues subsequently touched upon in this book. I wish to thank Robert Postel for facilitating my emotional grasp of the issue of alternatives.

I gratefully acknowledge the help of Ms. Barbara Teising in typing the manuscript.

My publisher, Keith Irvine, has been nothing less than thoughtful in the tiresome pre-publication process.

My final thanks go to Irving Thalberg—for his philosophical discussions on free will, for reading drafts and making stylistic corrections, but most of all for bearing with me and giving no end of encouragement.

Preface

Habitually dominated by men, and excluded from high-level participation in the social system, women are usually thought to be, and indeed often believe themselves to be, inferior to men (Chodorow 1971). Anthropologists, therefore, have traditionally taken note of the female only in passing, and the men and women of the societies studied have offered us little information on the women's realm. Thus the role of women has been accorded little consequence.

This book is a response. It presents an analysis of the roles and relationships of a group of Ghanaian women living in Accra. It specifically focuses upon the power that these women exercise in their choice of roles and the manner in which they carry them out.

Ghana is a modernizing society. Essentially this means that the roles people play and the spheres of activity they engage in are diversified. This leads to non-traditional patterns of economic and social behavior. The lure of the urban center is the promise of greater opportunity. But city dwellers come from traditional societies, carrying with them the old system of norms, values, and behavior. Traditional societies, as Philip Foster (1965) has pointed out, were structurally well-integrated and organized along lines of lineage. Status was tied to ascriptive criteria of age, sex, and lineage origin. Unlike the Western world, there was no ideological fiat to support recruitment by achievement. Compromises were made between purely ascriptive criteria and personal fitness. In fact, however, traditional societies resembled our own, where in theory no bounds are set to individual achievement, but in practice limitations are strictly enforced.

In Accra, the number of roles that can be played continues to expand. To what extent can such a society accomodate its female members ? Is the woman's sexually ascribed role giving way to one that is based on achievement ? Does a woman have any options to change ? Modernization was fostered by colonial governments, who also introduced a Western system of institutional differentiation and hiring on the basis of performance. Individuals were to be awarded recognition according to achievement, but, as had happened when traditional patterns were followed, some were judged to be more worthy than others.

A growing number of Third World researchers believe that modernization and urban living have eroded the woman's role. For example, in urbanizing areas of Morocco's Middle Atlas, there has been stricter seclusion of women (Maher 1974). According to Germaine Tillion, the French ethnologist, at the beginning of the 20th century a rule was instituted which required North African women who had to leave the harem for any reason to cover their faces—but only in the city. The veil was symbolic of the men's fear of allowing their women freedom in the city, a fear which led to their cloistering them more than before. This situation is a caricature of descriptions by others of conditions in some other parts of the Third World: despite what one might hope and expect, the woman's role has not only not expanded with the onset of modernization, but, on the contrary, has in fact declined.[1]

This holds true in Accra. No matter what their backgrounds, women are forced into the same sexually-defined roles. And they are still relegated to the domestic sphere, due to what Georg Simmel (1955) has called their "peculiar" functions as women. Even their major economic role, as market traders, is traditionally female. Yet, in the city, they are robbed of the buffers which cushioned them in the hometown, when they lived within a culture of women,

---

[1] Boserup 1971; Gugler 1972; Brain 1976.

family, and familiars. In the town they live among strangers, spatially isolated from the extended family. This is certainly characteristic of all African towns and cities (Little 1973). There may, indeed, be a greater number of arenas for expression, but that does not alter the fact that most of them tend to be closed to women.

Educational and occupational opportunities, which can provide both money and the chance to participate in public decision-making, are not theirs to choose. And the traditional support of women by men continues—to a degree that is exaggerated both by consumerism, and by conditions of life in a cash economy. In the city, the woman is far more financially dependent upon a male companion than in her hometown, where expenses are usually minimal, and responsibility for any excessive spending more easily accepted by her kin.

More important than the financial aspect is the woman's dependence upon a man for her adult status. Kenneth Little (1973) affirms that African urban women, literate and illiterate alike, share the desire for independence. "These women are not always clear about specific goals, but one aim appears to be held by many. They want to be able to decide their destiny, and, if they feel like it, to be independent of men altogether" (Little 1973: 28). But this insinuates that perhaps the women can obtain control over their destinies in general, and independence from men in particular. The fact remains that individual women must have options for alternatives, and be able to act upon them, in order to gain such independence. All too often this is not so, as we shall later see.

My analysis is based primarily upon research among women living in Adabraka, a popular low-rent neighborhood in Accra. Most of these women are new to urban lifeways; some barely have the chance to experience them. They are held back from this susceptibility by a combination of social, cultural, and psychological factors. They are no more able to renounce primary traditional roles than they are able to settle upon a constellation of new ones. Thrown together daily with women to whom they are unrelated, they must develop new forms of interaction. There is interplay between the physical and social environments. The compound becomes the woman's locus of orientation to urban living. Finding themselves even more dependent upon men for status and subsistence, they also have to manipulate relationships with them. Role negotiation, either with men or other women, however, is severely limited by the traditional social structure and the traditional content of relationships.

The neighborhood of Adabraka is neither clearly bounded nor self-contained in the way that a rural village is. Just as my informants' work, friendships, organizations, and so on, took them to other parts of the city, so did mine. I visited with the families of some of the women in their hometowns. I left my door open to anyone who wished to visit. I became involved in negotiating family disputes. And, as a single woman, I spent time with Ghanaian men. Thus, many of my observations are culled from Accra at large, and then further substantiated by the Adabraka women.

Adabraka is not portrayed as a microcosm of Accra, in the sense of representing the larger whole. While it is, of course, a part of the city, with characteristics that one associates with the city, it is by no means typical of anything other than itself. While it may be that it is no more than an arbitrary subdivision of Accra—both from the viewpoint of city planning and of anthropological research—it has nevertheless evolved a sense of its own identity as a neighborhood. Essentially, it is a sub-system of Accra, with linkages to the city as a whole. It is equipped as a city area with paved streets, street lights, a few traffic signals, and some specialized shops in place of, and in addition to, kiosks. The intricacies of the social system of Accra are also reflected in the behavior and attitudes of Adabraka residents. Thus intangibles, such as loyalties, and tangibles, such as primary institutions—both of which help to develop neighborhood cohesion—are lacking. Hometown allegiance and continuing identification with hometown people are more important to the individual woman than the identity she gains by her Adabraka situation. Those compound residents who happen to be of the same hometown, or of the same ethnic group, often associate closely both spatially and socially; they thereby differentiate themselves as a group apart from other residents.

The women protagonists of this study were chosen on the basis of length of residence in Accra.[2] The women were approached both

---

[2] Adabraka is not old enough to have housed women, for any length of time, who are past middle-age. Furthermore, Adabraka is continuous with the larger social system of Accra, so that residence in another part of the city may not explain one's reactions to the neighborhood—how one orients oneself, one's attitude

formally and informally—alone, and in the company of others. They were asked to discuss their options in daily life, both before coming to the city and after; their relationships with men and women, family and friends; their reasons for coming to the city in the first place; their sense of control over their different sectors of activity; and their new roles uniquely suited to the urban scene, which they had to learn.

The aim of this study is to find out whether the roles that the women of Adabraka play have been substantially affected (a) by the change from a rural to a city setting; (b) by the socio-cultural, political, and economic attributes of the city itself in conjunction with the women's own reactions to it. As such, the baseline for change is the traditional pattern as practised in hometown areas. Three sources have been used: (1) The ethnographic literature, supplemented by archival material; (2) Verbal accounts by informants and assorted other people; and (3) Visits to traditional areas.

The book falls into two sections. The first, consisting of Chapters I—IV, beginning with a theoretical review, places Ghana's "everywoman" in her socio-cultural and physical context. The second, composed of Chapters V—VII, analyzes her attitudes and behavior. As a woman, her situation is, of course, comparable to that of her sisters the world over. Therefore, illustrative material, the bulk of which is African and Western, has been drawn upon. The whole is drawn together in the conclusion by means of the ideas expressed by one of the women, and by the synthesizing eye of the anthropologist.

---

towards local urban environments, etc.—but it would account for a more general reaction to the city as a whole. Finally, in order to ensure so far as possible that length of residence in the same urban center is a common factor, I have included only those women who have lived in Accra at least since their 22nd birthday, if not earlier. Clearly there will be certain basic discrepancies in attitude between those born in the city 40 years ago, and those born elsewhere 40 years ago who have lived in Accra or Adabraka for 18 years. It is not, however, too much to expect that before the age of 22 one's perceptions, attachments, and self-image do not stop developing.

Perspectives on Autonomy

This chapter sets forth the theoretical framework for a book that is essentially a study of power: the extent of the power of the Ghanaian "everywoman" to choose among alternatives, to make her own decisions, and to implement them. The concept of autonomy employed by Schlegel is particularly apt. Autonomy (unlike status) defines woman not in relation to man, but "to control over her own person and activities and her meaningful contribution to society beyond breeding and feeding" (Schlegel 1972: 23).

In evaluating any woman's power or autonomy we must recognize that she does not operate in a void—that she is a social being in a socio-cultural context. Thus, while much of her behavior ties into the uniquely ethnic (in this study, Ghanaian) aspects of her being, she also has much in common with other women the world over by virtue of the fact that she is a member of the female sex. Moreover, her total social role—her rights and duties relative to various other members of her society—is a composite of several social identities.

In this study I examine autonomy in the context of spheres of interaction. I begin with two questions: (1) Does the urban

23

Ghanaian woman have options in choosing spheres of activity ? (2) Do her options for behavior vary relative to the sphere within which she is operating ? Each individual participates in various socially significant activities and operates in several social dimensions, acquiring in each a particular social identity which, as Ward H. Goodenough has phrased it, "makes a difference in how one's rights and duties distribute to specific others" (Goodenough) 1965: 3). And since all values and beliefs affecting how individuals interact in daily life are not operative at the same time, the same individual participating in several situations may exhibit inconsistencies of behavior—a phenomenon which E.E. Evans-Pritchard refers to as the principle of situational selection.

It has been suggested by Paul Bohannan that roles are complexes of expectations, separate from the individuals who activate them (Bohannan 1963). The duties inherent in an identity relationship (involving two people) are owed not to the individuals concerned but to the social identities invoked by the relationship (e.g. merchant-customer, parent-child, landlord-peasant, teacher-student, doctor-patient). The rules for identity selection are such that there can be confusion when two social identities involved in an interaction do not match.

Inasmuch as an individual is involved in several identity relationships simultaneously, his total being may be conceived as a composite of the several identities appropriate to a given situation. Goodenough calls this composite the "social persona". A.L. Epstein refers to the totality of relationships in a bounded area of study as "the social field," and breaks the totality down into subsets of relationships (e.g. domestic, commercial, political) that are internally cohesive but relatively (though never completely) independent of each other (cited in Mitchell 1966: 57). Through this device of regarding certain subsets as discrete, observers have been able to speak of traditional female activism in one sector and reticence in another.

Most of the literature on West African urbanization is based on the premise that African town life offers both men and women increased access to status and opportunity.[1] The standard thinking

---

[1] For examples of this point of view, cf. Tanya Baker and Mary Bird (1959); Kenneth Little (1959, 1959a, 1973); Daniel McCall (1961); Leonard Plotnikov (1967); A.W. Southall (1961).

is that the towns afford alternative life-styles not available to rural women, and that urban women face fewer restrictions in the occupational, domestic, recreational, and political domains.[2] The network of kinship relationships so important in African traditional life retains some influence on urban women (and men), but its functions are modified to suit the changing scene; in particular, there is a breakdown of the extended family as it proves no longer adequate to satisfy its members' needs.[3] Since the family has been the basis for political, legal, economic, and social action in most traditional societies,[4] the generally accepted scenario assumes that a transition in family structure means that the role of women should be changing as well.[5] Writing in 1971, for example, Philip Mayer took the position that, in the case of southern African women, East London is an escape from subjection to men, a place "to be free," a place where one may improve one's status through achievement. Similarly, the participation of urban West African women in the

---

[2] Because women were not a "hot" topic until quite recently, the literature exemplifying this "standard" view is scanty. It was promoted informally and appeared as an implicit assumption in works on other subjects. As indicated in the Preface, the establishment view that women have greater social, economic, and political freedoms in changing Africa is being increasingly challenged by current research.

[3] Cf. Joan Aldous (1962); Alison Izzett (1961); Kenneth Little (1973).

[4] Some psychoanalytic writers not only view the family as the basis of all realities of social life, but also maintain that everything outside of the family is a disguised form of family. See, for example, the article by Weston La Barre (1951) cited in the Bibliography.

[5] Among a select group of West African secondary students, T. Peter Omari found it significant that, with reference to polygyny, the marriage contract, and care of children, "the women have a more radical bent against the family institution than the men" (Omari 1960: 207). Such a sample—limited to secondary school students—is not particularly representative of women of the area as a whole, or even those of Accra. I found, for example, numerous informants who speak of the nuclear family as the ideal but who, in practice, maintain the tradition of "lending" out some or all of their children to be reared by female kin. Similarly, many among those who were monogamously married accepted their husbands' philandering as a traditional male privilege.

city's economy is usually cited as evidence of their independence. Indeed, "establishment" views of urban occupational opportunity exemplify points germane to the issue of autonomy. The term "independence" is used to capture an essence which seems to characterize these women—that is, as assertive and economically mobile in trade.[6]

My own view—supported by the writings of Vanessa Maher (1974), Josef Gugler (1972), and Christine Oppong (1974)—is that, at this time, the change in status experienced by urban women is not necessarily positive. In fact, as the story of Adabraka shows, women are far *more* dependent on men in the city than they are in the village.

One reason so much that has been said and written about West African women misses the mark is that no distinction is made between hawking (trading in the market and street) and all other commercial transactions. Hawking is entirely handled by women. Distribution and sales in stores, shops, supermarkets, and street stalls, which is more lucrative in the long run, is the male's domain (cf. Mintz 1971). When trading is the major occupation open to women, and every other woman is trading in the same limited stock—food, textiles, petty goods—any one person is precluded from making a killing on the market unless she is extraordinarily shrewd, unique in her approach, an early arrival, or has a great deal of starting capital.

In describing a woman as a trader, most writers on the phenomena of African urbanization do not consider how she went about getting her capital, how she chose what merchandise to sell, if being a trader was her own decision, or if she needed another's permission. The stringency usually demanded in description and analysis of the make-up of a society is not maintained here. Hearsay of male informants is accepted uncritically, and analyzed within a context of Western notions of "success." Why should anyone continue to work, day in, day out, twelve hours a day, five and a half days a week, if she were not doing well?

---

[6] Cf. Abner Cohen (1969); Kenneth Little (1959a, 1974); S.F. Nadel (1942).

[7] In my own experience this was so. I mentioned in passing to a prominent Member of Parliament that my neighbors were suffering as a result of climbing food prices. He insisted that, appearances to the contrary, the women are

The Public and the Private: Myths and Realities

Perhaps this ethnographic perspective arose in part because of the *public* nature of trading. Michelle Rosaldo and Louise Lamphere, in their introduction to *Woman, Culture and Society* (1974), note that there is an unexamined belief in most cultures (including our own) that women's lives are less interesting than those of men. Rosaldo also is mindful of the sharp contrast in many cultures between the "domestic" activities of women and the extra-domestic or "public" associations open to men. In consequence, it is men's activities that are accorded value and authority.[8] By extension, a woman seen operating in public, or skilfully manipulating a public business deal from behind the scenes, is accorded status by ethnographers—however specious her autonomy.

Although our immediate concern is not with the relative condition of status, status interacts with, reflects and is reflected by autonomy. Development of female public status may hinge upon a balanced division of labor. This is the thesis of Sanday (1974), who asserts that women must produce beyond mere subsistence and be organized in groups to achieve high public status. Leavitt (1971) would concur, pointing out that all elements in the social structure are integrated into, and reflect, the respective society's values and institutions. Thus *the* clue to the woman's status anywhere "is her degree of participation in economic life and her control over property and the products she produced"[9] (Leavitt 1971: 278).

Yet, status-accruing public activities (such as modern employment and politics) are generally associated with men, while women, in their roles as mothers, become primarily absorbed in domestic activities. Rosaldo (1974: 23) defines the domestic (or private) domain as "those minimal institutions and modes of activity that

---

wealthy. I pointed out that a trader in fried food is often lucky if her profits reach 50 cents a day. "Why should she be doing that for so little money?" he retorted.

[8] Cf. Cynthia Nelson (1974); Michelle Rosaldo (1974); Nancy Tanner (1974); Judith Van Allen (1972); Evelyn J. Michaelson and Walter Goldschmidt (1971).

[9] Both of these factors appear to be related to the kinship system. Thus, where descent is reckoned along the male line, men have a greater part to play in the economic sphere. As a consequence, women would have little autonomy beyond the domestic pale—if they had anywhere. The reverse would be true in matrilineal or possibly even bilateral societies.

are organized immediately around one or more mothers and their children.'' This public/private dichotomy is viewed by most participants and many observers as arising from the essential nature of the sexes; women are identified (often in a demeaning way) with domestic life, men with larger issues. This pattern has also been observed by others. Schlegel, for example, tells us that ''it is perfectly obvious that at all times and places most women center their activities around the domestic sphere and most men either center their activities around a community-wide or society-wide sphere or use the domestic group as an economically and socially productive unit...'' (1972: 23).

This separation of the sexes is found to some degree in countries of the Mediterranean area. For example, Ernestine Friedl (1967) chronicles the stress on sexual segregation in the Greek village of Vasilika. The men of Vasilika were found to have far greater access to public roles than the women; most of their work was carried on outside the home, and expressed high male prestige. Although the men might shop for household essentials, this was not strictly a domestic chore, since it involved doing something regarded as inappropriate for their wives—going out to negotiate in public.

Islamized societies present a more extreme example of the separation of the sexes into two distinct worlds and the confinement of women to the home. This practice originates in the Koranic precept that ''men shall have the pre-eminence above women, because of those advantages wherein God has caused the one of them to excel the other, and for that which they expend of their substance in maintaining their wives'' (Sale 1940: 77). Thus, in Algeria the locus of most women's activities is still mainly her home or that of a friend; women also follow the Middle Eastern custom of spending time together at sexually-segregated baths. As in Vasilika, the husbands or fathers do the shopping on market days. In urban areas, while women could go out, the colonial presence introduced greater limitations in the women's role, symbolized by the wearing of the veil (Heggoy 1974; Tillion 1966). Indeed, in the conservative Middle Atlas of Morocco, women are excluded from the public sphere for reasons of morality. Many town husbands require that their wives live in virtual isolation. The domestic role becomes all-absorbing, and secluded women turn simple chores into grand projects to occupy themselves (Maher 1974).

Jerome H. Barkow, writing in 1972, compares two Hausa groups in Nigeria—one which has been Islamized, and one which has not. The Muslim group lives in a village, the other lives in the bush surrounding the village. The situation of their women differs in several ways, especially in the freedom of movement accorded married women. In the Muslim group, the wives are secluded (i.e. required to remain indoors during the daytime and to cover their faces outside the compound); they rely upon unmarried girls to undertake tasks which take them outside the compound walls. Despite their seclusion, however, most of the Hausa with whom Barkow worked had some sort of craft or trade activity from which they derived income. The non-Muslim women in the Nigerian village are, of course, far freer; they are not secluded and may attend the market. It is Barkow's view, however, that it may be an oversimplification to conclude that Islamization has lowered the status of the village women; "it would, perhaps, be more accurate to say that it has increased the separation of the sexes, so that their status systems are more independent" (Barkow 1972: 328).

Some observers maintain that there is a carry-over effect between the public and the private spheres, noting that "status" in one affects "status" in another. In her study of Vasilika, for example, Friedl (1967) asserts that it is beside the point that the women in Vasilika are tied to their domestic domiciles; rather, she emphasizes that the village women hold a powerful position within the family, and that family life is the most important structural and cultural factor in the village. In such a situation, she contends, domestic power distribution must have consequences for societal power distribution. Since the kind of power she describes is informal and the data impressionistic, it is unclear whether her hypothesis can be substantiated.

Cynthia Nelson carries the point somewhat further, arguing that the public-private dichotomy distorts reality. She objects to "...the whole question of the 'power' and 'the political' and why this should be linked to such notions as 'private (domestic)' and 'public (political)' " (Nelson 1974: 552). It is her position that Western social scientists have assigned "private" and "public" labels to the worlds of women and men respectively, thereby invoking their own cultural biases and distorting the concept of "power."

Throughout the world, including the United States, association with a man is a more assured route to higher status for a woman than personal achievement. In some societies, this takes the form of bearing male offspring. In fact, in Algeria, this has been the woman's primary role. Upon marriage, the authority of the father, uncle, or older brother is replaced by that of the husband. Reporting on the evolution of the status of Algerian women, Heggoy (1974: 451) writes:

> To gain any real position in her new family, she needed to give birth to a son. All her life she had been trained to expect this.... Through a son she might eventually gain a voice in policy matters and in the community. The more sons the better. Many sons would establish a woman's reputation and authority.

In Latin America, Stevens (1973) has found that middle class women are encouraged to follow the *marianismo* ideal. This ideal has its origin in the Roman Catholic movement of special veneration to the Virgin Mary. Behaviorally, *marianismo* implies humility and sacrifice, patience with sinning men, submissiveness to male demands, and respect for the sacredness of the mother figure. This saintly ideal is contingent upon motherhood and is associated with the rendering of homage by adult male offspring.

A second form of status-giving association with men, which will be shown to be significant for Ghanaian women, is the sexual. Kathleen Gough (1971), for example, notes that among the Nuer, women gain power by attaching themselves to men of aristocratic lineages. Carol Hoffer (1972) describes a similar route in traditional sectors for mobility in Sierra Leone. In the United States, it is still the case among the middle class that a woman's station in life is a function of how good a marriage she makes. "I can be anybody, anybody, anybody," the American poetess/corporate wife Pat Bailhe writes (1973: 38). "It just depends on whom I marry." When *a*, if not *the*, primary social identity of a woman derives from her marital relationship, it does not seem peculiar that much of her time and energy should be devoted to the focus of its activity—the household.

In his study of the domestic power structure in two Ivory Coast ethnic groups, married both polygynously and monogamously, Rémi Clignet (1970) suggests that the more dependent others are upon an individual, the more power the individual has; thus, the greater the woman's financial independence (and the less her dependence upon her husband), the greater her power in household decision-making. Christine Oppong (1974) has similar findings for urban Ghana. In her research among families of matrilineal senior civil servants, she found that the division of power in such families depended, for *both* spouses, upon their respective contribution to the family of such resources as education, occupational status, and income. It is also the case, however, that few of these African women have the education needed for occupational status equivalent to that of their husbands.

The indirect power of women in situations such as these is increasingly recognized by ethnographers, but remains difficult to measure. Women may appear to be passive actors, shunted back and forth and playing out their "fated" role. Some ethnographers, however, take the approach that women use that role to manipulate situations to their own ends—thereby exercising an indirect kind of power. Female strategies include role-bargaining and financial machinations. In Louise Lamphere's scheme (1974), strategies are "economic" when they center on the exchange of goods and services, "political" when they influence men in authority. "Access to economic resources, the ability to withdraw goods and services, and even sheer defiance give women unassigned power, or increase their influence over husbands, sons, and brothers" (Lamphere 1974: 111). This is the type of political and economic power that Van Allen (1972) describes. Less obvious is the influence wielded by married Portuguese peasant women, studied by Riegelhaupt (1967). Legally excluded from political participation, and hence limited in their economic activities, these women nevertheless were influential over the decision-making of the men in the village. They were in contact with other women on a daily basis, primarily through agricultural work, whereas their men worked in isolation away from the village. Furthermore, the women made outside contacts through trading and domestic service. Trading kept them in continuous contact with urban life, while their relationship with their "patrons" (female town-dwellers who employ village girls for domestic service) gave them contacts not available to their husbands. Thus, access to information through other women, and through non-local "patrons" "give women key positions in local life, despite the barriers of the formal institutions" (Riegelhaupt 1967: 120). For example by putting pressure on the *junta* wives, they could even effect local changes.

Cynthia Nelson (1974: 553) is intrigued with the power of Middle

Eastern women to "levy sanctions" as a means of influencing the behavior of others. She delineates three possible situations within which a woman has such levying power: as a structural link between kin groups in societies where family and kinship are fundamentally important in daily life; as a member of a women's association which exercises some form of social control; and as a practitioner (real or imagined) of the supernatural.

Nelson is persuaded that Middle Eastern women do achieve their own objectives through the influence they wield over men. She ascribes the truism that they live in a segregated world bereft of political power to the "male-centered bias" of most ethnographers of the area (usually European or American males, whose access to the inner lives of the women has been very limited). In considering ways in which women have the capability to increase their potential for negotiation, she cites the example of the Bedouin of Cyrenaica and the Negev.[10] While women in these two areas have no control over property, they are critically involved in how it is manipulated. They mediate between husband, on the one hand, and father and brother on the other, making demands on all three. In situations where they play a number of roles simultaneously, their potential for negotiation is increased. Witness the case of the Negev Bedouin:

> A marriage link acts as a very effective communicative device between groups because the woman who conveys the communication is so intimately bound up with both her husband and sons and with her fathers and brothers. She has the interest of both groups at heart and would suffer most from an estrangement between the two groups. At the same time she is on the inside of both groups and *thus able to assert her influence over the sections* through the men to whom she is closely connected, as well as through women (Marx 1967 cited in Nelson 1974: 555).

How Role Bargaining Works in Ghana

Both the theoretical and empirical data briefly surveyed here reaffirm that the preponderance of women in the countryside and in

---

[10] Abner Cohen (1970) has analyzed the role women play in the stratification system of three Arab-Muslim villages in Israel. Nelson (1974) probably would not question Cohen's facts but might take issue with the points he chooses to emphasize and the assumptions he makes in his remarks on female behavior.

the towns in most parts of the world remain tied to a domestic role. The women I came to know in Ghana were no exception. Excluded from public decision-making, most women must still resort to indirect means to bring their influence to bear in the "public" domain. They are dependent upon men socially, politically, and economically; their status derives from attachment to men. Control of the domestic mechanism and child-bearing are important in themselves, but what degree of autonomy does the woman have in choosing to forsake this primary role?

My concern is not with the importance of the woman's role relative to that of the man's or with male/female equality *per se.* Rather, my emphasis is upon the woman's power to decide and to act, and also the power to choose *in what area* to act. In theoretical terms, I am interested in deviations from traditional models of thought and behavior as they facilitate the evolution of new models.

If we assume, as I have suggested earlier, that the roles played by two interacting people are not identical with the players of those roles, but are shaped by social customs and expectations, then it follows that a variety of interactions are possible. The selection among alternative social identities made by each person is in a sense a form of bargaining.

Homans (1958) has noted that behavioral responses are a function of certain values; behavior incurs costs and there are different behaviors open. Similarly, Goode (1960: 488) has written that "in his personal role system, the individual faces the same problem he faces in his economic life: he has limited resources to be allocated among alternative ends." Identity relationships must be evaluated to determine their price—how much to allot to each and what to expect in return.

In Ghana, role bargaining—the interplay of needs and demands—gives every relationship a peculiar "contractual" quality, characterized by consumeristic concerns. Thus a value is placed upon a relationship in terms of what the contracting party feels she can exact from the other, and what she must give in return. The specifics of the relationship are policed by an unwritten cultural rule of reciprocity.

Bargaining goes on both between woman and woman, and between woman and man. Since a woman's generalized status as an adult, however, is tied to her relationship to a man, it is in this area that her bargaining power must primarily be brought to bear. She follows an appropriately Ghanaian pattern, which is consonant with the syncretism that urban Ghanaians have fashioned out of their traditional values and behaviors, on the one hand, and the more flagrant aspects of Westernization on the other. In her quest for mobility, "everywoman" wields power covertly, through the traditional institutions of home and market, but in accord with the urban modifications of both. She sells herself to the highest bidder; the price corresponds to the bargain contracted.

Is the ability of an urban Ghanaian woman to participate in various identity relationships limited by her sex ? In other words, can she contract relationships for which there are no traditional models ? Banton (1965) has noted that the basic roles of a woman in any society usually depend upon her relationship to men of her society, whereas a man's basic roles depend more heavily upon age than upon marital status. But he has also depicted a role continuum, on which roles exist and may be activated independently of one another. The more complex the society, the greater its tendency to manufacture diversified roles. The continuum starts with basic roles, depending primarily on sex and age. It goes on through general roles (e.g., occupational) and ends with independent roles (e.g. recreational). What is of interest here is the degree to which an urban Ghanaian woman can operate, independent of (or in spite of) her basic roles. To what extent do her basic roles leak over into the others, thus affecting their attributes or determining them?

Since identity relationships are based upon the specific social identities of the participants, social identities must be evaluated *if* a choice is to be made by a participant. "Everywoman" must decide how much she is willing to pay (e.g. in terms of accepting or rejecting her basic roles) and balance that against what she will receive in such areas as autonomy in decision-making and activities; she must balance the alternative she is capable of *conceiving* against what is socially accessible and acceptable. The principle of negotiation, as applied to identity relationships essential to the woman's social persona, allows for manipulation of the terms without actually changing the structure of such relationships. New social identities and new identity relationships *supplementary* to those previously established are forthcoming. Those which *replace*, however, are not.

My evidence suggests that the Ghanaian woman may select

among alternatives of role behavior, but only to a limited extent. It appears that she does not have ready access to independent roles. In order to understand why this should be so, it is necessary to move to a more fundamental level and reflect upon the notion of "liberation" itself.

The Stages of Liberation

Liberation, particularly in the Western world, has become a loaded term. It does not denote an absolute, for it is problematical to speak of the total liberation of a human being. Indeed, in the West, the women's liberation movement grew out of the increasing sense of disenfranchisement and deprivation experienced by women vis-à-vis the situation of their male counterparts. Even on a more specific level, within the life of any one woman, her "liberation" in one area is measured relative to her liberation in another.

What I had in mind when I first began this study was to investigate the decision-making powers of Ghanaian women in their various spheres of activity. "Independence" or liberation was tentatively defined as the right to make decisions and implement them. Implicit to this definition is the notion of *option*—the effective ability to do or not to do a given act.

Liberation connotes, at a minimum, some degree of change. In a given society, there is a code of behavior whch incorporates norms, values, and so on. Such a code, which we might consider to be "culture," is manifest in the individual's expected or appropriate responses. This culture forms a baseline for change. In this sense, liberation connotes a move away from the accepted norms, a move toward a state of normlessness.

It is my contention that in modernizing Ghana, the liberation of women from traditional activities and their entry into new activities are both still equivocal. The fact of a woman selling on the street, or attending a place of business, may or may not be significant, just as the fact of a man and woman cohabiting says nothing of the content of their relationship. The economic situation of coastal West African women exemplifies the reality that liberation is a relative state, both within and between different areas of activity. Because woman have the mere freedom to pursue an occupation, they are freer or more liberated than if they were sequestered. And because some women *do* exhibit a drive toward success in their economic endeavors, they also exhibit a greater independence from certain cultural strictures.

My corollary belief, at the inception of this project, was that a woman's options vary, depending upon which persona she desires. Given these options, I posited that new social identities should emerge, with old restraints on the ebb, if they had not already vanished. The new urban woman, as I perceived her then, would be able to set up new identity relationships, different in context and content from the old, as a result of the new identities open to her. Her options would include that of graduating from those social identities bound to her basic role as female; she would be given the opportunities to engage in new roles, in accord with her capability.

What I have discovered, and return to throughout this study, is that the ability to conceptualize alternatives is a crucial measure of an individual's sense of power or free will. Liberation, as I now see it, requires not only that the individual realize that there are options, or alternatives. In addition, she must understand that choice among these options should depend on *her* definition of her own potential, *her* definition of the status she desires in the world. The individual must be capable of perceiving alternatives to her existing situation, and she must be capable of making rational decisions about these alternatives, if she is to "progress"—that is, depart from the traditional mind-set and enlarge her horizons in terms of activities, ideas, and relationships.[11]

Yet in my research I kept coming up against the absence of this ability. When I, as an outsider, visited an informant and tried to elicit a response, I was not always successful. Was this a deficiency

---

[11] This discovery is akin to Daniel Lerner's hypothesis of the "mobile personality," set forth in *The Passing of Traditional Society* (1958). He portrays traditional society as nonparticipant: people are deployed by kinship from isolated communities, there is little economic interdependence, horizons are limited by locale, and decisions involve known people in known situations. On the other hand, a highly empathic capacity is required of the individual who participates in modern, industrial, urban, literate society. Lerner defines "empathy" as the "capacity to see oneself in the other fellow's situation" (1958: 50)—indispensable to someone moving out of the traditional situation. He must meet new people, recognize new roles, and engage in new relationships. The empathic capacity involves psychic mobility—the ability to adapt oneself, incorporate new roles, and identify personal values with public values.

in me, or was it that the power of imagining alternatives, of fantasizing options that might subsequently be acted upon, of having opinions, was either lacking or repressed ? As time went by, it became increasingly apparent that this power to imagine alternatives could not be evoked, that the impetus for change—for liberation—is still lacking. I was reminded of the thesis that Jean Paul Sartre develops in *Being and Nothingness* (1943). He speaks of any state or act (be it the social structure of a society or the psychological state of an individual) coming about in reaction to what is not—the paradox of being growing out of nothingness.

The individual who cannot imagine alternatives has no claim to freedom. Action for change comes from imagining that which is not, imagining the possible.

The Persistence of
Traditional Attitudes

While the women of Adabraka are individuals, each with her own story to tell, they also have much in common. Their shared worldview is not so much a product of the homogenizing effect of the city as it is of the traditional belief system that continues to shape their social identity and identity relationships in the urban setting. In portraying this traditional baseline, I will sometimes borrow from the ethnographic literature, but it is primarily the women's responses and my own observations that enable me to single out five elements of the traditional system that are extraordinarily important in determining the values and lifestyle of Adabraka. These are reciprocity, polygyny, seniority, lability (a state of emotional volatility), and fatalism.

Many aspects of this worldview are so fundamental as to be present in societies throughout the world. The uniquely Ghanaian character of the elements is reflected in the manner of the individual expression and the society's institutional and social structure. I suggest that the tenacity of these attitudes accounts for the oneness of women and their subordinance in the authority structure.

Evans-Pritchard's (1965) observations on the position of women in "the" traditional situation of "simple" societies is helpful in establishing our framework. Marriage exists as a given; there is no such thing as an adult woman who is unmarried or childless by option. She has no choice between marriage and "career," she has little time for social activity, and given duties are assigned to married life. Every woman can have a husband, and it has never occurred to her to desire something else. The concept of romantic love is non-existent. Because women have few illusions about marriage, they seldom suffer consequent disappointment. Indeed, the sexes do not really intrude upon one another. Outside of the home, they operate as independent entities, and there is a clear sexual division of labor. The sense of companionship in a marriage is weak and there is relatively little merging of personalities. This lack of intensity holds for family relationships in general. Instead of an exclusive nuclear family, there is an extensive kinship network.

Authority lies in the hands of men. Even in matrilineal societies[1] the ultimate authority figure is male—the mother's brother. In the simple society, a woman may complain if she feels a lack of respect, but it does not occur to her that her overall status should be changed. She views her status not so much as being *lower* than that of men, but *different* (Evans-Pritchard 1965: 52). It is in this context that male ascendancy is the accepted norm.

The five fundamental elements of this traditional system found to be operative in Adabraka are considered here as discrete units for purposes of introduction; however, it will soon become evident that they are intricately interwoven in the structuring of social relationships. Reciprocity, the traditional etiquette, ensures that each person receives his/her due. Polygyny gives males primary

---

[1] According to Schlegel (1972), matrilineal societies are not only less common than patrilineal societies; they are also restricted to the "middle rank" of socio-economic and political development. She notes that Evans-Pritchard (1965) maintains that none of the "great" civilizations of the world have been matrilineal, while Kathleen Gough (1961) has gone still further in asserting that matrilineality is unsuitable and that matrilineal extended families tend over time to dissolve into more elementary family units. On the other hand, Mary Douglas (1969) reasons that matrilineal descent provides a good system for the recruitment and organization of property-managing groups in conditions of economic expansion in "any situation in which competing demands for men are higher than demands for material resources" (cited in Schlegel 1972: 142).

access to positions of power and authority. Seniority accords first priority—in deference, decision-making, interaction—to the elder. More abstruse than the others is lability, a peculiarly opportunist and ephemeral assessment of, and relation to, people. It connotes a certain emotional instability, and the mutability of relationships with others is a natural consequence. The fifth component, and the one that ties the system together, is fatalism—the unquestioning acceptance of the status quo. If things are to change, one must have patience and wait.

The continuity of traditional attitudes in urban Ghana is partially due to the continuity of rural-urban exchange. Through the persons of migrants and traders, rural people experience exposure to urban lifeways; if and when they come to the city, they have had previous acquaintance with urban practices. By the same token, the exchange has kept the city-dweller from losing touch with his roots. Far more than the people involved are aware, tradition retains a firm hold on their lives.[2]

Reciprocity

I begin with the most general and perhaps most widely practised of the five attitudes. Reciprocity may be thought of as the maintenance of contracts. Paul Bohannan (1963: 156) defines a contract as "an initially voluntary agreement between two or more people to carry out certain obligations and gain certain rights, when these obligations are not part of any other relationships in which the contracting parties stand to one another." Thus kinsmen would not make contracts with one another unless the rights and duties implied by the contract were distinct from those inherent to the kin relationship. A contract is a means of creating a bond, a social grouping.

In Ghana, as in the United States, a person is expected to

---

[2] Perhaps this tradition-bound outlook will change as more people permanently live in cities and education is expanded. In her study of conjugal family units among élite civil servants in Accra, Oppong has found that attitudes and patterns of adaptation to urban life depend on parental experience, spatial and social mobility, and particularly the generation of education. It is among the third generation of educated people that "processes of functional individuation and conjugal cooperation [as opposed to kin obligations] appear to be most marked" (Oppong 1974: 157).

reciprocate when he has accepted several dinner invitations from the same individual. When a gift is given, some kind of thanks is due. The major difference is how such debts are repaid. In "Middle" America, there are many acceptable ways in which the expression of return may be made, whereas in Ghana such acts are more formalized, and their nature is heavily influenced by the social roles involved in the transaction.[3] Although the concept of reciprocity is applicable to all societies, its special significance in Ghana lies in its pervasiveness, its explicit charter, and its interaction with the other four elements of tradition.

Ghanaians have a strong commitment to hospitality, courtesy, and cooperation, based upon reciprocity. In the folk setting, this is maintained in the respectful spirit accorded any hallowed tradition. As a woman walks to market, she passes many people with whom she has a history of connections, both direct and indirect. It is rude to pass without acknowledging each in turn, and they must respond in kind. In Twi, this is spelled out in a linguistic exchange—*"a ye ko"*, *"ya e"*—a simple acknowledgement.

The family system of relationships is the model from which reciprocal behavior is learned. In earlier times, when a person stayed in one village or town most of the time, those with whom he or she came into contact would primarily be kin. When friendship came into play, the kinship metaphor would be extended to cover the relationship. Behaviors associated with the actual relationship would be internalized and become a matter of course. In time, the friend might be incorporated into the family through such fictive kinship, with all traces of the original relationship vanishing (Evans Pritchard 1940).

Accordingly, guests in one's home were relatives or, at the least, would have been referred by relatives. For example, among the Asante, guests receive prior attention in every home:

---

[3] Formalized reciprocity is not only found in traditional societies. Stiff and literal adherence to the rules of etiquette is also found in the history of the upper classes in the West, notably in the Victorian era. Here we have an example of parallelism in the development of customs; some aspects of Western culture encountered by the Ghanaians with the coming of colonial rule were new to them, while others already present in Ghanaian traditional culture were reinforced by contact with the British.

...custom demands that he devote his whole time to their comfort. They must return home with all praises for him. Nothing should go amiss in his hospitality. It is not good manners to ask the visitor or 'stranger' when he intends to leave. That is tantamount to expressing the wish that he should leave your roof (Tufuo and Donkor 1969: 69).

The visitor knows he will not be denied entrance. He knows what to expect of his host, and the latter also knows what he will receive for his pains. Formalization reaches an extreme in visits paid to chiefs. For example, one is expected to bring a gift of liquor (usually schnapps) and assume a certain posture in order to make a request.

In its most crass form, reciprocity imputes a concrete value to any transaction or interaction. If one party gives or does something to (for) another, there is an "equivalent" return to be made, contingent upon the role relationship. One does not receive something for nothing. Everything is given a concrete worth. Inherent in reciprocity is the quality of trust—trust in a *just* return. In Ghana this is not left to chance; the demands individuals make on one another are explicit.

It is always intriguing to see what happens to institutions when they are introduced out of context. In Accra, the rituals of meeting and greeting, taking leave of people, and related interactions, are studiously maintained. This puzzles and enchants outsiders, insofar as it is incongruous with theories of urban alienation. Only on closer study does it become apparent that the ritual as practiced in the streets of Accra is hollow. As in the folk setting, one never neglects to greet an acquaintance, a neighbor, or a friend, because it would be rude to do otherwise. But the gesture here is perfunctory.

The values implicit in the term *Akwaaba* (welcome) carry over in a more genuine way in the daily lifestyle of the urban Ghanaian's room, compound, and immediate neighborhood. Just as the compound is the home base of the extended family in the traditional milieu, there is always room in its urban equivalent for one more. If there is a shortage of beds, mats can be found for sleeping; food can always be stretched. Another child may not be wanted, but it is accepted happily if conception occurs. Loyalties within the family circle are not to one person but to many. "One person brings forth, but not only one person nurtures or educates the child," in the words of the *Gbese Mantse* (the traditional paramount chief of the Gbese area of Accra). Every family has its room or rooms, but it does not live behind closed doors. A hanging curtain and/or radio provide privacy without cutting off the sense of contact. Children grow up in this spirit of openness and welcome, enjoying free rein.

Household etiquette in the city still closely parallels that of the folk setting. Not to welcome visitors is an insult, but ongoing work is not dropped. By the same token, immediately on sitting down, visitors reach for either the omnipresent picture album, or a stray magazine. There is an internalized system of filtering out disturbances; life is with people, and life goes on in accomodation to that fact. It was an enigma to Ghanaian city dwellers that Sonny Liston, the American boxer, had lain dead in his room for days on end before he was found. Even in the city, how could anyone live in such isolation ? In terms of the family versus the individual, priority goes to the family. Just as one is always welcome in the family home in the hometown, so one must always welcome hometown kin if they appear in Accra. Children often become pivotal in reciprocal relationships through the institution of fostering. They may be sent off to a grandmother or to a barren female relative—either of whom is expected to be pleased to raise them.

Fostering involves some interesting paradoxes. On the one hand, as Janet Pool observes, "motherhood is the source of power and prestige" for African women (1972: 255); on the other hand, children are systematically sent off to be raised by someone else. The explanation of the paradox is that custom opposes "packing off" children to just anyone.

In her work on the Gonja of northern Ghana, Esther Goody (1969) found the outstanding feature of fostering to be its pervasiveness and its major function the reinforcement of kin ties. Although a disproportionate number of the Gonja fostered were from broken homes, fostering is "a culturally patterned alternative, not a necessity" (E. Goody 1969: 59). Furthermore, the child is never sent to someone who is only the affine of a parent's sibling. "The foster-parent/foster-child tie is a direct one, based on the reciprocal relationship of service and training with respect to tasks which are central to the adult sex-typed role in this society. Men take their kinfolk's sons, women take their kinfolk's daughters" (Goody 1969: 63).

Fostering serves several useful functions. It may further the moral and technical education of the child, alleviate parental responsibility for daily needs in a large family, and/or provide labor for the foster home. Like parents and other kin involved in the child's socialization, foster parents are regarded as reference models. On the other hand, as Maher (1974: 133) has also observed in the Middle Atlas region of Morocco, fostering on the whole seems to be keyed more to the interests of the involved adults than to those of the child. In Accra, some loosening of the ground rules for fostering suggests that we are witnessing an example of how a traditional custom can be modified in its transplantation to the city. For whereas in Gonja tradition fostering does not take place until the child "has sense" (i.e. after the age of four or five), children of élite Accra dwellers are fostered at an earlier age, and even by strangers (Christine Oppong 1974). If, even in a traditional setting like Gonja, people sometimes stretch the customary limitations and send their children to a wide variety of kin, it is to be expected that in the city, where tradition and modernity are in more open conflict, greater alterations would take place.

In present-day Adabraka, application of a kinship metaphor to non-family relationships and adherence to prescribed behaviors based upon a contract of just return are exemplified in several ways. These include the observing of kin obligations (through visiting, financial help, general begifting, and the fostering of children); the negotiation of close relationships (primarily between men and women, though also among women as they develop the concept of "friendship"); and the initiation of contacts with strangers, as they develop the concept of "neighborliness."

Polygyny

The practice of being married to more than one woman at a time is common in traditional societies. Customary in orthodox Islamic communities of the world, it is also widespread (and fully integrated with other institutions) in rural Black Africa. In the rural economy, the more wives one has, the more land can be planted and the fewer laborers have to be hired. With all the chores that a rural wife must carry out, co-wives help alleviate the burden of domestic work (Leavitt 1971). The desire for many children is also a stimulus for plural marriage.

It is a commonly-held view of Africanists that the incidence of polygyny differentiates the rural from the urban sector (Southall 1961; Pool 1972). The arguments offered are worth noting. In the city, the household has limited need for manual laborers, and each additional wife is an additional expense; better health facilities reduce infant mortality rates; there are alternative symbols of status available for the urban dweller; and polygyny is forbidden by the Church, an institution that carries considerable weight in urban areas. Indeed, Kenneth Little maintains, in *African Women in Towns* (1973), that urban African women are not only liberated from polygyny, but from the traditional strictures of marriage itself.

I would argue the opposite. Although polygyny in a literal sense may be on the wane in urban centers, the practice continues through informal arrangements. Just as it used to be prestigious to have multiple wives, now it is so to have a wife and girlfriends. A man's peer group encourages such behavior, and wives remain accepting and fatalistic about man's ways.

This new/old lifestyle is reflected in the relevant laws, or lack of them. In 1961, during the Nkrumah regime, Ghanaian legal reformers failed in an attempt to reconcile native and European marriage, divorce, and inheritance laws. The White Paper produced in the course of this effort was interpreted by some as favoring polygyny, since it accepted the existence of plural marriage and specified that all of a man's children (including those from unregistered wives) would be eligible to inherit. Others interpreted the White Paper as a progressive step towards enforced monogamy, citing the stipulation that only one wife would henceforth be registered and eligible to inherit. Ironically, there was more concern among women about the implications of the proposed registration of a single wife than about polygyny itself. "If one considers that polygyny in one form or another is going to persist for some time, the more pragmatic concern of some Ghanaian women that men should be made responsible for *all* the women by whom they have children is as feminist in its way as the demand for genuine monogamy" (Vallenga 1971: 148).

Although a comprehensive Civil Code based on this European-oriented White Paper was not enacted into law, intermediary structures have evolved which combine both traditional and modern aspects. For example:

The sessions of the local Presbyterian churches have adopted methods for settling marital and family disputes which are somewhat similar to those of traditional courts... Further, the local courts themselves have retained some traditional characteristics. The outcome of decisions made in such settings may differ from those of a traditional chief's tribunal, but the methods are familiar ones to the participants (Vallenga 1971: 127-28).

There is a more important sense in which modernizing Ghana still functions as a polygynous society, and this is the continuing institutionalization of male pre-eminence. The distinction between male and female sexuality has been made in many cultures, for example Victorian England. According to traditional morality, men are sexually undisciplined and women weak. Consequently, it would be assumed that a man and a woman alone together are sexually involved. By extension, a man finding himself in such a situation would assert his right; hence the institution of chaperonage.[4] Where polygyny is practised, the distinction between men and women is telescoped. In rural Africa, men believe it their right to have access to many women, while insisting that the women maintain a standard of chastity (Southall 1961). In traditional Ghana, intercourse and conception were prohibited until the girl had completed her puberty rites (e.g. *Kpemo* for Ga, *Bara* for Akan, and *Dipo* for Krobo). This was a functional substitute for chaperonage, since marriage followed soon after the rites, thus almost assuring a legitimate birth. In any case, the young woman's range of associations was stifled.

Another facet of the sexual distinction is embodied in menstrual restrictions. As Schlegel points out, "Many societies see menstruating women as dangerous to men, to sacred objects, and even to crops or livestock, so that in these societies there is the added inconvenience of watching the menstruating women so that they do not inadvertently cause mischief" (1972: 24). In rural Ghana, husband/wife contact at such time is prohibited. Among the Akan, for instance, the "unclean" woman must stay out of her husband's sight. She may oversee preparation of his meals, though she can do none of the work. At the end of her period, she goes

---

[4] In comparing permissible sexual behavior in the United States with that in traditional societies, Margaret Mead points out that Americans have given up chaperonage—thus placing "our young people in a virtually intolerable situation, giving them the entire setting for behavior for which we then punish them whenever it occurs" (1949: 279).

through a ritual cleansing. It would be to the man's advantage in this situation, as in farming, to have another woman in reserve. Again the woman is subordinated, her autonomy stifled.[5]

Women have been enshrined in tradition. For example, the Ga have a proverb, "the fetish does not possess a fool," and, since the fetish only speaks through (possesses) women, it follows that they are accepted as the wiser sex. But the fact remains that Ga women, and Ghanaian women in general, have authority only within their own sexually-based groups; moreover, they are legal minors within the traditional group as a whole. Linguistic characterizations among the Ga express this: female things carry the pejorative label of "left-handedness."[6] The Ga major lineages have male and female sections. The male head serves as representative to the other lineages; old, respectable, well-versed in custom, he receives rents and lineage profits. The female head, on the other hand, is responsible for household order; she settles small disputes and takes large ones to the male head (Mills Odoi 1961). Her field of activity is the domestic sphere. Among the Krobo, a proverb reminds us that a woman does not own (or inherit) a house. This means that she is inferior, since she is prevented from becoming the head of a kin group (Huber 1963). Matrilineality is the key to Asante social organization; however, the lineage has a male head, chosen mainly by the older men and women, especially the former. It is his duty to watch over the welfare of the whole group, and he holds custody of

---

[5] Referring to those who have systematically investigated menstrual restrictions (Philip M. Bock (1967), Clellan S. Ford (1945), William N. Stephens (1961), Frank Young and Albert A. Bacdayan (1965), Schlegel (1972) notes that only Bock assumes that the tabus mark the superiority of women, rather than their inferiority. Schlegel halfheartedly suggests that men also suffer from the restrictions, and that the seclusion may come as a monthly vacation for the women. It does not seem to me that a man with another woman in reserve would suffer greatly; moreover, since polygynously married women alternate in their wifely responsibilities, the need for a "vacation" is doubtful.

[6] Throughout the African continent, and in much of the non-Western world, the left hand is traditionally reserved for toilet activities; it is improper to eat with the left hand, extend it in greeting, and so on.

[7] She is menopausal, no longer a woman in the strictly sexual/reproductive sense of the word.

the male ancestral stools—the sign of status and authority. The head is assisted by an *older* woman,[7] who is the Queenmother in the royal lineage. Her functions relate to *female* rather general matters; she is overseer of puberty ceremonies, caretaker of female morals, and family peacemaker (Fortes 1967).

The honor which accrues to the woman is in her roles as housewife and mother. Both roles depend on her tie to a man. Indeed, many tribes have no concept of the single adult woman, nor even a word for such a state of being. In Ghana among the Talensi, Asante, and Fante, celibacy is traditionally non-existent and considered abnormal (Gaisie 1968). Marriage is regarded as "the normal state of life for every adult. They cannot conceive of anyone voluntarily refraining from marriage throughout life" (Fortes 1967: 225). According to R.S. Rattray (1927), marriage among the Asante was regarded as the natural consequence of birth and puberty rites, and involved far less ceremony than these prior events. As a Krobo proverb phrases it: To marry is the woman's vocation; her status is tied to that of her husband.

Marriage and motherhood are closely tied. In fact, it has been repeatedly noticed by ethnographers that the bearing and rearing of children is central to African marriage (Paulme 1963). Among the Asante, for example, the mother-child tie is the keystone to all social relations:

> Childlessness is felt by both men and woman as the greatest of all personal tragedies. A barren woman is looked upon with pity not unmixed with scorn. She feels an outcast. And the lot of the childless man (*okrawa*) is equally hard. However rich he may be he feels that there is something seriously lacking about him if he is sterile (Meyer Fortes, quoting T.E. Kyei, 1967: 262).

In her survey of marital practices in Ghana, Niger, and Upper Volta, Pool found that "most women marry with the hope and expectation that they will bear a number of children, for in this way they will gain self-respect and social status."[8] Not only does fecundity reflect upon the woman, it also reflects upon the husband as an expression of his virility.

Indeed, the social stigma associated with being (or having) a barren wife is so great in most traditional areas that Ghanaian women will spend any amount of money to procure native

A group of Akan women in traditional ceremonial dress.
(Photo: Deborah Pellow)

medicines believed to encourage conception (Cardinall 1932). Contraception is an extreme measure which the Talensi, among others, find appalling. Among the Asante, abortifacients may be used only if the mother's life is in danger. The importance of children cannot be overemphasized, not only as sources of status but also as domestic helpers, as aids in maintaining kinship ties, and sources of support in old age. An illegitimate child always has a home; Adangme fathers are said to encourage their daughters to conceive (though after *dipo*) so that the child will be a part of his household and work for him. There is virtually no adoption, other than that of orphans; children are regarded as too valuable to relinquish, except temporarily for fostering. There is no cultural alternative to motherhood.

Ghanaian women know that their husbands, boyfriends, and fathers possess special rights by virtue of being men. Traditionally, a woman who marries falls under the complete authority of her husband. Among the Akan, for example, children were (are) an asset, and thus the wife gave allegiance to the man who fathered them; among the Northern tribes, the man's authority was complete with payment of the cattle bride price and subservience on the part of his bride was expected. Among the Ga, the wife lived with her own matrilineage, but complemented her husband's tasks in his occupation (Greenstreet 1972).

This double standard carries over into modernizing Ghana. As long as the man takes care of the basic needs of his wife, she has little recourse against him. She owes him obedience, and must accede to his requests when they fall within her wifely domain. Her

---

[8] Is this so different from the situation in the United States ? Admittedly, adherence to the "Motherhood Myth," which reached cult-level proportions among Americans in the 1950s, has levelled off. Men and women alike are choosing to be *single* parents, and some women have chosen not to have children at all. The phenomenon is, however, still confined to a minority of the population. In general, even though women despair of their child-centered existences, they have not relinquished the role: "The motherhood minuet is taught freely from birth, and whether or not she has rhythm or likes the music, every woman is expected to do it. Indeed, she *wants* to do it. Little girls start learning what to want—and what to be—when they are still in their cribs" (Rollin 1971: 353).

behavior in such areas reflects upon her husband. In a positive sense, it brings him a good name; unsatisfactory behavior, on the other hand, is justification for divorce. In his autobiography, Kwame Nkrumah recounts that, in the 1930s, a woman who said to her husband "Don't be silly," gave him grounds for divorce.

One of Pool's findings in her survey of urban women in Upper Volta and Niger is that the man may not only have many women, but also has more of a right to choose his wife than do women to choose husbands. Only a small proportion of the women surveyed felt that women should also have such a right, and those who expressed such an idea were primarily under 30 years of age. She found mutual consent more prevalent in urban Ghana. This form gives the woman the latitude of the customary tie, with the addition of the choice factor and freedom from worry about traditional polygyny. Such unions, however, appear to be short-lived, perhaps due to their lack of formal definition. By age 25 most Ghanaian women are in customary (traditional) marriages, "where the status and rights of a wife are more closely defined. Marriage remains as an ideal everywhere, even for the prostitutes of Niamey" (Pool 1972: 246).

The shared frustrations of the wives in a given polygynous marriage do not in practice lead to mutual solidarity, either in the traditional setting or in urban areas. The Ga, for example, have always tried to keep their families together, but the level of antagonism between wives does not always make this feasible. Among the Asante, the vast majority of non-royals currently have only one wife, and the usual practice is for a polygynist's wives to live separately (Fortes 1967: 281). The reason is indicated by the term co-wives use to refer to one another: *kora*, meaning "jealous one." In Accra, including Adabraka, the wives of polygynously wed men are generally housed apart, and here again the word commonly used for co-wife ("rival") is indicative of the reason. This tension also exists between the wife and the husband's girlfriend. The basis for rivalry is competition for the man's favors; in urban as in traditional life, he is the authority and the dispenser of "goodies."

Urban marriage is characterized by the same low level of husband-wife "togetherness" found in traditional society. The whole concept of a man and wife sitting down to a meal has always been foreign.[9] The rented compound room life-style of Adabraka, where houses are not designed with a dining area in mind, does not encourage movement toward this pattern. Man and wife rarely party together either. Once the first child is born, whether the marriage is polygynous or monogamous, the man (but not his wife!) begins to wander. Since it is "unthinkable" for a woman to voluntarily refrain from marrying, the unhappy wife makes the best of the situation; any husband is better than none.

Seniority

Seniority connotes the ranking of people relative to some quality, and acknowledgement of such rank through language and behavior. In traditional societies, seniority often takes the form of respect for age. Deference to the elders is closely tied to the ritual of ancestor worship (Abraham 1962). Here again we encounter a reciprocal "bargain"; by maintaining proper homage and respect, one would enjoy the recompense of weal. The expression of respect involves the same behavior accorded the venerable deceased when they were still alive, for in life they were the authorities.

Writing of the Yoruba of Nigeria, William Bascom (1942: 37) reported that:

> ...all inhabitants of a compound except for the outsiders are ranked into a graded series according to their relative seniority, and the kinship terms which are used in addressing relatives either by descent or by marriage must show proper respect for the status of a senior person.

In some instances, the determination of seniority is closely related to the principle of relative age. In others it is quite distinct from it, involving such factors as the reputation and character of the person addressed; the closeness (and hence extent of intimacy) of kinship between the speaker and the person addressed; the speaker's arrogance or humility (i.e. respect for the position of the other); and whether the person addressed has children.

The traditional method of reckoning seniority and the attendant

---

[9] If we use the behavior of the paramount chief as a model of Asante tradition, it is significant that even today the paramount chief and his wife or wives are not permitted to dine together. Ga chiefs also take their repasts alone. These forms are, of course, only the ceremonial remnants of the "pure" traditional model.

behavior have by no means disappeared. In modern, industrialized countries, ethnic pockets often maintain the principle as part of their cultural tradition. The mainstream of the society, however, has usually reinterpreted it in meritocratic terms, and age and experience may be bypassed. Traditional seniority may be vestigial only, emerging in the form of proverbs or tales of "how it used to be."

In African cities, where the "old country" is a matter of miles away, there is great carry-over. In *Politics in an Urban African Community* (1958), for example, A.L. Epstein analyzes two conflicting systems of authority in a mining town in the Copperbelt region of what is now Zambia. Because the workers belonged to many tribal groups, the mine officials instituted a system of Tribal Elders to represent the workers to the officials. Since the majority of the Elders were in fact related to the lineage of chiefs, the traditional authority was carried into the industrial sector. When a strike broke out, however, the Elders were powerless. Their backgrounds and skills were relevant to the traditional context, but they did not understand the issues that precipitated the strike; the situation was further complicated because the striking workers identified the Elders with the mine officials. The Elders regained their former role after the strike was settled; however, their authority was rejected once and for all throughout the mines five years later, after new disturbances arose at a different mine. The African Tradeworkers Union emerged and gained overwhelming support for its insistence that the system of representation by Tribal Elders be abolished.

There is no doubt that traditional authority continues to shape everyday behavior in Adabraka. At family gatherings, it is the eldest male (the family head) who pours the libations. When a divorce is desired by either a man or a woman, and the marriage was performed in accordance with traditional law, the plaintiff must go to the senior family person and, for a court of higher appeal, to the elders in the hometown. If their opinion is that the plaintiff has no case, the marriage may not be dissolved.

As a matter of basic courtesy, parental guidance is always requested before embarking on a new venture, and even in daily comings and goings. If the biological parents are not alive, or if the individual is living with other guardians, the respect and allegiance is extended to them. As the father of one of my interviewees said to me: "You must listen to your parents; they are *gods* and their advice should be followed." The Adabraka women had a very concrete understanding of what is proper and why. The right to control or at least influence one's decisions is accorded first to one's parents or guardians. The basic rule that one must "always listen to those older because they know better" embraces, secondarily, husbands and boyfriends.

It is generally accepted that, if nothing else, a person owes his life to his parents, for they *bore* him. "Maybe he [the father] is an old man and old are trouble, but you should take him as your father and if he talks you anything, be patient." It is bad to insult one's husband, an informant explains, because "when you marry, he [the husband] becomes your father..." But it is even worse to insult one's parent. "If she insults her husband, the husband has to sack her; but as for the father, he gave birth to her, she can't do it."

There is inevitably some conceptual confusion between the respect due to age and that due to sex, and it is this confusion concerning behaviors of deference that ties together the principles of seniority and polygyny. As one informant phrased it, "Here in Ghana, men they like to think that when they say something to woman, the woman must take it more than they think." But if she gives *him* advice, she continues, he, as a man, will never listen. Decision-making in general, it was agreed, is a function of age. My attempts to compare age and sex elicited some hair-splitting responses. Some women felt that if one is offered counsel by both a man and a woman, one should listen to the woman if she is older, for her wisdom and experience are greater. If the man and woman are peers of the woman seeking advice, some would suggest listening to the one with the greater wisdom. Although many accept that "it is necessary for a man to advise a woman," others opted for listening to the woman because "women are my mothers."

In former times, when responsibilities between men and women were more clearly demarcated, it was not necessary to distinguish between the older man and woman in determining who deserved the greater measure of respect. Even though a family consisting of the usual male and female members lived under the same roof or within the same household, all domestic matters were referred to the senior woman. The counselling of *older* women, considered conducive to peace and harmony, was also accepted in public matters. (As was noted earlier, older women are no longer sexual—i.e. childbearing—beings.)

By deferring to another, by showing respect, the individual is engaging in reciprocal interplay. Women recognize that there are rules of etiquette with other women, as with men. It is just that the consequences of a breach are of a different order. When sex is added on, the dimensions of the interaction change. Among the Hausa of Northern Nigeria, the wife is expected to respect her husband and not call him by name—although this rule relaxes with time (Onwuejeogwu 1969). The Krobo woman calls her husband "father" or "owner" as a token of respect and obedience (Huber 1963). Many of the Adabraka women demonstrate respect by addressing their husbands as "Mr." And in accord with Bascom's description of how seniority is observed through appropriate kinship terms, the Adabraka women address their female elders as Auntie or Miss, and their peers as Sister. One of my informants continuously shuffled her feet when in the presence of an elder, or whenever asking or answering a question; she always preceded her statements with "please" and explained that one should use the expression *"me pa wo kyo"* (I beg you) in asking a favor of an elder.

Respect for one's elders, when carried to an extreme, rules out any chance of exercising one's free will. Even for mundane matters, such as procuring a new job, there is invariably some one person or group of persons to approach for advice, permission, or just as a formality. To determine the best avenue or best activity at a given time, much less to shape a course for one's life, is inconceivable. The lesser decisions are either left to chance or sought from others, who themselves follow a model set down in tradition. For example, marriage is accepted as a given, and one marries the man one's family picks. And *their* choice in turn is based upon traditional guidelines.

To explore these traditional attitudes, I posed hypothetical situations to my informants. The power of fantasy, of spinning imaginary tales and situations, connotes the recognition of alternative courses of action. This power was lacking in these women, who could not see the point of trying to think in abstract terms. Typically, even questions relating to alternatives (the choice factor) *within* traditional roles elicited no response. To ask a woman of Adabraka whether she wants to marry is devoid of cultural content; and when you set the question aside and ask her *whom* or what kind of person she would like to marry (educated, non-educated, professional, laborer, handsome, etc.),[10] she will say only that it is not up to her to think about such things.

What their outlook demonstrated to me is that women coming to Accra still go from the dominion of one authority figure to that of another—from the home of their parents to that of the husband. Young women sometimes take up residence by themselves upon completion of school and the start of a job. I found that this occurred far less frequently in Adabraka than I had expected. The reason is not that there are no jobs or places for the women to live; rather, there continues to be a strain between the loosening of restraints associated with urban opportunities, and the maintenance of tradition (especially the tie to family and lineage) expected by the hometown folk. And most women, young or old, still think more than twice before bucking the traditional guidelines. Given the prospect of moving from the hometown to Accra, only three of my informants insisted that they would ignore their parents' prohibition and come. All of the others to whom I talked told me that they would let their own daughter, in the same situation, move—even while accepting that they, as their parents' daughters, could not. They generally, however, appended a condition (such as job hunting, or marriage to a specific person) that would justify the move, so that it would be clear that the daughter was not relocating just to run around.

In sum, traditional subordination continues in the city. Because of the social necessity to marry, and the correlation of male sex with seniority, women are particularly affected. We cannot assume that men and women have equal access to full participation in the world beyond the compound wall. In fact, women have even less autonomy in the halfway house of Adabraka than they did in the traditional setting.

---

[10] When I asked informants how they came to know (how they met) their husbands, the response was often strained; only through cajoling and/or elaborate explanation of what I meant was I able to obtain genuine replies. Professor Victor Uchendu recently pointed out to me that traditionally in West Africa women are *introduced* to potential spouses by a relative. In the city, this sequence has been translated into a question of morality: loose women seek men out on their own, rather than being introduced by relatives or friends. Thus my question was initially interpreted as implying a lack of virtue in the informant.

Lability

The concept of lability is borrowed from psychology, where it is defined as "flexibility"—connoting pliancy or adaptability (Kretschmer 1972: 379)—and as "plasticity." More specifically:

> ...A thought or intelligence factor in the sense of the ability to undergo restructuring; embraces agility in thinking, readapting, discovering and deducing the essentials from stable structures... Ability of other parts of the organism *to act as substitutes and take over functions* where there has been partial failure (Haase 1972: 17—emphasis added).

An individual exhibiting lability is "easily moved or changed; not stable; not rigid; free in the expression of emotion, or quickly shifting from one emotion to another" (English and English 1958: 286).

Drawing upon this traditional psychological usage, I have adapted the term lability to connote an individual's ability to *substitute one person for another* in the sense of shifting a given emotion from one person to another. When lability is present, relations have a mutable quality—what Evans-Pritchard (1965) perceives as a lack of intensity. The person who plays out a certain role may be replaced by any other individual capable of undertaking that particular role.

Radcliffe-Brown (1924) was the first to explain kinship extension in his discussion of Bantu family relations: mother's brother behaves as a male mother and father's sister as a female father. In Ghana, children may be cared for by a variety of persons. Among the Krobo, for example, any nursing woman in the compound may feed a child. Children are the pets of all. At least until the age of five, they may accept food from anyone. As is indicated by the importance of the mother-child bond to the Asante social system, this sharing of a supervisory responsibility does not mean that Ghanaian children lack love and attention. They are brought up as small adults rather than as children once they reach the age when they can fend for themselves. Even for infants, cuddling does not occur in the context of our "children's hour," since they accompany the mother and training is not restricted to the house or to a special children's area set apart. The sharing of parental rights and duties has also been described for the institution of fostering.

In Western societies, on the other hand, the mother's role customarily devolves upon one person; in fact, as more and more married women go into or return to the job market, there has been much discussion of filial deprivation—the assumption being that no one can substitute for the mother in the love and care of her children.[11]

In Ghana, unlike the West, kinship bonds are emphasized at the expense of conjugal bonds (Fortes 1962). I suggest that traditional society structures with this emphasis both create and are sustained by lability. The strongest bond is that of siblings, of whom there are often several in a family. The child in an extended family is not oriented toward "a" central figure. He grows up learning to depend equally upon any one of several different persons standing in a certain relationship to him. He may be steered in and out of several family situations as a result of divorce and remarriage or fostering. Even if he remains in a single household, it is likely to contain family members in addition to his parents and siblings. The intense emotions that Western parents project onto their children are in Ghana diffused through a whole network of persons. The child does not have the same opportunity to develop affective mechanisms,

---

[11] Writing about the situation in the United States, Lois W. Hoffman cites numerous studies which show that the working mother of a school-age child, particularly in the middle class, "makes a deliberate effort to compensate the child for her employment...and the dissatisfied mother, whether employed or not and whether lower or middle class, is less likely to be an adequate mother.... The very idea that maternal employment brings emotional deprivation to the school-age child has not been supported..." (1974: 152). In the case of infants, too, there is little solid evidence for this conclusion. It seems that a one-to-one relationship with an adult is imperative for intellectual and emotional development, and there is some evidence of a need for cuddling and environmental stimulation. But the studies in this area were carried out in understaffed institutions; possibly with increased staff, greater attention to the infants, etc., the outcome would be different. Furthermore, no evidence was found "that the caretaker has to be the mother or that this role is better filled by a male or female.... Child psychologists generally believe that there must be at least one stable figure to whom the infant forms an attachment, but this theory is not definitely established; and we do not know whether the periodic absence from the infant that is likely to accompany maternal employment is sufficient to undermine her potential as the object of the infant's attachment" (Hoffman 1974: 154).

and therefore movement from relationship to relationship is fraught with less tension and anxiety. Ronald Cohen (1972: 46-51) notes the same behavior in Northern Nigeria.

This has ramifications in adulthood. Interpersonal relationships in urban Ghana are often marked by low emotional content and a "commercial" approach. One tends to regard as interchangeable those persons who carry out a given function relative to oneself. Roles are roles.   Given this conditioning, it is not surprising that women continue to adapt to polygynous unions as easily as men. This is not to say that every relationship is invested with exactly the same amount of emotional content as every other. Clearly there is a range, just as there is a range in the "liberation quotient" for women. All of my informants agreed that in times of trouble one can always go to kin, particularly those in the immediate circle. But (as with one's mother's sister) the concept of "kin" might not run along strict biological lines. There seemed little doubt that the attachment is greater to a family member than to a spouse.

Just as a child is fed on demand in Ghanaian society, so a Ghanaian adult may seek to receive on demand; in any case, it does not cost anything to try. When emotional intangibles are removed from the content of a relationship, the interested party is after something other than the whole persona of the other, and his own persona is not invested in a given exchange. The bargaining concerns a particular role or activity. As long as the person occupying a role in a given transaction fulfills his/her end of the deal, the contract is kept intact. When one of the participants does not reciprocate in accordance with the rules of the game, the other can go elsewhere. There is neither the sense of binding oneself to one person who will carry out all, nor of "selling one's soul." The relationship is priced in terms of what the contracting parties feel that they can exact from each other, and what they must give in return. The specifics of the relationship are lent support from the more generalized rule of reciprocity.

Marcel Mauss (1966) uses the term "gift" to signify anything involving a trust. A relationship of trust, a reciprocal relationship, involves a time lag, during which one person (the recipient) is in a position of debt to the other (the giver). The disequilibrium continues until repayment is made, and then the cycle begins anew. Bestowing a gift (or "dash" as it is called in West Africa) in effect sets up a contractual relationship; the recipient is expected to and expects to fulfill his side of the bargain in due course.

Consider the strong mother-daughter relationship in Ghana. By raising her child properly, the mother knows that she will not suffer in her old age. By the same token, the daughter knows that an occasional dash and proper respect will accord her the right to entrust her children to her mother's care. There is another way in which a "gift" in the sense in which Mauss uses the word, is important to this reciprocal relationship: it is a way of paying respect. Displaying respect (even if only as a polite formality) is a part of many "contracts," and may involve dashing, appropriate phrases, and accompanying behavior such as posture and stance.

The various elements of a reciprocal relationship need not be, and in fact traditionally are not, accompanied by an investment of emotion. Let us consider courtship and marriage as an example. In the introduction to *African Systems of Kinship and Marriage* (1967), A.R. Radcliffe-Brown reminds us that, in order to understand African marriage, we must remember that the institution of marriage as it is perceived in England today has resulted from recent social developments. Before the 18th century, romantic love was conceived of as taking place *outside* of marriage, as depicted in the songs of troubadors. It was less than two centuries ago that the concept of love within marriage began to evolve as the idealized norm. In customary African marriages, this is not yet so. According to Radcliffe-Browne (1967: 46), "the strong affection that normally exists after some years of successful marriage is the product of the marriage itself conceived as a process, resulting from living together and cooperating in many activities and particularly in the rearing of children. " The arrangement of the marriage itself is a bargain struck by others than the bride, however, and traditionally includes the payment of a bride price. The more desirable the woman (the more she embodies revered attributes, or the higher her social status or that of her family), the higher this bidding price. In urban Ghana, registered or church marriage carries a higher price than customary marriage—not because of the requisite fees, but because of the added status and the necessity for extra show.

According to William J. Goode (1963), *all* courtship systems are market or exchange systems. They differ from one another with respect to *who* does the buying and selling, which characteristics are more or less valuable in that market, and how open or explicit the bargaining is. In a conjugal family system such as our own, mutual attraction in both courtship and marriage acquires a higher value.

Fatalism

As Richard Taylor defines it, "fatalism is the belief that whatever happens is unavoidable... [it] provides the basis of the attitude of calm acceptance that the fatalist is thought, quite correctly, to embody" (1974: 59). The fatalist regards the future in the same way that most of us ordinarily think of the past; we accept that past events are beyond our power to replay, while a fatalist would say that they never were within our control. Fatalism is based upon the presupposition that all statements about past, present, and future events are eternally true or false. In Taylor's words, "Nothing *becomes* true or *ceases* to be true; whatever is truth at all simply *is* true" (Taylor 1974: 68).

I construe fatalism to be an unarticulated attitude among Ghanaians, correspondent to the reasoned thought of philosophers. In Ghana, as well as in other African societies, fatalism derives from traditional religious beliefs. The relationship between man and God is thought to be direct and exclusive, as is suggested in the following Akan sayings[12] cited by W.E. Abraham in *The Mind of Africa* (1962: 58):

> There are no sidepaths to the destiny that God has appointed for one.

> A sensible man does not try to change the words that God has spoken beforehand.

> If God has not fixed one's death, and a human being tries to kill one, one does not die.

The Akan believed that man has an aspect called *okra* (literally, mission), and it is the *okra* that represents the destiny that God has appointed for man:

> The *okra* is the guiding spirit of a man... by being the bearer of destiny, [it] lends its name to signal good luck and signal bad luck,

---

[12] I follow Abraham (1962) in his use of the Akan as a paradigm of African societies in general.

both being thought in a way to be deserved, or at least unavoidable, and perhaps fitting.... The *okra* was conceived to be automatic in its functioning, even when it gives advice which is good or bad. Its advice does not arise from any interest, but from the ineluctable unfolding of the destiny appointed for it (Abraham 1962: 59-60).

This sense of powerlessness in arranging one's life—in altering that which is fated to be—persists in the modern sector. The Adabraka woman's social identities and identity relationships stay within the traditional mold. She does not perceive the city's opportunities as hers for the taking. For one thing, not very much has been made available to her; more significantly, she holds herself back, for she does not think in terms of change.

The women are fully aware of the restrictions placed upon them as women in their social system, but they do not consider that it might be within their power to change this system or to leave it. And I would argue that this is why they stay put—*not* because they believe that they are doing so well for themselves. When polygyny is a cultural given, for example, how can one stop it ? A woman's life is controlled by her husband's coming and goings, his assignations, his marriages. As one informant summarized the situation: "If he likes to marry another woman, how can this woman tell him: 'Don't marry' ? He will happy [*sic*]. Her husband feels to marry, she can't tell him: 'Don't marry.' She [he] will happy, that's why." The statement is followed by the familiar fatalistic shrug.

Although some women maneuver their way into advantageous positions vis-à-vis men, the benefits are temporary. "Free will" can be exercised only within narrowly defined limits when a woman's adult status (as a member of society) is at stake. A woman may defer marriage, but ultimately she submits. It is part of her life experience. Similarly, bearing children is part of a status in life. And to ask how many children a woman *wants* is irrelevant.

Although we are concerned here primarily with Ghanaian women, it must be noted that women are not alone in sitting back while nature takes its course. Men also conform to traditional patterns that promote neither risk-taking nor individual assertiveness in new ventures. The go-getter is rare; both sexes wait for success or change to find them, rather than setting out to attain it.

To speak of the pervasiveness of fatalism in Ghana is another way of saying that the power of negation is stifled—the drive to negate that which *is* in order to create something that is not, something new. The person lacking this power is not free to imagine himself or herself in situations other than what has always been; and the fatalist thinks, why bother ? The acceptance of this worldview neutralizes the diversity of the women under study. It constitutes the basis for a social system, supports its maintenance, and retards change. It causes the women to act as a conservative force.

The Impact of the West

Another crucial factor affecting the position of women in modernizing African societies is the lingering impact of the Europeans who superimposed their role over that of traditional institutions during the colonial period. In the case of Ghana, this cultural overlay is British. Although a succession of European powers vied for trade hegemony beginning in the 15th century, Britain was clearly predominant by the middle of the 18th century, and Ghana (called the "Gold Coast" until independence in 1957) was officially declared a British colony in 1874. With the shifting of British administrative headquarters from Cape Coast to Accra in 1877, Accra became henceforth the central locus for the spread of English as the language of education, government, and commerce, as well as for other alterations in the social system.

Any assessment of the changes that have taken place in Ghana as a result of the British association must take into account not only the model for behavior presented by the colonizers, but also the Ghanaian's interpretation and selective assimilation of this model. Since we are here specifically concerned with the role of women, we must turn back the pages of history to look briefly at the lifestyle of Victorian women in England. More importantly, we must see how the colonizers transported the Victorian concept of woman's role to the colonies, adding new forms of social, political, and economic discrimination to those already existing in traditional society. Above all, however, we are concerned with the ways in which the melding of indigenous and imported ideologies shapes the role of women in today's Ghana.

The term "Western model," as used throughout this book, refers to the British-inspired behavioral components of the Ghanaian social structure. These include various superficial aspects of lifestyle adopted by members of the élite and propounded in the daily newspapers. Sometimes, as we shall see in subsequent chapters, "Western" and traditional attitudes clash. When the social assumptions of the two interacting models are similar, however, they become mutually reinforcing. This mutual reinforcement has been particularly evident in the definition of the role of women.

"The Lady": A Victorian Ideal

In medieval Europe, domestic service was universally accepted as an important part of education for the daughters, as well as the sons, of rich and poor alike (Aries 1962). The bourgeois household, which the married woman oversaw, was not just a home; it was a center for whatever business activity the family conducted, and was not infrequently composed of the immediate family, servants, apprentices, and unattached relatives. In those days before the development of training schools, a boy could apprentice out to a given household, his choice dependent upon the kind of occupational training he sought. Girls were trained from childhood in household tasks, but given the nature of the establishment these were important not only to the immediate family but to the community as well. Thus domestic work was a public as well as a private service.

The nuclear family, a product of the transition from the medieval (preindustrial) to the modern (industrial) world (Wittner n.d.), altered the European woman's role—changing the character of domestic work, while at the same time undermining its primacy. The routine work formerly undertaken by the young unmarried girls of the extended household now fell upon the individual "housewife" (Clark 1920: 11-12). By the end of the 17th century, factory production and the decreasing economic importance of the domestic establishment had widened the division between men and

women and also between women of different classes. As leisure
became a new possibility for upper-class women, their economic
and political importance diminished. A growing literature
delineating "proper" female roles encouraged the women of the
higher social strata to retreat into dependence upon fathers and
husbands (Wittner n.d.). Meanwhile the wives and daughters of the
poor were forced into a different sort of dependency—that of wage-
earners in a work force administered by men—and became
increasingly vulnerable to exploitation (Clark 1920).

In 18th and 19th century England, it was commonly believed that
woman was by nature subservient to man. Her only way of rising in
the world was through marriage. The "natural" position of woman
was ascribed to two factors, the first being physical constitution.
Thus Alexander Walker, writing in the 1830s, proclaimed that:

> the man possessing reasoning faculties, muscular power, and courage
> to employ it, is qualified for being a protector; the women, being little
> capable of reasoning, feeble and timid, requires protection. Under
> such circumstances, the man naturally governs: the woman naturally
> obeys (Quoted in Banks and Banks 1972: 23).

Even many gifted women shared with their sisters a conviction of
their inferiority to men. Elizabeth Barrett, responding to Harriet
Martineau's efforts to enlist support in raising women's status,
wrote:

> let us say and do what we please and can... there is a natural
> inferiority of mind in women—of the intellect... not by any means of
> the moral nature... the history of Art and of genius testifies to this fact
> openly (Quoted in Sampson 1965: 54).

The second factor was divine providence. Fundamentalist Christian
doctrine traced woman's inferiority back to the Book of Genesis
and Eve's creation from Adam's rib, and it followed that
"resignation to her lot was the only recourse of a woman with true
Christian humility" (J. and O. Banks 1972: 23).

The duties of the perfect wife were to her husband: she was
expected to create a home environment that provided shelter from
the harsh world. In return, her husband had a duty to support and
protect her, providing a comfortable maintenance for her as his
dependent. Her obligations, however, went beyond her husband to

her role as a mother: the noblest aim of her existence, in the eyes of many, was " 'to generate beings who, as women, may tread the footsteps of their mothers, or, as men may excel in the higher virtues which these, to them softer and sweeter occupations, render it impossible that they should themselves attain' " (Walker, quoted in Banks and Banks 1972: 61).

In mid-19th century England, the drive for social esteem among the middle and upper-middle classes was characterized by great display. Married women of this stratum[1] again underwent a change in life-style: one symbol of social status involved a transition from being the perfect wife and mother to being the "perfect lady." The woman's preoccupation with her appearance performed the function of exhibiting the family's wealth; indeed, it was her responsibility to do so (*Quarterly Review* 1847, cited in Roberts 1977; Veblen 1899). Conspicuous consumption and waste reached their heights in the 1870s and 1880s. While ambition in career and productive living were stressed as virtues for the man, an expensive and showy existence of domestic *leisure* belonged to the woman. She repudiated

> the purely domestic virtues precisely because of their association with a rather more lowly past. To the aspiring middle classes the kitchen was no place in which to demonstrate one's social prestige. The result was to emancipate the middle class women from the exclusively domestic role... [which], however, should not be confused with emancipation from dependence upon the male members of the family (Banks and Banks 1972: 12).

The middle-class woman was still the major administrator of the house, but she was freed from performing much of the actual work through the increase in the supply of cheap servants. Indeed, she spent much of her day outside the confines of her home, whiling away her time in frivolous activities. Although seemingly enjoying considerable freedom of movement, she remained under the authority of her husband, who was morally and legally her superior. In 1869, the year that John Stuart Mill published his treatise *On the Subjection of Women*, it was a woman who restated the majority view:

---

[1] The reference groups for "socially acceptable" behavior among the Victorians were the middle and upper-middle classes.

'It is a man's place to rule, and a woman's to yield. He must be held
up as the head of the house, and it is her duty to bend so unmurmur-
ingly to his wishes, that the rest of the household will follow her
example, and treat him with the due respect his sex demands' (Sarah
Sewell, quoted in Banks and Banks 1972: 60).

It was a period when a woman had no existence save through her
relationship to men. According to the 19th century writer Mrs.
Sarah Ellis, woman was a "relative creature" (cited in Basch 1974:
5). The essentials of the female being were that she was supported
by and ministered to men (W.R. Greg, cited in Basch 1974: 5).
Victorian essayists characterized marriage as the total
subordination of the wife to the husband, with the onus on the wife
to make it a success (Roberts 1977). Women were typically
portrayed as beings with humility, softness and timidity, intelligent
passivity, having a noble nature that needed a man in order to grow,
and needing protection and guidance (Calder 1976: 58).
Superimposed upon the doctrine of inferiority was the theory that
the sexes had different attitudes and roles. Thus, the man was
active, an architect, with intellectual capacity for creation, inven-
tion, and synthesis, while the woman was passive, the soul of the
house, with judgement only for details and trivia (Basch 1974: 5).

Whereas chastity, before and during marriage, was crucial to the
maintenance of a woman's respectability, the middle-class man was
subject to a far less stringent code. The Matrimonial Causes Act,
passed in 1857, decreed that a man could sue for divorce on the
grounds of adultery alone, whereas his wife had to prove desertion,
cruelty, incest, sodomy, rape, or bestiality in addition (Banks and
Banks 1972). Women were to be protected from writings or
conversation with sexual content, for such influences were
considered harmful to their constitution; furthermore knowledge
was perceived as corrupting. The sexual experience was regarded as
a passive one for the wife, who was to be the mere recipient of her
husband's base needs. The existence of prostitutes was rationalized
as being necessary because of the conflict between the organization
of society and male sexual appetites. The Contagious Diseases Acts
of 1864-67, enacted in the face of increasing prostitution, required
registration and medical examination of its practitioners.

The organization of Victorian society effectively ruled out the
possibility that a middle-class woman could support herself. The

standards of education for girls of this class were low. The emphasis was on the rudiments of French, reading, writing, arithmetic, and more general accomplishments—"in short the elements useful for a role of 'display' " (Basch 1974: 3). Even some would-be reformers in favor of educating girls accepted that the subjects and examinations could not be the same as those for boys, since women were not considered to have the power of intellect needed for rigorous studies. Instead, their education would further moral development.[2]

Employment opportunities for women expanded between 1851 and 1871, but these did not extend to fields that were traditionally masculine; moreover, opportunities for men were widening even more rapidly. The middle-class women who were engaged in paid work generally pursued some sort of literary career; it did not overly interfere with the role of wife and mother, and it was one of the few careers open to women. Moreover, it provided both money and a sense of vocation (Basch 1974: 42-43). Yet the image of "the lady" was reinforced by the ban on paid employment—"a ban so strong that many who wrote for publication, even though writing at home, did so under pseudonyms, or else signed their work simply 'By a Lady' " (Peterson 1972: 6). The one employment that would not cause a middle-class lady to lose her status—and which she might take up in the event that she found herself in financial distress—was as a governess (Peterson 1972). A married woman had claim only to her personal possessions, unless she was protected by a marriage settlement (mainly an upper-class phenomenon). The earnings of a woman separated from her husband were still legally his, until the Government Bill on Marriage and Divorce, enacted in 1858, introduced some protection for the property of a separated or divorced wife.

All in all, the spirit of the times was that household management and raising children were "good womanly work" and since "man has no aptitude for domestic duties" (Landels, quoted in Banks and Banks 1972: 46), woman must remain to carry them out. The married household was socially and culturally central; it was a woman's noble Christian duty, as well as her *instinct*, to be a true wife and mother. These assumptions were not perceived to be in conflict with the new trend to relinquish manual labor and the care

---

[2] See excerpts of Miss Dorothea Beale's speech in J. and O. Banks (1972: 47-48).

of children to servants.

Historians agree that 1860-70 marked a turning point in the Victorian era. During that decade, a number of feminist reforms were enacted.[3] Alternatives for the Victorian adult woman existed only in the doctrines of feminism—a movement which, in the view of J. and O. Banks (1972), was related to the rise in the standard of living. It is significant that this "New Womanhood" movement was confined to the middle classes. Ironically, it grew out of the "perfect lady" transition, since its leading members had the time and energy to put into their nascent cause because they had been released from domesticity; in addition, the movement represented a revolt against the triviality and humiliation of this new role. Middle-class acceptance, in the late 1800s, of limitations on family size also paved the way for "sustained argument about an alternative 'way of life' for the married woman." (Banks and Banks 1972: 26). As part of easing burdens of married existence, the feminist movement called for a revamping of prudish Victorian sexual attitudes and the double standard. Beyond this, it sought expansion of opportunities for education, employment, and income.

The Colonial Presence

Since the British carried with them to Africa a worldview that emphasized the propriety and public invisibility of women, it did not even occur to them that African women might be accepted participants in the politics of their societies. The British encounter with the Igbo of Nigeria is a case in point (Van Allen 1972; 1976). Igbo women possessed a traditional base of power which lay in their gatherings, *mikiri*, a political forum where women's interests were articulated. One of the primary functions of the *mikiri* was that of a market association. Rules were made there which applied to men as well as women. If, for example, a man mistreated his wife, violated the market rules, or permitted his cows to eat the women's crops, the women might engage in a strike or boycott to force the men to police themselves, or they might choose to "sit on" the individual

---

[3] These include the Second Reform Act of 1867, which had property qualifications but granted the franchise to women of the lower-middle class and a small privileged section of the working class; the Factory Acts of 1867; the passage of the Contagious Disease Acts in 1864-69; the public airing of birth control issues in 1868 (Basch 1974).

offender. This involved gathering at the guilty man's compound to dance, sing, call his manhood into question, bang on his hut, and rough him up. "Although this could hardly have been a pleasant experience for the offending man, it was considered legitimate and no man would consider intervening" (Van Allen 1972: 170).

The British did not take into account such indigenous institutions as the *mikiri*. Furthermore, they ignored custom in their appointment of Warrant Chiefs (as links between the Colonial government and the people), for it violated Igbo concepts to have one man represent a village. The women's resentment of the additional power given to the Chiefs by the British and of possible new taxation by the colonial regime culminated in the Aba Riots, or "Women's War" of 1929—an expanded form of "sitting on" a man. The British, having failed to inquire into the nature of the *mikiri* network, saw the riots as irrational. Their responses fell into a pattern:—

> ...*not* of purposeful discrimination against women with the intent of keeping them from playing their traditional political roles, but of a prevailing blindness to the possibility that women *had* a significant role in traditional politics and should participate in the new system of local government (Van Allen 1972: 176).

Indeed, most of the District Officers thought that it had been the men who had organized the women and were responsible for the riots !

James L. Brain (1976) provides further documentation on the erosion of women's roles as a result of British involvement. The government of post-independence Tanzania decided to set up village settlement schemes; President Julius Nyerere felt that until all Tanzanians lived in villages, they would not enjoy the benefits of modernization. Settlers could only join a village if accompanied by a wife, "rather as though a wife were a necessary piece of equipment" (Brain 1976: 271). Many brought common-law wives: the Luguru left their legal wives behind, so that they would not lose their land rights in the hills. In the event of a divorce, the common-law wife had no protection from traditional law, which guaranteed the legal spouse half of the proceeds from joint marital ventures. Yet *legal* wives had no rights in the settlement village, and all earnings from work went to their husbands. The women had no way to earn pin-money. Luguru and Kutu women had traditional rights in land, which gave them a good deal of economic independence.

These rights, however, were contingent upon use. Since most women could not utilize their holdings once they moved to the village, they lost them. Finally, no provision was made for the wife in the event of her husband's death. The design of the plans reflected the ideas of British ex-colonial civil servants who worked for the settlement agency. "These men were honest, hard-working, and sympathetic to Tanzania's development, but because of their background they were totally incapable of grasping what Nyerere had in mind" (Brain 1976: 268).

It was in the "new towns" that the colonial pressure was most obvious, manifest in the imposed Western system of stratification. These urban centers were transportation junctions for major European enterprises, the centers of colonial administrations, and the marketing and service centers of European settlers. Max Weber (1946) distinguished three base criteria which stratify a society simultaneously: the possession of economic goods and opportunities, i.e. class; the possession of social honor and prestige, i.e. status; and the possession of political power. According to prevailing Western ideology, social position is to be earned through achievement, as distinct from ascription. Ralph Linton elaborates:

> Ascribed statuses are those which are assigned to individuals without reference to their innate differences of abilities.... The achieved statuses are, as a minimum, those requiring special qualities, although they are not necessary to these. They are not assigned to individuals from birth but are left open to be filled through competition and individual effort (1936: 115-116).

If it is accepted that the general criteria for traditional roles in Ghana are ascriptive, based upon age, sex, and ethnicity (Apter 1968), then it would seem to follow that the rise of a new pattern of role definition through achievement should be a liberation from the past, especially for women. As we have seen, however, the Victorians did not reject ascription when it came to gender. In an achievement-oriented system, the avenues to upward mobility are education, occupation, and income. In Ghana, as in other countries where this system was imported, opportunities for participation by the local population were proffered mostly to men. This applied in particular to education (Du Sautoy 1958; Foster 1965).

During the first half of the 18th century, the number of Europeans in what is now Ghana was so small that they did not constitute a generalized reference group upon which the Ghanaians were motivated to model their aspirations. They did have a role in influencing cultural behavior in the towns, but this influence was limited to a tiny African minority.

> In the traditional societies of Ghana education was informal and was carried out by the community as a whole, with the child's own family playing the most important role. It was, in fact, identical with the process of socialization by which the culture of the society was passed on to the young generation. In such relatively homogenous, slowly changing societies such a system was adequate to meet the needs of the society. Consequently, when the first European type schools were introduced to West Africa, there was no popular demand for their services (Hurd 1967: 217).

Whatever demand for Western education eventually emerged did so not because European culture was perceived as having unusual intrinsic worth, but because of the vocational opportunities such training opened for some town-dwelling Ghanaians.

By the end of the 19th century, however, the British had come to constitute a generalized reference group, especially in the towns where their economic and political presence was most directly experienced. The range of occupations to which the resident British reference group addressed itself was limited, and Africans seeking upward mobility through these activities had to direct themselves to a fairly narrow range of educational options. Academic rather than vocational education was emphasized throughout the colonial period, and the colonial education system:—

> emphasized individual achievement as against corporate responsibility, the virtue of the clerical and technical career as against the agricultural. The pen, at least as far as status was concerned, was mightier than the matchet (Crowder 1968: 387).

A side effect of the direct relationship between adoption of European ways and ranking or employability in towns was that even those whose exposure to education was limited to the primary level came to reject their own heritage.

One of the attractions of academic education, as contrasted with technical training, was that it was not self-limiting. The demand for technicians and craftsmen was never large during the colonial period; skilled workers and artisans accounted for less than ten percent of the male labor force in 1948, including traditional craftsmen. The bureaucracy, on the other hand, expanded steadily under British rule, until by 1951 two-fifths of African salaried workers were employed by the government, and 18 percent of the African labor force were salaried workers. Academic training also opened up the possibility, however remote, of studying law—the most prestigious profession for Africans in the colonial period. In a sense, as Philip Foster points out in *Education and Social Change in Ghana* (1965), academic training *was* vocational training in these circumstances.

What of the women ?

> Although the colonial educational system offered considerably greater opportunities to men, in the first half of the 20th century proportionately more women were educated in Ghana... than in any other colonial African country (Smock 1977: 182).

However, there were great disparities in the education of boys and girls. Girls schools were built in the late 19th century, the first secondary boarding school opening in 1881. The fare offered was different from that of boys, including the subject of needlework (Graham 1971). Given Foster's thesis that the early schools (both government and mission) were created mainly to train Africans for clerical and other useful roles, it is not surprising that the education of males was different from that of female students. Moreover, it could hardly be expected that the quantity and quality of schools for females in the colonies would be greater than that available for girls in England itself. After all, we have seen that only a few English women of the mid-19th century were beginning to organize in pursuit of their rights to educational and economic parity with men. Thus, in the Gold Coast of 1918, the government and Wesleyan Mission schools were educating one girl for every six or seven boys; the Basel Mission, on the other hand, had a ratio of one girl to three boys (Graham 1971). The inequality of male and female schooling in Africa was not entirely a reflection of bias on the part of the colonial officials or the missionaries, however, since local populations were resistant to the equal education of the two sexes. In fact, even the boarding schools established by the Basel Mission and others to remove children from the traditional environment during the educational (and Christianizing) process trained young women in ways that reinforced traditional views of female roles. The emphasis was on courses in domestic economics and the Christian ideal of the well-domesticated wife as the center of a nuclear family.

During the economic depression of the 1930s, the Gold Coast, like most countries, was suffering from unemployment. The view expressed by the Chief Inspector of Labour at that time was that wage-earning opportunities for men were more important than similar ones for women; this "can be taken as typical of colonial government thinking even in 'normal' times" (Greenstreet 1971: 118). This is not to say that women did not work during the colonial period. In a letter of March 6, 1931 from the Secretary of Native Affairs to the Colonial Secretary, we read that women of some tribes hired themselves out to carry produce to neighboring markets or to assist in road construction by carrying light loads of gravel. Women were not, however, employed in lifting heavy weights, in mining, stevedoring, or the coaling of ships. These jobs were for men only. Where custom provided no model, the colonial government created new legislation. Thus, on the one hand, the ban on female employment in heavy and dangerous trades was not a part of colonial law, but instead derived from custom. On the other hand, under Ordinance 54, Cap. 101 of the Gold Coast laws, night employment of women was prohibited.

It was in the growth of the retail sector that women's economic advance was most significant during the colonial period (Smock 1977: 183). Colonial supervision helped eliminate restrictions on trade items that women could carry while also enabling them to trade in more distant rural markets. Central markets were established in towns, enabling women to rent stalls, regularize, and expand their trade (Smock 1977: 183-4).

In a sense, the situation of African men during the early colonial period was comparable to that of women in more recent years. When the British set up their administration, African males were the inferior status group to which they turned to staff the lower rungs of the bureaucracy and the urban economy. As training, experience, and changes in British policy enabled African men to advance in the hierarchy, some of the lower level jobs were opened to women.

Contemporary Syncretism

It has been fashionable in recent years to blame the colonizing power for all of the imperfections of postcolonial African society. There is no question but that the British helped prevent, or at least inhibited, women from preparing to participate in the modernization of their colonies, but it is also true that African "converts" took over where the British left off. The early élite of the Gold Coast was made up of families whose members monopolized the commercial and political posts created by British colonialism. They adopted English names and the Victorian style of life, including the institution of the nuclear family (thereby eroding extended family ties and support). They nominally accepted Christian teaching and values such as marriage based on love (in consistent with tradition) and monogamy (promoting girlfriends and prostitution). Bourgeoisification became the style for "the modern mode." In contemporary Accra, the standard of conformity is that which most nearly approaches the European way. Few Ghanaians would admit to a desire to live abroad, but the "been-to" (the colloquial expression for one who has been abroad) has a status all its own. He has gone away and brought back the Gospel. He has learned the etiquette required for acceptance by Westerners.

The term "Westernization" carries with it the notion of modernizing change. While much of Accra's present system is Western in form, the dynamics are traditional in content. Values, attitudes, and behaviors are still in the process of crystallization. The superficial indications of Westernization notwithstanding, traditional customs continue to insinuate themselves into daily living. The majority of the people still adhere to the ingrained formal patterns they or their parents learned as children in the hometown, and the informal patterns they have incorporated along the way. Selective espousal of old and new create contradictions, adding to the general confusion of the urban scene.[4]

---

[4]A.L. Epstein (1964) complains that there is a tendency among urban anthropologists to disregard the existence of an urban social system, and to see the city as a mere conglomeration of people from different regions and cultures. In fact, such a system must emerge, and undergo considerable ferment in the early stages. For African migrants with no urban experience, some customs may need to be altered. Similarly, European norms are often inappropriate, because

An example of British colonial architecture in Adabraka.

(Photo: Edward S. Ayensu)

There is, for example, an explicit code and form to follow in bureaucratic dealings. The standard procedure is that anyone wishing to see the Principal Immigration Officer at the Ministry of the Interior must be referred by one of the lesser officials; the Principal Officer handles only special cases, and only after the preliminary legwork has been done. If the dossier relevant to a particular case has not been located or processed according to the prescribed form, the rule is that one must wait until these steps have been properly completed. Crosscutting these "Western" bureaucratic procedural steps, however, are such traditional patterns as ethnicity and patronage. The result is that rules are selectively enforced. Even though the Principal Officer knows that his job entails carrying our x, y, and z in sequential order, there will be occasions for choosing to do otherwise. When a fellow ethnic or the son of a friend is involved, technical form be damned.

of the mixture of backgrounds present in most African cities. The imitation of certain features of the colonizing society is part of the reorganization of the amalgamating cultures into a coherent whole.

In no area of Ghanaian life is Westernization more pervasive than in attitudes towards consumer goods. For men and women alike, the imported Western product is invariably accorded greater worth than the indigenous, whatever their relative intrinsic value. A woman wearing Manchester cloth (from England) or else Dutch Wax cloth (from the Netherlands) has more status than a woman wearing local Tema cloth. Watches, whether they keep time or not, are worn as pieces of jewelry and as symbols of status. Women carry purses, often empty, while they tie their money in the traditional manner in the corner of the skirt cloth.

Baako, the anti-hero of Ayi Kewi Armah's novel *Fragments* (1971), engages in a brief exchange with a veteran Ghanaian "been to" while on an airplane returning to Ghana from abroad. When Baako asks his fellow passenger if he doesn't find it hard to return home, the response is unfaltering:

> "Oh no. No. But I understand you. I have learned to take precautions myself. There are important things you can't get to buy at home. Every time I go I arrange to buy all I need, suits and so on. It's quite simple. I got two good cars on this trip..."

> "You see this," Brempong brought out his lighter, "Where in Ghana would you find a thing like this ? Sharp eyes...." He leaned back completely and his voice relaxed to a quiet sound just above a whisper, "You just have to know what to look for when you get a chance to go abroad. Otherwise you come back empty-handed like a fool, and all the time you spent is a waste, useless." A loud, forced guffaw broke the easy tenor of his voice. "But if you come back prepared, there's nothing to worry about" (1971: 73-74).

While women no less than men have fallen victim to this feverish fascination with Western styles and material possessions, the basic patterns of their lives remain remarkably unchanged. Women are the last to be hired in the urban job market. To rise above subordinate wage-earning occupations to which they have been limited (Colette LeCour Grandmaison 1969; Oppong et al. 1975), it is necessary (though possibly insufficient) that they possess either a high level of Western education or specialized training. Age and ethnicity continue to carry weight in job recruitment, but "wrong" ethnicity is a lesser hurdle than sex. If Ewe tend to meet with discrimination in hiring practices and later become more "acceptable," for example, it is the male Ewe who are first accomodated. That this is not a simple case of one-sided bias, but something deeper in the society, is indicated by the response of female students to the introduction of mass education: the overwhelming demand was for "sewing, cooking and housecraft classes, as well as instruction in child welfare" (Du Sautoy 1958: 107).

In summary, urban Ghanaian women operate in a society that has nominally accepted the achievement-oriented Western stratification system, but in which a residual system of traditional attitudes continues to place constraints on their own concept, and society's tolerance, of their autonomy. This fusing of old and new values has tended to increase women's dependency on men, and their acceptance of this dependency.

Adabraka and its People

A woman's perceptions of social reality and her place in that reality—roles, aspirations, satisfactions—are governed in part by the sector of society to which she belongs. This is particularly so in the case of Adabraka, where we might well expect the extent of one's behavioral autonomy to vary with ethnicity, education, urban experience, etc. The women of Adabraka affect, and are affected by, each other, as well as the physical and larger social environment within which they interact. Hence the utility of considering them *in situ*.

How Adabraka Came To Be

Once ensconced in their administrative headquarters at Accra, the British became aware of not only the outright hostility between members of different ethnic groups,[1] but also the striking as well as subtle differences among ethnic traditions and law codes. In planning for the expansion of Accra, therefore, the colonial

---

[1] Cf. Secretary of Native Affairs 1806: Extract from an interview at Christiansborg Castle, when Chief Okajo and others met with the Governor on December 8, 1903.

government found it convenient to think in terms of ethnic communities.

In 1908, the Governor, Sir John Rogers, presented plans for a number of town sites to the British Colonial Secretary. These were intended to alleviate sanitary conditions in the city.[2] Adabraka, one of the sites, was conceived as a kind of *zongo* (strangers' quarter) lying on the Kibi (Nsawam) Road, which runs north from the Ga section. (*See* Map of Accra, page 4).

People of diverse origin had already begun to filter into the area. In the late 19th and early 20th centuries, after the abolition of slavery in Brazil in 1831, many blacks from that country migrated to West Africa. Those settling in the Gold Coast, who called themselves Tabon, were accepted by the Otublohu—one of the Ga peoples[3]—and eventually received from them land and a stool;[4]

---

[2] In 1908 there was an epidemic of bubonic plague in the old section of Accra. The government concluded that sanitary improvements were essential if another epidemic was to be avoided. They sought to demolish some of the houses in order to improve ventilation and actively encouraged resettlement in new town sites such as Adabraka through consultation with the local chiefs. Adabraka was established on April 24, 1910, as reported by Edward Hall, the Acting Director of the Public Works Department; some Ga did resettle there. It was intended to accomodate "two Hausa tribes viz.:—the Fulanis and the Yorubas and also dispossessed Ussher Town (Ga) people." Most of the latter were not inclined to settle in Adabraka. Two years later, the Sanitary Engineer remarked that those reluctant to resettle "are nearly always of the poor class, or of a class such as the fishermen whose occupations confine them to the town. It can be seen from the type of houses now being erected that those who do go are of a better class, who appreciate the advantages of a healthy well laid-out township" (Secretary of Native Affairs 1348/12: Sanitary Engineer L.C.S. Wellacott's remarks; December 4, 1912).

The large plots (160 feet by 82 feet) were left with room for extension southward "as those are the only ones for which there is likely to be any demand." (Secretary for Native Affairs 1348/12; letter/report of Mr. Hall; April 27, 1910). And the smaller depth (58 feet 6 inches by 60 feet) of the plots for the Hausa and Fulani was thought necessary "in order to limit the number of buildings on a plot and successfully cope with the tendency of the Hausas to overcrowding" (*Ibid*).

[3] "The Otublohu quarter consists of the progeny of a colony of Akwamu people from inland, who, on account of a quarrel with their own people, came and allied

A balcony view of a street in the Liberation Circle area of Adabraka.
(Photo: Deborah Pellow)

their present-day descendants claim Ga citizenship while also maintaining their identification as Tabon.[5] In addition to the

themselves with Accra and were given a place to live" (M.J. Field 1937: 88).

[4] "Stool" is analogous to throne, save that it is consecrated after the chief's death and becomes a shrine for his spirit. The Ga adopted this custom from the Asante.

[5] There does not seem to be a formal set of currently practiced traditions distinguishing the Tabon from other Ga; rather, there is an informal acknowledgement by each individual Tabon of his or her heritage. According to Mrs. Bossman, the Queenmother of the Tabon, they only get together "when there's necessity for it... whenever there is anything, or we wish to organize ourselves, to do something for somebody, or anything..." She maintains that they are so fused with the Ga that hardly a house in Accra exists where there is no one of Brazilian descent. "We don't have any custom, because if you're taken away hundreds of years ago...if you want to have custom, then you must look for Brazil. So we do the Ga custom." Ga functions are attended, often as a group.

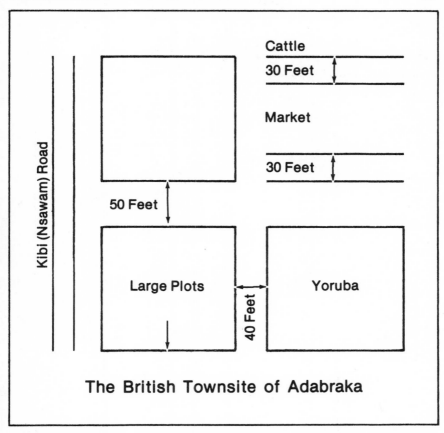

The British Townsite of Adabraka

Tabon, some Hausa also drifted into the vicinity of what would one day be Adabraka. These Hausa did not set up communities as such; rather, each man built his house, lived with his wife and children, and worked the small plot of land on which they lived. As the story goes, some of them would wander about with their hands out, saying "*adabaraka*," i.e. "give me a little something" (literally, "for the sake of blessedness"). They became known as the "Adabraka people" and in time the area took on the name as well. (This explanation of the name's origin, and much of the material that follows, is based on the recollections of Mr. Henan Annan, a retired "educationist" and longtime resident of Adabraka.)

Those for whom the area was intended—mainly Ga, Yoruba, and Hausa—were wary of committing themselves to live there. The Hausa, for example, felt that the plots were too small. When the British began to divide up the land, some civil servants built houses.

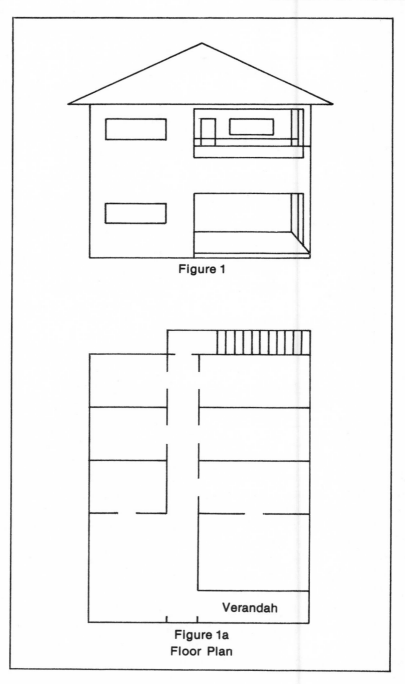

Figure 1

Verandah

Figure 1a
Floor Plan

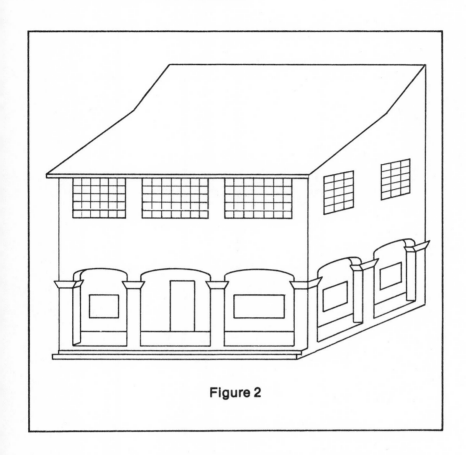

Figure 2

The government built a few sample dwellings, on which others were modelled: the one compound house (bedroom and hall plan, with enclosing verandah), and two small single houses (one bedroom, hall, kitchen, and bath; slanted roof). (*See* Figures 1—5, on pages 84-88, for floor plans and exterior views). Many of the houses in those days, however, were small tin-roofed structures of sun-dried bricks. In the 1930s architects came in with different blueprints, and well-constructed multi-story buildings were then introduced. The Colonial Administration banned the construction of wooden buildings, ostensibly for fear of fire. This ban held until the late 1950s, the early period of self-rule. Then wooden housing was erected next to the more substantial type.

Mr. Annan recalls the Adabraka of his childhood:-

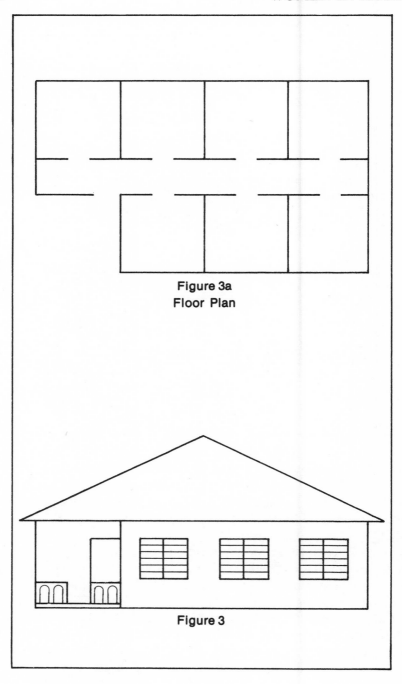

Figure 3a
Floor Plan

Figure 3

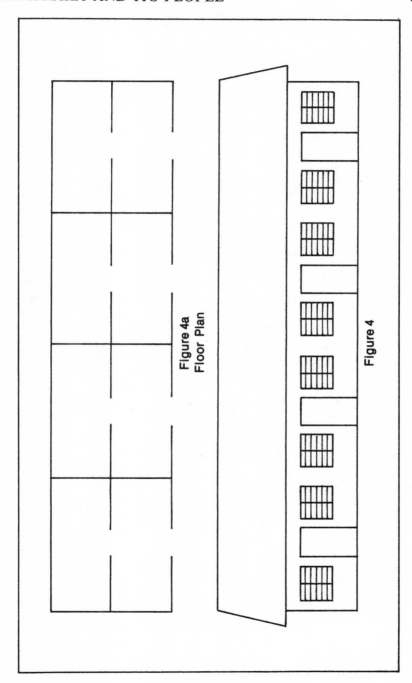

Figure 4a
Floor Plan

Figure 4

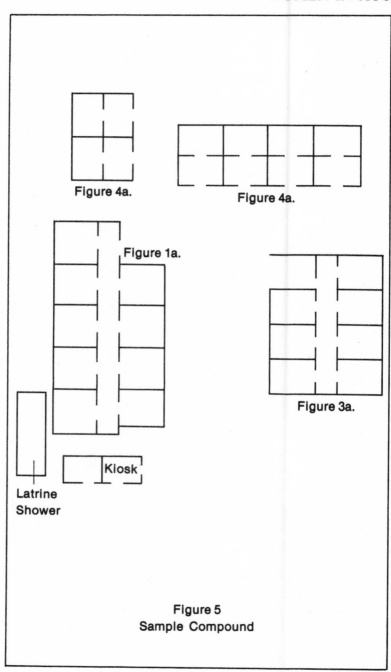

Figure 4a.

Figure 4a.

Figure 1a.

Figure 3a.

Kiosk

Latrine
Shower

Figure 5
Sample Compound

Round about 1914, 1916, there were wolves after 6 o'clock round about this side. I actually heard them when my grandmother was staying in one of the [previously-built] wooden structures here. At that time, I used to come on weekends to visit her. At 6 o'clock the doors shut and you heard the wolves.... Everybody is frightened. Gradually the road was repaired and people travelling on it to Nsawam, and the animals were frightened away. This was in '16 and '18. And during that time, water was scarce in Accra. And people came all the way down to this side of Adabraka, called Anetaibu. There they collected water.... And at 12 midday, you see that the whole place is damp. There are so many wells and people used to go there to collect water.... At that time there were not so many people living here. The whole of this side was bush. Then, people began to build and all of this gave way to modern houses and Adabraka began to look like as you see today.

As late as 1931, most of Adabraka was still bush. There were only two buildings along the main road: the police station, and the house (built in 1925) of a Mr. Bossman, a noted barrister whose widow is the Queenmother of Tabon. The Kibi Road had not yet been tarred; during the day maybe seven lorries would pass. The site, selected by the British planners for a market served, during the early 1920s, as a quarry for stones to make a breakwater at Jamestown Beach. In 1923, Korle Bu hospital was opened, and in 1925 Achimota College was founded. Korle Gonno, a townsite southwest of Adabraka, began to take shape. Bridging the lagoon, it housed some of the site workers.

It was through the efforts of A.K.W. ("Kojo") Thompson, while he was a member of the Legislative Council, that Adabraka Market was actually built, in 1926-27. Kojo Thompson argued that Salaga Market, in the old Ga area, was too distant.[6] Makola Market was somewhat closer; however, it was fairly new and not yet as popular, having been inaugurated in 1922. Yet the women of Adabraka refused at first to sell their wares at their new market, preferring to continue going to the main one at Salaga.

As time went by, Adabraka became a very mixed community. People who wanted to live a quiet life, for the most part civil servants, began to buy plots there. Later on, others came as well.

---

[6] This was perhaps a mile and a half to the southwest, in the heart of Jamestown.

A scene in Adabraka market.   *(Photo: Edward S. Ayensu)*

"For instance," remembers Mr. Annan, "my grandmother was advised for health reasons to live at Aburi [20 miles north on the Akwapim Ridge]. But because it was far, the doctor advised her to come to Adabraka because it was airy." Many Kwahu and Asante moved in because of trade. The Kibi (Nsawam) Road became paved. This made Accra easily accessible to residents of Nsawam and Kibi (25 and 80 miles north of Accra, respectively). During the early 1930s, there was only one shop (near Boundary Road, the other major north-south road running parallel to the Kibi Road); it was later to become the location of the United Africa Company.

Here is how Mr. Annan summarizes Adabraka's development during the past four decades:

Before, by 6 o'clock, you can't come from the central to Adabraka, because there were robbers on the way to take away all of your possessions and go away with it. But now, people walk up and down all through the night. It is only in recent years, from the 1930s when the city began to expand, has Adabraka been anything other than residential. It was with people flocking in that it became a commercial center. Before, it was impossible to do business here—you had to go to Accra. It was only getting to the '40s and '50s that you begin to see shops. When the roads to Nsawam and Kumase were paved, and also when congestion got too bad, people began to flock in. Quite a lot of shops, petty petty shops, were opened by the indigenous people themselves.

While Adabraka today bears little resemblance to the *zongo* planned 60 years ago, it continues to attract a diverse population because of its proximity to the business area of Accra and the availability within its environs of reasonable rental housing.

The People Who Live There

Although Accra is located within what was historically Ga territory, the migration process has significantly molded its demographic structure. Indeed, one of the striking features of southeastern Ghana is the movement of people around and through the cities (Michael McNulty 1966). An Adabraka compound contains diverse types of people; the same is true for a given street and the community as a whole.[7] My work was carried out in five sub-areas of the neighborhood (*see* Map of Adabraka, page 5, and Appendix I, pp.229-38): (1) Obuadaban Terrace, named after a house on Liberty Avenue (a major north-south thoroughfare in Accra). It is an area of untarred roads. (2) Liberation Circle, named after the circle a block north on Ring Road, commemorates the coup of February 24, 1966 which deposed President Kwame Nkrumah. The Circle area is always bustling with activity—the Orion Movie theatre is located there, as is the Lido Dance Hall, and numerous kiosks, shops, and spots for foodsellers. (3) Tuxedo Junction, named after a local bar, and (4) Adabraka Market, its namesake obvious, border each other, about five blocks south of the Circle area. Both of these sub-areas are far more congested than the others—they fall within the bounds of the original site plan and construction, whereas the first two are of more recent vintage. (5) Finally, Asylum Down, lying across Kojo Thompson Road, (the other major north-south thoroughfare), takes its name from the local mental hospital (the only one in Accra).

For a number of reasons, Asylum Down has a far lower

---

[7] This section's demographic profile is based on the responses to questions asked in a preliminary census of adult women living in houses systematically chosen in five sub-areas of Adabraka. See Pellow (1974) for tables and statistics.

residential population than do other sections of Adabraka. First, much of its housing was built to accommodate nuclear families; there are fewer occupants per dwelling than in the traditional-style houses (i.e. those with single rooms opening onto a long hall). Secondly, compounds in Asylum Down are better spaced. There are many vacant lots and the few blades of grass which survive among the abundance of rocks provide grazing fare for goats. This sub-neighborhood is somewhat off the beaten path, besides being newer than Adabraka proper; it is also distinctive in that it is one of the few inner-city neighborhoods considered acceptable to Europeans.[8] Although many of its roads are unpaved, much of its housing is quite new and Westernized in style.

Ruth Simms Hamilton (1966: 51) deals in part with Adabraka. She describes the neighborhood (which is more specifically Asylum Down) as:

> ... a good residential area. It is occupied by a number of Syrians, Lebanese, Indians and a smaller representation of Europeans and Americans. They live in the northern segment where most of the large modern homes are located.

While some of the houses I visited in Asylum Down did contain aliens,[9] I did not find Hamilton's description to be in complete agreement with current conditions, perhaps because of the departure of many aliens from Ghana as a result of the 1969 Aliens Compliance Order.[10]

While still a popular area, Adabraka is now predominantly African in character and population. The majority of Adabraka women were not born in Accra. They come from towns large and small, near and far, speaking a variety of local languages and

---

[8] This is not to say that Accra is segregated; in point of fact, it is not. Most Europeans who come to Accra are either with their country's foreign service or a business enterprise, and are usually provided suburban lodging by their employers. They are joined by Africans who are in a similar situation, or who have a good income. Indeed, moneyed Africans would not choose to live in the inner city, except as part of an established extended-family household, because of the prevailing materialistic ethos—big suburban house, flashy car, and so on.

[9] Since this piece of research is concerned with the roles and perceptions of Africans, non-Africans were not included.

"The residents of Adabraka have not yet made the total leap to urban ways." A kid stands beside a dismantled kiosk in this Adabraka street scene.   *(Photo: Deborah Pellow)*

---

steeped in different traditions. Many have maintained noticeable ties with farm life. Goat kids frequent the streets, particularly in unpaved areas, and cocks crow from scattered compounds where chickens are tended. Hamilton's figure for the proportion of migrants in Adabraka's population was 72 percent (1966), as compared with 57 percent for Accra as a whole. As noted above, the city's non-Ghanaian migrant population was probably greatly depleted in the early 1970s because of the Aliens Compliance Order.

---

[10] The Aliens Compliance Order of November 18, 1969, enacted to nationalize businesses and provide more occupational slots for Ghanaians (i.e. anyone whose mother was born in Ghana), resulted in the departure of more than a million persons—Africans (mainly Nigerians), Europeans, Lebanese, and Indians. See Nelson Addo (1970).

At any rate, migrants from within Ghana abound in Adabraka: the neighborhood includes not only Ga and Akan (Kwahu are heavily represented), but also a sizeable Ewe contingent and a variety of Northerners (e.g. Hausa, Dagomba, Dagbani, Buzanga), of whom the Hausa seem to predominate—in impact if not in numbers. When a given compound houses more than one ethnic group, clustering may be physical (with respect to room location) and/or social.

One migrant woman I came to know was Lizzie, 21, who had moved from her Kwahu hometown to Accra, a distance of 100 miles, when she completed commercial school. She came to Accra to work, and lived with her sister in a chamber/hall on Obuadaban Terrace. Their bungalow building and two adjacent buildings of the compound contain Kwahu only. That same year, her mother's second husband died; the older woman left the hometown and she, too, moved in with her elder daughter. Lizzie moved "upstairs" (to the main building), where mostly Ewe and a few Kwahu are housed. The landlady is a Nigerian who does not live at the compound. She apportioned the three sets of toilet and shower facilities according to ethnicity. While Lizzie lives upstairs and her mother, sister, niece, and nephew down, all of her social and domestic activities within the compound focus around the sister's room and the Kwahu residents.

A few doors from the Adabraka Market mosque is a Ga-owned house, where rooms are rented to Hausa and Mossi by a retired school teacher; according to information offered up gratuitously by a teenage neighborhood boy, she is rumored to be a witch. It is said that if anyone takes a mango from the tree in her garden, she will work her witchcraft on the guilty party. Consequently, none of the local residents will live there for fear of her strange ways. Those who do rent her rooms are not usually "urbane." They are either as yet uninformed about the local lore—perhaps because they speak no Ghanaian tongue—or have no choice.

There are no ethnic clusters embracing an entire street or sub-area. Many Hausa live around Adabraka Market, presumably because of the mosque and Koranic school, or vice versa; however, they hold no exclusive claim to this section. Directly opposite the mosque are three compounds. One is composed of Ewe, Hausa, and Buzanga; one is an Adangme family house with Akan, Ewe, and Ga as tenants; the third is a Ga family house, exclusively so. The

Hausa, together with a smattering of other Nigerians and other Northerners, are followers of Islam. This gives them a cohesiveness which no other ethnic group in Accra possesses. Most holidays and *rites de passage* bring them together, from all over the city.

Polylingualism among Ghanaians is common. It is not unusual for an "illiterate" to be fluent in three or four African languages. Thus most newcomers to Accra can make their way in transactions such as marketing. Those who stick to their own might be seeking nothing more than the comfort of interacting with others with whom they have a mother tongue in common. Often a woman's ethnicity is defined by her language—e.g. "She is a Twi," meaning a Twi-speaker (an Akan). Those whose language backgrounds do not include southern Ghanaian languages learn them—a task facilitated by living in mixed compounds.

In Adabraka, where different ethnics live side by side and among each other, objections to strangers[11] are not prominent at the daily small-group level of functioning. The neutrality of Adabraka is reinforced by the percolating effect of Western ways, including education and fluency in English. As one might expect, the younger women are better educated than the older. Similarly, while younger, better-schooled persons tend to be English-speakers, this is less true of older, uneducated ones. The mean level of education lies in the Middle School range. A goodly number go on to train in specialities, but very few pursue a university degree.

One might reasonably expect that there would be a homogenization of opportunities in the nontraditional areas of a developing country where nationalism is promoted over tribalism. This has not yet happened in Ghana. Certain ethnic groups simply will not touch certain occupations and may not have access to others. Night-soil collectors, for example, are assumed to be Northerners, and most night watchmen are from Mali and Upper

---

[11] Stereotypes concerning various ethnic groups abound; they are often at least implicitly pejorative. Kwahu are called the Jews of Ghana, because of their reputation as good businessmen; Ewe are feared and avoided for their supposed "bad magic" and thievery; Asante (who assert their absolute cultural superiority) are often referred to as warmongering and cruel; Krobo, who established themselves against great odds and whose chiefs still wear a dagger, are also considered cruel; Ga are criticized as allegedly dirty, worthless, and lacking in culture. And so on.

Volta, although they are slowly being replaced by Northern Ghanaians (notably Fra-Fra, easily recognizable by their featherlike facial scarification, and one of the most discriminated-against Ghanaian groups). Similarly, Asante do not engage in manual labor. These are common categorizations, articulated by the average citizen.

Women suffer a similar fate. Adabraka women work primarily in the traditionally female areas of trading and domestic crafts (*See* Appendix I, pp.229-38). Salaried employment in some of these areas—for instance, working as a seamstress in a department store factory—gives a modern twist to traditional work. Yet these women have done little branching out into new occupational areas. They do not earn much money, although the same is true for the majority of Ghanaians. According to the 1969-70 Ghanaian *Statistical Yearbook*, the average monthly income for all industries is N₵ 42.89.[12] An Adabraka trader might earn N₵20 to N₵30; a salaried woman, e.g. a clerk with Middle Form Four education, earns between N₵35 and N₵45. This is in a city where neighborhood chamber/hall accommodations run about N₵ 15 a month, and where it costs approximately N₵ 60 per annum to send a child to secondary school—more than most can afford.

Components of Neighborhood Life

All societies evolve a set of institutions which are congruent with the respective socio-cultural system. The institutions and behaviors promoted both gain credibility from tradition and work to support the new system. They provide models while incorporating the interactants. Within the traditional setting, there is a sense of cohesion and familiarity. Institutions—the weekly market, annual festivals, the political hierarchy—and kin-based behaviors tie the members together as part of an extended kinship network. Urban life is fundamentally different. It owes much of its appeal to the inherent anonymity and compartmentalization of people and activities that it entails. The local sense of belonging may not only be absent, but not even sought.

Adabraka is in the tradition of Gutkind and Southall's "urban village"—"more urbanized than the ordinary rural village, but still

---

[12] From November 1967 until late 1971 the Ghanaian new cedi was valued at US$0.98.

not strictly a 'town' (1957: 100). Personal repertoires of familiars are far more limited than in the hometown. The fragmentation is accompanied by the dream of mobility, the anonymity with the possibility of behavioral flexibility. The residents of Adabraka have not yet made the total leap to urban ways, but neither have they remained "country folk." Thus certain physical, institutional, and behavioral inconsistencies have emerged. Ties to respective hometowns are still strong. A woman born in a town within striking distance is not considered an Adabraka woman. She is of that other town, and her allegiance belongs there. The more accessible the town, the more often she will travel there, to the extent that she can juggle her schedule. In a sense, this splits her existence. More often than not, if it were not for such exigencies as employment or marriage which necessitated migrating, she would have stayed in her hometown; there she would continue to play an integral part in the institutional and behavioral network.

When one enters a traditional hometown for extensive transactions or with a desire to settle, it is customary to greet the chief formally; it is in his power to facilitate one's acceptance within the community. Adabraka has no comparable patron. An Accra-wide Hausa chief presides at festivities of that ethnic group, and adds further support to its cohesion, but other immigrant groups have no traditional figurehead. Technically, Adabraka falls within the jurisdiction of the *Gbese Mantse*. His territory, however, runs all the way up to Achimota, some 12 miles distant, and he does not have any sub-chiefs whose immediate responsibilities lie beyond the Gbese quarter.

In many West African urban areas, traditional structures have been replaced by voluntary associations that guide the newcomer in adjusting to town life. These religious, social, benevolent, or other groups may be traditional, modern, or a combination of the two (Little 1965). There are, however, no such associations circumscribed by Adabraka and exclusive to its residents.[13]

---

[13] The Hausa women have two Accra-wide benevolent associations. The larger of the two is *Zumunchi*, defined as "we all love ourselves and we will all make one and we will help ourselves," and referred to as "meeting." It was formed in 1968 when a group of women were at a *suna* (a ceremony similar to an outdooring held seven days after a baby's birth) and one suggested that they get together on a regular basis. They began meeting at Cow Lane (within the Hausa *zongo* in

The neighborhood contains several churches, including Presbyterian, Methodist, Anglican, Roman Catholic, Christian Scientist, and those of several revivalist sects. There are religious associations, such as the Presbyterian Women's Fellowship, affiliated with individual churches. Membership in these associations and these churches is city-wide; by the same token some neighborhood people worship elsewhere. Recently a Twi-speaking congregation of Presbyterians was established in central Accra, joining another already active in the outlying area of Kaneshie. Many Twi-speaking people from Adabraka attend, complaining that the service in the local church is too long: because more than half of the 700-person congregation consists of Ga, the service is conducted in English and Ga, while announcements are made in English, Ga, Twi, and Ewe. Two blocks north of the market are the earlier-mentioned mosque and Koranic school, frequented in the main by Hausa and other northerners.

Commercial activity thrives on several levels. Within an eight-block square area of Adabraka may be found, among other things: provision stores, drinking bars, chop bars, tailors and dressmakers, photography studios, carpentry shops, beauty salons, cleaners, petrol (gas) stations, plywood stores, radio/television/photography mechanics, car mechanics, and record kiosks. Most of the shopkeepers commute, however, and there is no association of neighborhood merchants. The streets also teem with women selling prepared foods, perhaps something as simple as roasted plantain with groundnuts on the side; or *kenkey*[14] with fish and pepper; or rice and stew. All manner of fried snacks are also sold, most

---

central Accra), each contributing sixpence weekly for chairs and a canopy. Most of their meetings are for births, and include much singing led by four vocalists. There are four leaders, chosen by the group, who have a male spokesman or "linguist." The *zumunchi* begins with Islamic songs and prayer, led by four *malams* (Muslim clerics). The mother of the child for whom the *suna* is being held provides food. Any problems, such as a member's illness, are discussed.

14 *Kenkey* is the typical Ga starch, which everyone in Accra, Ga or otherwise, eats regularly. It is made from fermented maize, which is ground, cooked, formed into balls, wrapped in dry corn leaves, and then boiled again. The resulting food has the consistency of heavy pastry dough, and is eaten in kneaded chunks with fried fish and pepper, or with stew.

An Adabraka record kiosk. *(Photo: Deborah Pellow)*

heavily flavored with pepper, some with ginger, and all fried in copra oil. One could eat an entire meal by stopping at several roadside coalpots or tables. Petty traders are also numerous. Small kiosks sell everything from needles and thread to Heinz's salad cream to nightly fresh bread with margarine; and itinerant tradesmen, such as watch repairmen, shoemakers, and upholstery repairers, set up work on the side of the road or under a tree. Some of these small businesses duplicate market items—on the chance that, for example, a woman might need two tomatoes for her stew after the market has closed for the day.

The majority of the neighborhood merchants (as opposed to traders or hawkers) are men—80, out of 139. For men and women alike, the ethnic groups predominating in trade are Kwahu, Ewe, Ga, and Fante. These numbers do not take into account the women who appear on street corners at odd times. If one does not run a business from within walls but merely sets up shop on a card table or next to a coalpot, hours tend to be flexible. Furthermore, some businesses, such as the trade of the local *kenkey* seller, are run from compound yards, and these are not visible from the street.

Small businesses and trading ventures may come and go, but Adabraka Market remains a fixed neighborhood institution. The market traders are almost all women, and their backgrounds reflect the ethnic diversity of the neighborhood. The market is centrally located within the neighborhood; it is one block square, ensconced behind stone walls. The street to the south is lined, on the market side, with women selling foodstuffs. The other side of the street is given over to small shops: Nat's Electric Shop, Namko Krandeng's Dressmaking Shop, Madame Christiana Brankua's Provision Shop (just barely meeting costs, because it was robbed and Madame Christiana could not afford to restock the store), Kotoka Tailor's Shop, Clinic of the Ghana Psychic Traditional Healing Association, two more provision shops, a bar, and a fish store (a cold store, as distinct from a provision shop).

The market is not paved, and during the rainy season it runs with water and mud. One half is arranged in north-south aisles, and the other in east-west aisles. Entrances are on the north and south sides. The only closed structure is near the north entrance—the meat section, operated mainly by Hausa or northern men. They are the only males working at the market, other than the charcoal sellers, whose stalls flank the meat section. On the other side of the meat sellers is a chop bar.

The women sit in covered stalls. Stalls are not as difficult to rent as in Accra's main market, but a woman generally does not relinquish her spot without good reason once she has set herself up. In the east-west division, they sell fruit, vegetables, smoked fish and shellfish, and petty goods. In the north-south stalls are found all of the starches—plantain, yam, rice, cassava, maize, etc.—and oil. Cloth sellers wander about; a few have stalls, although the main cloth market is opposite Makola in central Accra. There are a few seamstresses sewing, and other women selling various odds and ends, such as pots.

The market supplies all the fresh goods that a woman generally needs for meal preparation. Most families still do not own refrigerators, so women go to market daily—but not necessarily to the one at Adabraka. Just as women resisted selling at Adabraka Market when it was first opened, so now women hesitate to shop there. The market as an institution is as popular as ever; the market transaction is so engrained in the minds of the women that, even though they can go to U.T.C. (the United Trading Company) or G.N.T.C. (the Ghana National Trading Company) department stores, and pay less than street prices for certain items, they prefer the market. But many women who have the time prefer going to Makola, Salaga, or even Lagostown, rather than Adabraka. They complain that Adabraka is too dear, and the selection of goods (as in any local branch) somewhat limited. Even when a woman does go regularly, she does not necessarily patronize the same seller of a given commodity. Instead she trades with whomever has the best product at the most reasonable price on a given day: fearing that the day would come when the trader she patronized exclusively would have poor produce, outrageous prices, or nothing at all, and that others would then refuse to sell to her.

What about neighborhood public services ? An adequate description of Adabraka, Accra, and all of British West Africa must include the sanitation system. To the east of the market and alongside it sit the public toilets, a visual and olfactory disgrace. Every street is lined on either side with an open drain. These drains play an important part in daily life, substituting for facilities lacking in many compounds and public spaces. Men and children use the gutters to relieve themselves. Children bathe, or are bathed, alongside the gutter in front of their compound wall. In the early morning or late afternoon hours, it is common to see a frothy body or two, with a bucket of water in tow.

The gutter also serves as a garbage disposal. People walk along the road from food-seller to food-seller, stopping at one or several, and deposit their accumulated litter in the gutter. After cooking a

Children bathe, or are bathed, alongside the gutter which
runs in front of the compound wall.   *(Photo: Deborah Pellow)*

meal and cleaning the utensils, women toss the dirty water and
scraps over the compound wall and into the gutter. During the rainy
season, children may float home-made toys in the running water.
And, in a moment of boredom, a treasure hunt in the gutters may
turn up items of interest.

The community's sanitation problem is intensified by the general lack of flush-toilet facilities in homes. Most of the compounds in Adabraka still have latrines, and if there is any lapse in the pick-up schedule of the night-soil collectors, the air becomes heavy. Before the Aliens Compliance Order, the night-soil collectors were Liberians. Given the distasteful nature of their job, the old regime kept them well-paid and properly equipped. The job has now been taken over by Northerners, who walk through the streets every few nights in khaki shorts, barefooted, with tall buckets on their heads. They are employed by the city and live predominantly in the district of Nima, known for its hideous living conditions, and for rampant disease. Remuneration is no longer adequate to compensate for the nature of their job. One week these sanitation workers went on strike. With no one to work their job, the latrine situation in large compounds became unbearable. One young neighborhood boy went to relieve himself near the lagoon. Caught with his pants down, his mother was fined N₵ 20.

Many houses (compounds) do not have a water pipe in the yard. A common neighborhood sight is the self-employed, barefoot, khaki-clad Northerner, struggling along under the weight of two water buckets hanging from a pole across his shoulders. He wanders through the streets, selling water that he has drawn from public taps. Frugal women who do not have a spigot at home carry their own water, either from the public tap or from a neighbor's yard. The taps, like the gutters, are popular centers for children's water play.

Adabraka is never free of odors. In addition to those of the gutters and latrines, there is the smell arising from the heavy pepper content of food cooking. Moreover, the steaming radiators and burning oil of the lorries add another layer to the odors. The major form of public transport, the lorries are known as "trotros," since they used to cost thruppence ("tro") to ride. The traffic congestion is indicated by the fact that, at the time of my residence there, three of Accra's six or seven traffic lights were in Adabraka.

As for recreation, the Roxy Cinema, purveyor of popular Indian and "spaghetti Western"[15] films, also hosts live concerts by popular African groups. Dan's Milk Bar, Ghana's only ice cream parlor, was built on the main road in 1970, and has become a

---

[15] Westerns made in Italy on a low budget.

A variety of small businesses are to be found in Adabraka.
Here women are seen handling a load of pineapples.

(Photo: Edward S. Ayensu)

---

gathering place for the younger set. The most important social
centers, however, are the bars where locals gather to drink and
exchange gossip.

In the north section of Adabraka and around Liberation Circle
are a number of good African craft shops, two French restaurants
run by Lebanese and frequented in the main by non-Africans, and
one of the three movie theaters patronized by the expatriate
population. Further south, still in Adabraka, there are "boutiques"
carrying European apparel.

In describing Adabraka's physical and social character in such
detail, I do not mean to suggest that it is not also an integral part of
Accra. There are no particular features of the community's
institutional structure to set it apart as a distinct entity—no local
political system, either traditional or modern, no self-sufficient
market or business system, no genuinely localized voluntary and
religious organizations, no striking physical features such as the
style of houses. If this neighborhood has a common denominator, it
lies in the very diversity of its inhabitants.

The Urban Compound

When people come into the city, they must find a place to live, one which does not involve long-term commitments. In contrast to the traditional way of life, the city situation is a transient one; great investment need not be put either into one's living space or into the people with whom one interacts. Not only might a woman find herself in a new home, away from her family, in a strange city, but she is also in a living situation over which she has very little control. She lives wherever she can find a room.[16] She must alter her behavior to cope with distance, in both physical and social terms.

She may narrow down her choice to a particular section, such as Adabraka, because of convenience, ease of transport connections, friends, etc. The rental of rooms is carried out through informal networks—someone hears of something, or someone in a compound moves out and a friend of someone else is told and moves in. Or a new arrival may merely walk up and down the street, knocking on doors and inquiring after vacancies.

In the Enumerator's *Manual of the Ghana 1960 Population Census*,[17] a house or compound is defined as:

> ... a self-contained building unit. It is a structurally separate and independent place of abode. The essential features are separateness and independence. An enclosure may be considered separate if it is surrounded by walls, fences, etc., so that a person or a group of persons can isolate themselves from other persons in the community for the purpose of sleeping, preparing and taking their meals or protecting themselves from the hazards of climate such as storms and the sun (Quoted in Caldwell 1967: 63).

There are houses in Adabraka that were built primarily for the

---

[16] If a family is present, the question of extra room simply does not arise. There is always room, even if there is not. Mr. Ofori, the husband of one of my informants, complained bitterly to me. His pregnant wife, their two children, and he, occupied one small room. His wife's cousin, somewhat removed, arrived without warning or money and moved in without shame. She did provide minor household assistance.

[17] Streets have names throughout the urban area, and house addresses are reassigned at each census. Adabraka residents, however, do not heed street names and most do not even know the number of the house they occupy.

immediate family, but most have come to incorporate strangers as well. Thus, housing can be characterized as predominantly rented compound rooms. The establishment of Mercy Foulkes-Crabbe,[18] one of Adabraka's picturesque and esteemed inhabitants, is a case in point. Mrs. Foulkes-Crabbe's house is a large and gracious British colonial-style structure, sitting one block south of Adabraka Market. The compound originally housed this building only, but Mrs. Foulkes-Crabbe had two more buildings constructed after she retired from her job at Cape Coast. All of the tenants in the new rental buldings are strangers to her. Her compound is typical in its heterogeneity of residents.

The greater the number of rooms a household can afford, the smaller the number of people sharing each room. My survey (*see* Appendix I) yielded the following results on the average number of people per room in different types of housing: 3.4 for single-room arrangements, 3.3 for 1.5 rooms, 2.4 for 2 rooms, 2.3 for 3 rooms, 1.7 for 4 rooms, and 1.6 for 6-room accommodations.

John C. Caldwell notes that:-

> Many more Ghanaians now live in large town houses containing a considerable number of rooms. In one sense, this has represented a surprisingly successful attempt to carry a village way of life to the town. Living, in a town like Accra, with a population over a third of a million, has in many cases not meant leaving the communal life of the village for residence in small lonely quarters in the town. This is especially true of richer families with interests in cocoa or other lucrative fields rather than of poorer immigrants from further afield (1967: 67).

The large town houses have indeed perpetuated the appearance of a communal life, and Caldwell's point certainly holds true in the

---

[18] Mrs. Foulkes-Crabbe has been a force in educational reform and Accra-wide community affairs. In 1966, at the age of 70, she founded the Women's Society for Public Affairs, the purpose of which is to promote the cause of women in all sectors of public life. The members of the Society include such prominent women as Dr. Susan de-Graft Johnson, Supreme Court Justice Annie Jiagge, and Regina Addae, owner and operator of a public relations agency. These are the fortunate few, the ones who are usually interviewed for newspaper and magazine articles about the emancipated West African woman.

A lorry, or truck—known colloquially as a *tro-tro*, since they used to cost thruppence (*tro*) to ride—stops to pick up passengers. *(Photo: Edward S. Ayensu)*

sense that individual rooms or sections of houses occupied by families; but my sample does not indicate that entire families often occupy such houses.[19]

Compounds differ in terms of size; the number, style, and age of buildings contained; the floor of the yard (concrete versus dirt and stones); the color of the houses; the location of the laundry lines; the presence of shrubbery and trees; the type of physical closure (a wall in front versus a small kiosk); the occupational paraphernalia (a *kenkey* seller's soaking maize and large iron pot, or the baker's igloo-like clay oven); and, of course, the occupants and their idiosyncrasies.

[19] The different nature of Caldwell's discipline, perspective, and methodology accounts for the differences in our results. A demographer is interested in population trends; I am interested in the grassroots reality that is revealed only by closer scrutiny. While his work shows few extremes, which become lost in large-population averages, mine runs the risk of small-sample bias. There are gains and losses on both sides; to my mind, anthropology has the advantage.

Most compounds contain more than one building. The main building, generally well-constructed, is often multi-storied, and always has electricity. The auxiliary structures are not necessarily electrified, and are often tin-roofed. Houses are usually brilliant shades of green, blue, yellow, or pink. Rooms are drab shades of the same. White walls are rare, both inside and out. In a building with several storys, an individual usually has only a small chamber; indeed, an entire family might share one chamber. Each of these opens onto a long hall, which connects with the yard or a stairway to the yard. In the long, narrow bungalows, each chamber is entered through a short hall, or antechamber, which has a door into the yard. In both arrangements, residents can go outside the yard without passing through the rooms of other occupants. Those living in bungalow-style family houses consider their living quarters to be the room within which they sleep and keep their possessions. (*See* Figures 1—5 on pages 84—88).

The fact that a woman lives in one room with three children and her husband, in a fly-infested compound with graffiti on every available wall, need not imply poverty. One's station in life—real or hoped for—can be displayed through appropriate symbols. In England, as George Orwell reminds us in *Keep the Aspidistra Flying* (1936), identification with the middle class was publicized by keeping an aspidistra in the window. In Adabraka, the key indicator of bourgeois aspirations is the vase of artificial flowers; almost as significant is the photograph album, readily accessible in the event of a visit. Wall spaces in Christian homes exhibit calendars or a classic portrait of Jesus Christ ("Christ is the unseen visitor in this house, the welcome guest at every meal").

The more Westernized and moneyed the occupants of a dwelling, the greater is the variety of electric/electronic equipment in display—radio, record player, refrigerator. These are invariably the possessions of the husband (in the case of married couples), as are the hard furnishings. The women own their clothing, cooking utensils, work paraphernalia (such as a sewing machine), and their "boxes,"[20] which are piled up in a corner of the room, a pressed starch cloth between each. A couple with many household possessions may well be living in single-room accommodations,

---

[20] These are wooden boxes, which the traders use at the market for storing their merchandise. At home, women keep their worldly possessions therein.

quite possibly adjacent to a couple with nothing more than the barest minimum of furnishing, i.e. something to sit on, a bed, and a wardrobe.

Money is not the only factor here. Ethnicity,[21] even among long-time urban dwellers, also dictates décor. It is traditional among Hausa for a mother to give a daughter upwards of 50 porcelain tureens when she marries. These are piled atop a wardrobe. While they are a form of ready cash, they are sold only *in extremis.*[22]

A compound yard serves any number of functions. It is a general socializing space, enclosed by the buildings and/or a wall. If a woman selling prepared food lives in a given compound, the yard almost certainly serves as her kitchen and very often as her take-out shop as well. Every block or two, for example, there is at least one *kenkey* seller. Most of them do not bother to go out into the street to sell—their residence is known and patrons come there.

Indoor living space is invariably small and crowded; even in the chamber/hall arrangement, the sitting area (the hall) is only about four feet by ten feet. Inside it is hot and crowded; outside, it is airy and roomy. Thus, most people are impelled to spend a good deal of their free time outdoors.

It is rare for residents to do much visiting in each other's rooms, unless kin live there, or it is a family house; private corners in the yard are easily found. Since the day begins early and ends early, it is not uncommon to have a visitor at seven o'clock in the morning; it is less common much past nine o'clock at night. Some, but not all, compounds have an outside light. The sun begins to set a bit past six o'clock, with very little seasonal variation, and within ten minutes it is dark. Smoldering coals used in cooking give off enough light for

---

[21] M.J. Field (1940) has noted that Ga compounds are ugly and that there is no material cultural baggage. Their fishing boats, in contradistinction to those of the Fante, are not painted. A sophisticated man might cram European junk, such as Victorian vases, into a spare room. He might put out money for a "fine" compound for himself, but certainly not for his wife or women kin. And the women never do so for themselves.

[22] This is also true for other Northerners and may have originated in Islamic custom. In Ibadan, the Hausa women are heavily cloistered (in *purdah*), and must conduct their business in trade from behind compound walls; this they do with the help of young children—their own or those of others. Earnings are converted into porcelain pots, which are piled in the house (Abner Cohen 1969).

outside eating and chatter.

The yard also serves as a playground for the children, though they are perfectly at home wandering in and out of everyone's rooms. There are no barriers to their incursions: because of the heat, shutters and doors are left open (with a curtain hanging) as late as possible, and then closed only out of fear of thieves. As Mr. Annan puts it:

> In the olden days, say in the central area there, my grandfather had built a house. Say about four or five rooms. He gave each of his children a room. They would marry and have children, and if they liked they would build an extension to the house. And stay there, because in the good old days, they would say—"What, you going to stay outside ? At night when the thief comes in, and you shout, who will hear you ? Who will come to your aid ? So build near us." That is the reason for the slums in Accra—and in the whole country. For fear of thieves or anything that can break out during the night...

There are those who will not travel, because they are afraid of thieves breaking in. Although it would be in the interest of everyone in the compound to go after a thief, people do not feel that they owe their first loyalties to their compound-mates. Neighbors look out for each other only to the degree that a very ritualized etiquette demands.

Compound apartments do not include kitchen and toilet/bath facilities. The compound yard is "everywoman's" kitchen, though each occupies her respective spot. Some compounds have either a lean-to or a proper building subdivided into a few rooms, each of which functions as a kitchen and is usually shared. These are generally used for storing utensils, since very few women cook indoors because of the heat. The stove is a small coalpot—a wrought-iron container, similar to a hibachi, which is stoked with coal; the cooking receptacle is then placed on the red-hot coals. Rarely far away is a large wooden mortar and pestle used for pounding *fufu*,[23] as well as another for pounding palm nuts to prepare palm nut soup.

When one has to go to the toilet or bathe, she must cross the compound yard. There is a separate latrine and shower room—more than one of each in larger compounds. Bathing is done out of a bucket. The shower room has a hole in one of the corners for the water to drain; this also serves for urination. Despite the preparations required for bathing, Ghanaians are fastidious about personal cleanliness and most bathe twice a day. When there is a water pipe in the yard, it is generally to one side of the compound. This promotes further outside interaction.

With so many of the house's facilities centralized for all to share, visual involvement, at least, is great. Living here is with people, and privacy is a very relative thing. Under these circumstances it seems judicious to consider loud radio as a barrier, since it muffles sounds as well as entertains. No compound is without at least a G.B.C. (Ghana Broadcasting Corporation) box radio. This is wired to receive one station only and goes on automatically when programming begins.

In summary, Adabraka functions as an address of sorts, but not the primary source of identity, for the women with whom we are concerned in this book. It is a physical location with a name but no institutional structure of its own. Although there are longtime residents, the area conveys a sense of being a stopping-off point for new arrivals. Some folks pass on to other places, some settle in the neighborhood, but all learn in the compounds a new set of behaviors that socialize them into the urban system.

---

23 *Fufu* is the characteristic Akan starch, which is eaten daily, in hometown areas at least, with the main meal. It is made by boiling plantain and cassava, or cocoyam (a root crop, related to yam) and cassava, or plain yam; when soft, the substance is put into a mortar and pounded, while small amounts of water are added, until the texture is that of soft putty or pastry dough. The mixture is formed into loaves or balls and has the appearance of unbaked bread. *Fufu* is eaten by breaking off small pieces with two fingers and dipping it into soup.

Modern Constraints in Access to Options

In Westernizing societies, education, occupational options, and income are the tools associated with mobility and changes in status. This chapter is concerned with the access of Adabraka's "everywoman" to those tools—the extent to which she is removed from traditional lifeways such that she may develop new social identities and identity relationships. Unless otherwise noted, all of the data in this and the following chapters derive from interviews with the sample women.

Education

The period from 1952 to 1966 was one of great educational expansion in Ghana, due to the establishment of new institutions and the absorption of private schools into the public system (George 1976). In 1961, the Nkrumah government initiated fee-free compulsory education, regardless of sex, for primary and middle school levels. Primary school normally begins at age six and lasts for six years. Middle school continues for another four years. Those students who succeed in a national examination at the end of primary school may go on directly to secondary school for the Fifth Form and if successful in a further examination at the end of five

112

Kenkey-seller (right) and friend   *(Photo: Deborah Pellow)*

years of study, to the more specialized Sixth Form.

In the 20 years following 1951, the number of educational institutions in the country increased, with the notable exception of primary schools.

Table 1*

Number of educational institutions:
School years 1951, 1965-66, 1971-72

Year	Primary	Middle	General Secondary	Commercial	Training	Teacher Training	University
1951	1,083	539	13		5	20	1
1965-66	8,144	2,777	105		11	84	3
1971-72	6,715	3,608	139	9	15	71	3

* *Source: George (1976: 202)*

Table 2[*]
Enrollment in educational institutions: 1968-69

| | Ghana | | Accra† | |
Level	Boys	Girls	Boys	Girls
Primary	564,266	451,191	36,704	37,975
	56%	44%	49%	51%
Middle	241,318	140,251	15,882	13,831
	63%	37%	53%	47%
Secondary				
Forms 1—5	32,286	11,620	6,870	2,634
	74%	26%	72%	28%
6th Form	2,186	420	349	30
	84%	16%	92%	8%
University				
Univ. of Ghana	2,092	353		
	86%	14%		
Univ. of Science				
and Technology	1,466	83		
	95%	5%		
Univ. College				
of Cape Coast	931	110		
	89%	11%		

[*]Source: Ghana Ministry of Education 1971: Tables 7, 16, 25, and 39.

† The enumeration district for secondary schools is Greater Accra, which includes the Ga Local Council area, the Shai Local Council area, Accra-Tema (Accra District), Accra-Tema (Tema District), and Dangbe. One must keep in mind that recruitment to secondary schools is national and that Accra area schools may have students from other regions, while Accra youngsters may be attending Central, Western, etc., secondary schools.

In 1965-66, primary enrollments peaked at 1,137,000; after the coup in 1966 they declined significantly to 948,000 in 1970-71, rising slightly to 960,000 the following year. One deterrent to primary school enrollment was the merging of facilities to eliminate duplication, thereby making it more difficult for some children to attend. Another deterrent was the introduction of textbook fees by the new government.

According to the 1970 Population Census (Vol.II, xxiv), the decade of the 1960s saw a decline in the percentage of girls six years of age and over who had never attended school—from 83 to 66. For the 6—14 year age group alone, the enrollment of girls increased from 33.3 to 58.4 percent. In the Accra district, the male-female ratio for compulsory schooling stood at 84.3 to 70.2 percent.

While the general expansion in educational facilities has increased the attendance of girls, there continue to be marked differences between the rates of boys and girls, and these become greater at each succeeding level. (*See* Table 2, page 114.) So we see that in the Accra primary schools, girls slightly outnumber boys. But by the Fifth Form, both in Accra and the country at large, the girls are outnumbered almost 3 to 1 and by the Sixth Form the imbalance increases to 5 to 1 (in Accra to a high 11 to 1). Women are disadvantaged at the secondary school level due to the expense (especially at boarding institutions) and the limited number of places reserved for them. Even the "co-educational" facilities are overwhelmingly populated by boys. While university education is subsidized by the Government (all students attend on scholarship), admissions are at a premium and entrance is highly competitive.

> Because their schooling is likely to be of inferior quality, the women who do have a chance to attend secondary school are also not as well prepared for the examinations and for university work. Since the era of educational expansion is drawing to a close, it does not seem likely that many more facilities will be provided for women (Smock 1977: 199).

Thus in this system which consists of a broad base of elementary education, a selective secondary structure and an even narrower apex of higher learning, women are still within the lower levels of the pyramid.

The continuing imbalance in education for men and women is due to two earlier-mentioned factors: the imported British structure and the persistence of indigenous attitudes. The perception remains strong that a greater risk is taken in educating females than in educating males. Despite the elimination of matriculation fees for primary and middle school, textbooks and uniforms must be purchased, and of course secondary school costs are high. What if the young woman begins secondary school and then quits because of failure or pregnancy, or graduates and cannot find work appropriate to her training ? Her family will have wasted funds that could have been put to good use. A compromise solution to training girls for urban work is to send them to vocational school. During the decade of the 1960s, the Government and private sector focused more attention on vocational training. All Government vocational training schools and centers have been co-educational. "Although the majority of those taking advantage of the facilities offered are males, a growing number of females have been attracted and have shown preference for certain courses" (Greenstreet 1971: 127). While providing an education, vocational school differs from secondary school in its goals and the status it carries. In commercial school, for example, one learns those skills requisite to competent clerical work. Secondary school offers an academic course of study only. Vocational school is less prestigious, but it is also less costly and more appropriate to occupational possibilities than is secondary school.[1] Thus, when a Ghanaian woman (unlike the middle class Victorian lady) is educated, she is expected to do something with her education. The cultural assumption that she will not finish, or that she will not be able to get a job anyway, then becomes a rationale for *not* educating her. It is not surprising that urban families with superior educational and occupational backgrounds have been more likely to take a positive position toward secondary and university education for female offspring than have those less privileged and less worldly.[2]

In studying the women of Adabraka, I was particularly interested in exploring with them the value that they placed on schooling,[3] the

---

[1] Smock (1977) notes that employment such as clerking, typing, dressmaking and baking, for which women gain vocational training, is not expanding rapidly enough to absorb job applicants.

[2] A striking finding of Foster's study (1965), however, is that children with rural backgrounds and low levels of parental occupation and education are well-represented in élite secondary schools.

[3] Some confusion arose because I neglected to define my term "school." To my informants, this term always had a Western connotation, with the limits set by

extent to which their parents had helped or hindered the education of each, and the correlation between the educational situation of the women in my sample and that of their parents.[4]

Levels of education among the women with whom I worked run the gamut. Few of the mothers and most of the fathers of 38 of the women considered here had received some formal education (mostly middle school). Most of the respondents, on the other hand, had at a minimum completed much of the middle school course of study—at least enough to be able to read, write, and speak English. The middle school curriculum is designed to give students the basics of formal education. This will be the end of academic exposure for the large percentage of middle schoolers who turn at this point to some kind of on-the-job training program (apprenticeship) or commercial trade school, as well as those who drop out because of pregnancy, inability to pay the fees, or lack of motivation. The "new" women in my sample who had attended secondary school came from mixed educational backgrounds; in each case, their siblings had been accorded the same educational opportunities extended to them. While it seemed to me that nonacademic training in a specific skill is viewed by Ghanaian men as restrictive, all of the women who had been training in a trade, such as sewing, spoke in positive terms of the importance of having a skill that enabled them "at least" to earn a living.

Fifteen out of the total 39 interviewed were functionally illiterate (had experienced little or no schooling); their ages ranged from 23 to 64. All of the illiterates had illiterate mothers and, with two exceptions, had been prevented by parents from going to school. "My parents were ignorant about school"; or, "at that time, you didn't send girls"; and, "because we were many and my parents couldn't afford to send us all, so they sent the men to school and not the women." Their parents had not been consistent in their

---

the individual's ken. Thus to an illiterate it may connote Middle Form Four; to a middle school graduate, it can mean Secondary Form Five or possibly even university. For example, Adisa, one of my informants, doggedly insisted that she had never been to school. In fact, she had been to Koranic school (she is Muslim), leaving at age 14 to marry.

[4] Here foster parents or nonparental guardians stand in for biological parents when appropriate.

actions with regard to their other children. Such behavior often
seemed to be a function of the era in which the crucial choices were
made. In one case, the woman was among the older children in her
family, and those following her had opportunities not available to
her because times had changed or because they did not have heavy
household responsibilities.

Decisions about education may also be a function of ethnicity.
One example is provided by the Akan, a matrilineal people whose
customs stipulate that a father's responsibilities (including those of
providing appropriate education) are to his sister's children rather
than to his own. (Oppong's research [1974] suggests, however, that
the conjugal unit among élite Akan is increasingly modelled after
the Euro-American pattern, and that the man who maintains his
traditional obligations to school his kin at the expense of his own
children encourages tension in his household). Another case in
point is provided by Adisa, a Muslim of Adabraka, who explained
why Muslims have reservations about sending their daughters to
European-style schools: "Only they should read the Koran. It is not
good, they say, to go to school, because a woman mustn't work. If
you marry a Muslim, he'll insist that you stop work. You may only
sell near your house."

What were the less educated girls expected to do rather than
attend school ? In general, they were to be prepared for adult
responsibilities that would be carried out within the confines of the
house. Auntie Rose, for instance, had to stay at home because her
mother needed her to help care for the other children.

Although the number of informants with whom I worked
represented only a small segment of the population of Adabraka,
there could be little doubt that their stories were typical of the
community in the sense that gender rather than financial limitation
per se was more often the decisive factor in determining who was to
be educated. Four of my informants said that they would have gone
to school except for the fact that there was no one to pay; in each
case, further questioning established that the needs of a male
sibling were accomodated at the woman's expense.

Call it fatalism, call it an absence of conceptualized
alternatives—in either case, most of the women with little or no
education shrug their shoulders. At the time they were growing up,
girls did not go to school, so... Or, there was not any money,
therefore what could she do ? These women seem to harbor no deep

bitterness or feelings of denial. In most cases, they are not concerned about the inconsistencies between their lot and that of their brothers. Here again they accept the culturally prescribed roles that dictate what a man *can* do and a woman *cannot*. Jeanette, for example, is 39 and illiterate. She is the last-born of a family that included six girls and three boys, of whom only two of the girls were sent to school. She says that she does not know why her father (an Adangme, thus responsible for his own children) allowed these two and not her brothers or herself to attend. Her father's sister's daughter also went to primary school and even passed on her uniform to one of Jeanette's sisters; still, Jeanette's father said no. She discussed this with my interpreter and the latter said that when the two of them sit down and think about it they "could feel to cry—school is good." Yet it was clear that Jeanette had never given much thought to her educational possibilities, at least not once she had lost the chance for schooling as a child. Questioning her (and most of the others) was difficult for that very reason: it was as though choice about education were a conceptual category devoid of meaning.

The women still go along with the idea that males deserve preferential treatment in the area of education, although their acceptance is qualified. For example, financial obligations to kin are still felt, and a woman would help a younger brother who needed money to attend school, but not at the expense of her own daughter. Georgina, a literate girl of 19, phrased the general sentiment this way: "I will send my brother because he is a boy," but if money were tight, he would have to wait until Georgina's daughter had finished.

The situation is far less clear-cut when a choice must be made between one's own boy- and girl-children. Most of the women believe that only the boys should be sent to school, or at least that they should have more education than the girls.[5] Some of them reason as follows:

Send the boys, because when grown up and you don't give them good

---

[5] Of the 17 who expressed inegalitarian views about the education of their own children, 10 are illiterate; these illiterates are mostly from 20 to 40 years old and, like the literates in this opinion group, comprise Ga, Adangme, and Akan (with one Northerner).

education, they will be roaming about. They will be useless. And if
you don't take good care of them, they will turn to thieves... As for
girls, their work is not very hard as the boys. Even they can sell or
learn some handiwork.

(Nineteen-year-old Dora, Fante/Krobo, literate)

Girls can do anything at all. Even when not going to school. But when
a boy is not going to school, it's not good... He won't get any work in
future to do very well... But a girl she can sell, do anything. But
nowadays in Ghana, everybody wants to go for education. Boys don't
want to sell. [Do boys sell ?] Yes, they can sell in bar and canteens,
which is all right. (Do you have to go to school as a boy to sell ?) No.
But girls, even when hasn't gone to school can sell.

(Twenty-one-year-old Faith, Ga, literate)

An oft-heard variation on this theme is the assertion that men have
a family to support whereas women just marry and are taken care of
by their husbands.

Possible pregnancy is offered up as another reason for stinting on
girls' education. The risk of an unplanned pregnancy is real and of
greater consequence in the city than in the traditional setting where
girls married early and were domestically oriented. Since school is
coeducational at least through middle school, contact between
young boys and girls is extensive and so the worst must be
anticipated as a possibility. This was on the mind of an informant
who planned to send her boys to secondary school and then to
London for university training:

We shall go to London and learn something. In London, when you
are going to learn something, you can learn it very well, but here, the
girls and the women worry my mind, that's why I want my son to go
to London. Don't want to send my daughter, because you spend your
time on her sending her to school, and then she gets pregnant.

A similarly harsh judgement of girls was voiced by a prosperous
Adabraka baker whose business is maintained by a number of
young apprentices. She used to bring girls in from her hometown
areas to live with her and learn the business. But, she said, girls are
worrisome and skittish. One went home to stay with her mother
after six months of training in Accra; two others who had been

there for a year and a half soon followed suit. In their place she brought in three Northern boys who proved to be much better. Once girls reach a marriageable age, she said, they become unpredictable. They may leave without giving sufficient notice. Boys are less troublesome and work harder.

My interviews indicate, however, that an increasing proportion of women believe that *all* of their children should be encouraged to attend school irrespective of their sex.[6] Any qualification made relates to the child, boy or girl, having the brains and the desire of continue. For, as more than one said, there is no way of knowing in advance whether a boy will do better academically than a girl or vice versa. As Auntie Viv puts it:

> Both of them will have the same, provided they can study. If not, find something one can do. Formerly, we thought that the woman's place is in the kitchen—that they need no more education. In fact, a woman can do more than a man: she can cook, study as hard, she can be motherly, with love for children. She cooks and feels at home—not so with men.

This last sentiment is still the exception rather than the rule, of course, given the relatively low level of sophistication prevalent among these women; indeed, it is not even shared by all of the women who have had a higher education.

Thus it was not surprising to learn that all of the children of primary and middle school age of members of my sample are currently enrolled, and that all of their offspring who are now older had at least been accorded the opportunity for compulsory schooling. For example, Auntie Rose (an illiterate Ga) has tried to send all of her children through Middle Form Four; her eldest boy, now 25, left midway, at which point his uncle took him off to another school in Kumase, and her first daughter failed before finishing. The older children (now in their twenties and more) of the few women with secondary school training had at least started secondary school.

---

[6] This group includes only two illiterates—one older, one younger— and a variety of ethnic groups—Ga, Adangme, Akan, Ewe, Northerners. Only five of the women are over 30.

Occupation[7]

The decision on whether to attend school is simply not in the hands of children; they are too young, or inexperienced, to know what is best. Granting that employability varies according to the type and extent of education that the individual has received, what sort of power does the woman (no longer a child) have in choosing her occupation ?[8]

Women have always worked; there is a cultural expectation that they do so. Thus, according to the 1970 Population Census, 61.1 percent of women throughout the country were employed, and only 2.4 percent were unemployed. And in the Greater Accra regiom, 56.6 percent were employed, with 5.4 percent unemployed.[9] Following the "natural order of things," women's economic pursuits tend to be restricted to occupations with the label "female" attached: occupational choice being severely limited by the attitudes of Ghanaian society (including the women themselves) which define women as domestic beings:

> Most Ghanaian women think their main vocation is marriage and child-rearing, though they may continue to work. Tension between the traditional idea that a woman's place is in the home and the new idea that a woman should have the right to a career and personal fulfillment does not appear to have arisen for the higher income earners who can financially afford to allow both partners a greater degree of freedom. In the lower income brackets, the primary object of a working woman is to supplement the meager family income. Though the men find the additional income a boon, they still expect their wives to manage the home (Greenstreet 1972: 353).

Consequently, it is taken for granted that women will usually undertake only those pursuits that do not conflict with domestic work. A notable example of such a pursuit is trading, an apparently

---

[7] See Appendix II for the listing of the sample women's occupations.

[8] In questioning the women about their choice of work, I had a great deal of difficulty in establishing the concept of "choice." This was particularly so in the situations requiring an interpreter. Pushing the question brought diminishing returns; the informant became confused and I became aggravated.

[9] The balance fall under the categories of Homemaker and Other.

inherited role.[10] The largest occupational category in Ghana, trading is still the potentially most rewarding alternative for an untrained or illiterate woman ("Women at Work" 1963). While Accra's occupational structure has expanded, women continue to be active in internal trade (trade in local market places). Thus, "over half the employment secured by immigrant females from other countries is in commerce, and the overwhelming majority takes the form of petty trading" (Caldwell 1967: 62). In Accra according to Little (1973: 45), nine out of every ten women gainfully employed is a trader.[11] Prostitution or domestic work (other options) do not carry the same degree of respect. In my survey population of 353 Adabraka women, 36 percent were involved in some kind of internal trade; among the sample group, the percentage is the same. It is probable, however, that many of the 101 professed housewives in the large population (29 percent of the total) also engage in some trading.

As noted earlier in this book, hawking is the exclusive domain of females. Not all trade is reserved for women, however. Butchers are still mostly Northern men, ostensibly because the skill of ritual

---

[10] Considerable coastal trading has gone on in what is now Ghana since at least the middle of the 15th century (*See* Florence Sai 1971). Because the men needed weapons and also took prisoners to exchange for goods, they originally did most of the trading, while the women stayed at home, minding children and land. According to "customary law (in either a patrilineal or matrilineal system) the children or a wife being dependents of a man, family life requires that a son should work with and for his father, and a wife with and for her husband..." (N.A. Ollennu 1962: 39). Property acquired with such assistance belonged to the man; however, man and wife often worked out an arrangement whereby the wife would take the surplus produce of their labour to sell, giving her spouse a percentage of the take. Markets developed to accommodate the increasing trade, and as they expanded so did women's participation in them. This market trade flourished under European colonialism as urbanization increased and the money economy was extended. At the same time, the colonial government created and accorded high status to clerical jobs to which only the men had access. With men taking specialized jobs, the market was gradually left to the women; by the turn of the century, this process was virtually complete.

[11] Little does not make clear which year he is referring to; from the context I assume that he means as reported in the 1960 Population Census.

slaughter is taught only to males. Before restrictions were imposed on aliens under the terms of the Aliens Compliance Order, Nigerians were active in trading; they did not trade on the streets in "common goods," however, but specialized in particular areas such as native art and handicrafts. Some still operate underground. Furthermore, men have a monopoly in the distribution aspect of marketing, as well as external trade (Sai 1971: see also Mintz 1971).

Despite the exceptions just discussed, traders operate in what is pre-eminently a woman's world. The concepts of "woman" and of "trade/selling" are strongly linked in the popular mind. This emerges in the semantic distinction the women themselves make between "work" and "trade" (or selling). "Work" seems to be the Ghanaian English word for "salaried job," whether held by a man or a woman. Many women, when asked if they work, or ever have, replied in the negative. Asked if they would like to work, their response was again no. But, I persisted, do you not sell in the market ? Now the response was affirmative. "I can feel [sic] to trade, but I can't feel to work." Work often carries with it the connotation of a world to which these women still do not feel privy—the world of offices, of white-collar positions that are associated with men.

Another reason that women prefer selling is also tied to domesticity: it can be combined with the care of small children. Market women with pre-schoolers simply bring them along, unless there is someone at home with whom to leave the little ones. Selling also makes cooking very convenient. By keeping a coalpot with her market goods, a woman can buy her ingredients on the spot, cook them there, keep them for mealtime later, send them on to her spouse, or do whatever else she might choose.

Not a single one of my actively employed informants gave even a hint of dissatisfaction or disenchantment with her lot. Their rationalizations include keeping busy (housewife Regina says, "When you are working, you don't feel lazy sleeping like that") and financial gain ("—If you have money full up this room," admonishes Auntie Rose, "If you don't work and add it, the money is gone..." and then you cannot buy cloth, scarves, etc.). Seamstress Joanna works "because of my child... Not all of the time can my husband give... You can't rely upon a man; you must do some small thing." Finally, Lizzie states concisely, "If I don't work, how can I eat ?"

Skilled manual labor in the modern job sector, such as car repair and trucking, is described by my informants as "difficult" and therefore men's work. The real problem appears to lie elsewhere, in the prevailing assumptions about which occupations (and hence which training) are appropriate for whom. Ghanaian women are certainly not incapable of hard labor; they maintain their households, carry heavy loads on the farm to and from market, prepare meals, raise children, and cater to their husband's personal needs. Much of their time is spent carrying out lengthy, tiring, and tedious tasks considered inappropriate for those of loftier capacities (i.e. men).

All of the women engaged in trading of one sort or another confirmed this notion. Selling oranges, for example, is considered a woman's job. Benedicta: "I can't say why, but I haven't seen a man selling oranges before." More to the point, Adisa: "Only a woman can feel to sell oranges, not men." Similarly, selling firewood is acceptable for women and old men, but not young men. Ekua: "Because you can take the wood, you can dress the wood—the young cannot feel to do it, because it is too simple."

Then there are kinds of trading that involve work that is too hard or dirty for men. Making *kenkey* is a case in point: "A man cannot do it. A man cannot put his hands into hot water to remove *kenkey*. All that petty petty work, a man cannot do it." Again, selling fried plantain is for women only, because "first time, you put the firewood and the pan and the oil. And grind the tomatoes and pepper and onions, and cut the plantain, that's why. Because of the pepper and the fire. Men don't like fire. They are afraid of fire." And, adds Auntie Rose's 18-year-old daughter, "people will say, "Look at the man selling *kelewele* (fried plantain)!""

Selling oil carries with it similar unpleasantries, which only women, and their daughters, are willing and (according to my informants) *able* to transcend: "At any time, men in Ghana cannot feel to sell oil, because at any time you wake up, you put on the fire before you sell it, that's why men cannot feel to do it... Because you will make dirty and is difficult for men."

In most cases, the division of work between women and men parallels the divisions between the household and the outside world. Only women work at the YWCA nursery school, because, according to Faith, when the children arrive in the morning the teachers "...must undress them, cook breakfast, and in the afternoon give them lunch, clean them: it is the care of women. A man can't do it; it is hard work." While men are not trained to cook or do most domestic chores, such duties are taken over by men when they are commercialized.

The references to fire in the responses of the women about their capabilities versus those of men in the areas of domestic work and selling seem to have symbolic overtones. I sense a bit of contempt—a feeling that women are more capable and that men claim their positions of superiority through ascription, not through powers of achievement. *But,* consciously at least, the distribution of rights is not questioned.

Although there is an element of choice within the established categories of possible female employment, a young woman rarely makes or implements the decision to engage in a given type of work entirely on her own. For one thing, she is often influenced by suggestions that play on the theme of tradition, that are proferred by a respected elder, that involve reciprocation for past favors, or that must be taken seriously in the absence of anything better. The person who gives the advice may be a parent (or substitute parent) under whose aegis the vast majority of Adabraka women I interviewed started out, and in whose occupational footsteps children have traditionally followed. One-third of the women have in fact gone into occupations identical to those of one or both of their parents, primarily in the area of commerce. While none of the women (one-fourth of the total) whose parents were farming people carried on the tradition, they have all kept to the accepted female areas—trading, making and selling *kenkey*, sewing—save one, who is a clerk / telex operator.

When the mother practices a craft, her child becomes an integral part of the operation, often participating in both the manufacture of the product and its sale. Auntie Elizabeth, a woman of 54, is a baker; her mother was a baker too. "At that time, I was very small, but I sell bread." After being socialized into the business, her mother died. There was not enough money to send Auntie Elizabeth to secondary school. With her background, it was convenient to apprentice her to a female baker. Subsequently she went out on her own. The mother of 19-year-old Dora is likewise a baker and makes porridge and doughnuts on the side. Dora and her younger sister have equal responsibility for baking, cleaning up, and selling. Dora maintains that she does not want to work for her mother, but *must* because her mother does not have the time and wants her to. Like Auntie Elizabeth, she learned at her mother's knee, watching and receiving formal instruction. Ekua, whose mother is a tobacco seller in a rural Asante area, came up through the ranks of trading. She is currently selling firewood, however, because her father, who moved to Accra, asked her to help him. All of the women either learning to sew or already employed as seamstresses followed the suggestion of a senior male relative—father or brother. Bebbe said that her father heard about a particular woman giving lessons and passed on the information to her. Auntie Atta said that she needed work when she first came to Accra and was living with her older brother, and he pushed her in that direction.

Aggie did not *choose* to leave the employ of her trader aunt any more than she had *chosen* to enter it. Her father decided that she was wasting her time in the kiosk and told her to see his friend, the headmaster at a local boarding school. "When I got there, I was applying for telephonist. But at that time there was no telephone there. And he said the kitchen has shortage of one woman. So I must go there and try. Even I told him that I can't do the work properly..." But the combination of filial respect and contacts made Aggie into a cook.

Another senior male who may be responsible for "everywoman's" gainful employment is her husband. They may work together, as their forebears did in the rural setting. Akosua sold alongside her husband in his store; Hope works alone, or with her young brother-in-law, *for* her husband. In both cases, the profits are the men's. Ruby's husband set her up in a little kiosk; she gets a small percentage of the take and does some trading on the side.

Finally, there are the special cases of reciprocation, a prime example being that of mother and unmarried-daughter-with-child. In general, the baby is easily absorbed into the household and the major responsibility for socialization falls to the mother (the child's grandmother). In return, however, the daughter is beholden—perhaps to work in her mother's business.

Of the eight sample women who work in the modern sector, only two have gone into non-clerical positions. One is a film editor for the Ghana Broadcasting Company, the other is self-employed as a sand and stone contractor. Helena, the editor, has been through Secondary Form 5; her father, a store-keeper, has also finished secondary school, and her mother, the manager of a canteen, finished middle school. Auntie Viv's parents were both secondary school graduates; her father had been a cocoa agent and her mother an auction buyer and seller. From the responses I received, it is unclear how parental expectations, together with the daughter's education, have affected "everywoman's" modern occupational aspirations.

A woman introduced by family into a particular occupation will tend to stay with it out of inertia and a sense of familiarity. Should, however, that same occupation become unprofitable, she may consider making a change. In general, this requires the support of another—someone who is senior to the irresolute one. Both customary and serendipitous contacts may also lead to a job. I met Mary, a graduating secondary school student, on the street. She was exuberant when I proposed that she work as my interpreter, but she felt it was not her place to commit herself to me; I had to meet with her family first. She was in the nominal care of her paternal aunt, because her mother was deceased and her father lived elsewhere in Ghana. It was her uncle—her mother's brother, an Adangme like herself—who came to see me in order to determine my sincerity and integrity, and to extract promises of helping Mary in mapping out her future. Only after gaining his consent could I employ Mary.

Ease of access to a job and / or ease in performance may also have much to do with the final choice. This applies both to workers in the modern sector and to those following more traditional pursuits. Selling oranges, for example, is preferred because one need not "put them to fire," which is more tiring.[12] Similar considerations were important to Lydia, who had been working as a seamstress for a department store just before she quit to give birth:

> I like working better than the selling. In selling, somebody will credit
> some, so they will say, come today. Today, if you went, he will tell

---

[12] The traders had not considered choosing between the different kinds of trading and, say, working in a chop bar. The women engaged in commerce could not suggest any comparisons that they might have drawn. For them, trading was a given; their decision related to which type to pursue. Among the traders, trading was in effect perceived as the most accessible of any occupation.

you another story, he will go away. Some of the aliens, they have taken my money away. So I like working. If you work you know that at the end of the month, you will get ten pounds then you will get ten pounds. But if you sell, and you credit, you have made your budget already. If you go, somebody will tell you another story. Then your money will be short. So I like working better than selling.

Lydia continued her remarks along this vein, admitting that she made more money when selling or sewing on her own, but complaining that it was not worth the troubles involved in collecting. And besides, she said, selling is more difficult. "If you go to work, you go and sit behind your machine and you can work. But when you're selling, you have to go and come."

Market women still command a great deal of respect. Those who have made it big have done so against great odds, such as having to establish credit when illiterate. But as Lydia said, it means coming and going. Women with market stalls arrive at opening time, about 7:30 a.m. Those who hawk on the streets adjust their work schedule to their stock-in-trade. A woman who sells porridge and doughnuts will be out on the streets by 6 a.m., since most of her trade is in breakfast customers on their way to work. Most bread sellers are out at night, along with rice, *kenkey, fufu,* etc. sellers. A *kenkey* seller like Fatima does the bulk of her business during the early part of the day, so must start cooking at 3 a.m. While there are variations, market women typically put in long, hard hours.

Since Ghanaian women are accustomed to long work days, if not in the market then on the farm or in the home, the hours of work and tedium are not always treated as an important consideration in the choice of occupation. A trader does not consider it burdensome to sit at the market all day long. Operating a stall, in any case, is more prestigious than hawking on the street. Rather, she evaluates the "hardness" of her work in terms of the effort required in preparing or selling the product. That this may be changing is suggested by the attitude of Helena, who is employed in a professional, Western position. Less willing than some of the more traditionally oriented women to put in a full day's work and then rush home to prepare supper for her husband, she complained that her hours were too long.

The last criterion for occupational choice to be discussed is the financial. Women may find some occupation difficult to enter because of the requirement for an initial outlay of capital. When a girl is apprenticed to a seamstress, for example, she may have to pay a fee even though she helps the woman in her business. The same is true for such crafts as hairdressing, baking, and catering. In earlier times, such arts or crafts were passed on through the family network. Today, a girl might do household work in exchange for instruction, depending upon her age. Some sort of reciprocity is always expected. If money is required, the father or a senior male relative takes over the responsibility for fees. A trade such as sewing also involves the expense of a machine. Without a sponsor, a young woman cannot consider occupations requiring such outlays.[13]

Among those interviewed, the idea of training had never originated with the apprentice girl. Either she followed parental example (as with the two bakers) or she followed advice leading her to the trade and the actual instructress. The father took responsibility for unmarried girls, unless he was absent or insolvent. In that case, a girl's operative guardian—in some cases her boyfriend—assumed the responsibility. The case of Georgina, a Kwahu, is a good example. She is an apprentice to a hairdresser. To work there five and a half days per week, for one year, she must pay NȻ 120—half at the beginning of her training, half upon completion. Her mother ekes out a modest living running a small provisions shop; her father has no spare cash, and in any event her mother's brothers would traditionally be responsible for educational costs, so she went to her "friend" (a well-to-do businessman) and he gave her the money.

For those going into business, starting capital is a particular problem. Sai (1971) found that 40 percent of her sample of textile and food sellers started out with less than N Ȼ 10, the lowest amounts of initial capital being associated with the food sellers. Certain other fields of trade, such as textiles, require greater initial investment. In Adabraka, I found that few traders started out with their own money. Most are set up by a "senior"—partner, older sibling, foster parent, husband, etc.[14]

---

[13] I have no firsthand information on the situation for male children. It is clear, however, that they are given encouragement in academic studies, that this involves a good deal of expense, and therefore that *someone* with both authority to give consent and the money to finance the venture must be called upon.

Those of my informants whose careers were not simply mapped out by their families displayed varying degrees of sophistication and self-assertiveness in their search for employment. Some had little idea where to start looking. Such problems were due in part to the absence of initiative (or independence) that is so characteristic of both men and women in Ghana. There is always someone older and wiser who can offer advice or connections, or both. A woman seeking work might merely ask around her local contacts, or (as in times past) seek out kin or a traditional leader who has connections at his fingertips, or to someone with greater access to the modern sector.

As a "European" (a word that in Ghana denotes a non-African), I was approached both by young women and by parents of young women. Among the latter was the father of Dora, my housegirl, who wanted his daughter (aged 19, with a year-old child) to follow his advice and finish school, or at least complete Middle Form Four.When she conceived, he claimed, he was not vexed; when she failed the examination, he understood. He did not want to cause her trouble, he continued, *but* he would be happy for her to stay with me. He asked me to teach her and show her how to be respectful and so forth, and then, when my "course" was finished, I could take her with me to the United States for schooling. "If only you could advise her well and show her the right way. I would be so happy." Similarly, when I was leaving Ghana, my interpreter approached one of my contacts, a well-known chief well-versed in the "American way"; out of deference to me, he found her a position through his network of contacts.

Despite the odds, some Ghanaian women do achieve real success. Auntie Viv provides a fine example. She began to trade at the age of 16, while she was at home on vacation from secondary school in Sierra Leone; meeting a man on the street selling hats, she bought a dozen, added a few shillings to the price of each, and sold them quickly. The same man suggested that she write to London to get more hats at cost. She ordered four dozen, C.O.D. It was Christmastime when they arrived, and so they rapidly sold out. Then she began to buy from UAC (United Africa Company). Still at school when the goods arrived, she asked her sister to pick them

---

[14] Repayment seems to be rare, especially to men. Appreciation is shown most often through dashing or labor.

up and put them on sale. When Viv arrived home, she dashed her sister a few shillings in return for the latter's efforts.

Viv subsequently trained in nursing and in teaching as well. In 1966 she went into wholesale and retail contracting in sand and stone. Each of these changes was made for reasons of financial gain. Along with her contracting business she is also involved in wholesale importing. She says, however, that the latter brings in little money because of the surcharge imposed by the government on imports and just gives her headaches: she must wander about the city collecting money owed her, a complaint similar to that voiced by many traders. In contracting, on the other hand, customers simply pay into her account, so she need only check at the bank every so often. She is continually thinking about how to improve her business; for example, she wants to put up a building near the quarry at Achimota to use as an office and as quarters for business guests. After that, she hopes to go into agriculture and bring in poultry. This would give her the opportunity to drop the importing business. Auntie Viv displays financial acuity and shrewd management. She has initiative and drive. Although she consults with both husband and mother, she will hear others out only to be polite; once she has made up her mind, she forges ahead. It would be overly simplistic to draw a direct casual relation between her success and her personal initiative; the opportunities were there. She, however, was also capable of recognizing and taking advantage of them.

Income

Despite generally low profits or wages, the anticipation of earning money is the overwhelming motive for choosing to work. It would be in keeping with traditional Ghanaian mores for men and women to receive equal pay for equal work, but high-paying jobs or professions are not readily accessible to women because of the discrimination inherent in both the British colonial and Ghanaian customary systems: "...women's average earnings are generally lower than men's because of the concentration of women in those branches of the economy where the average wage is below the national average" (Greenstreet 1971: 124).

The average reported income of the original population of 353 Adabraka women is N₡ 20.70 per month. This figure, however, is skewed, because almost 50 percent of the women pleaded ignorance of their earnings. Many in fact do not keep regular accounts, while others are afraid to reveal this information. In the sample of 39 women, the average reported income is N₵ 51.66 per month;[15] however, this too must be qualified. Firstly, it is impossible to confirm the women's responses. One who rents out rooms in her house reported her incomes at only N₵ 20 and two others refused to reply. Secondly, to ameliorate bias, I omitted from my calculations the numerous unemployed at one end and the one very high earner (N₵ 1,200) at the other. Finally, I could not figure in indirect income. In many instances when the individual works for the family, she does not receive a set amount of salary. Instead she is "dashed" or given money for specific needs. Generally, indirect payment is supplementary to basic subsistence needs, although one woman who sells *kenkey* for her sister is both fed and periodically dashed money.

Salaried women, for example clerks with middle schooling, earn between N₵ 35 and 46 per month. The secondary school-educated film editor Helena earns only N₵ 72 per month. Only one of my informants has bought a house with her own money, and she is a woman in her sixties.[16] All of the others either live in a house belonging to their own or their spouse's family or in rented quarters.

The romantic image of the market mammy, who carries her bundle in her bodice, applies to few traders. In her sample of 57 textile and food traders, Sai (1971) found that the 17 traders who owned their own homes (three owning more than one) did so as the result of 30 years of trading: 20 rented their homes or rooms at N₵ 3 to N₵ 6 per month; and the balance lived in family houses.

My informants would agree unanimously with Sai's finding "that

---

[15] About 25 percent of the women interviewed have no income or a negative income (i.e. apprentices); 36 percent fall within the N₵ 2-20 a month category (mainly traders); another 26 percent are in the N₵ 21-40 a month category (traders, dressmakers, and clerical workers); 10 percent earn N₵ 41-75 a month (in dressmaking, clerical work, and film editing); the contractor goes off the chart at about N ₵ 1,200 a month. The housewives fall into the first two categories, with any extra money received from their husbands considered as income.

[16] Auntie Viv could certainly afford a separate home, but her husband works in a different city and she has followed the tradition by remaining in her mother's house.

a woman had to work, even if she had someone to look after. This is a well-established tradition: all women had to work, on the farms, at craftwork (dress-making) or trading" (1971: 13). In rural life, the husband and wife worked together for the common good of the household. The husband was expected to provide for general maintenance, but often he handed over "chop money" (money for food) only. In such cases, the wife would quietly assume responsibility until better times. In town, however, she might be moved to make a stir and leave the marriage, for here the woman is far more financially dependent upon family or consort. Urban life involves a stream of subsistence expenses—rent, electricity, water, food. All of the women interviewed contribute in one way or another to such expenses, but it is not a cultural obligation for them to do so in the sense that it is for their husbands. When Ramatu's husband temporarily moved out on her, he refused to pay her rent. She poured out her troubles to her girlfriend Skenatu, also a Muslim. "Allah!" exclaimed Skenatu, "If he were my husband, I would go crazy, I would take poison. What ! That Ramatu should pay the rent, that she should be shamed !" Ramatu's only alternative, however, was to move in with her mother, and she was opposed to this. "In my country, if you live with your mother, you can't do anything. No going out, no cinema, no nothing." So she waited out her husband's return, although she would have been within her rights to leave him.

If the husband is not in a position to pay for children's school fees—either because he has no money or because he is obligated to take care of his sister's children and does not have enough money—the woman's small earnings come in handy. Secondary school fees, however, are often prohibitive. In this case it is mainly the extras—personal luxuries such as scarves for herself and sweets for the children—that provide the incentive to work. Most women believe that they cannot ask their husbands for oddments such as these. "Not all of the time can my husband give... you can't rely upon a man; you must do some small thing."

The expenses of the nonemployed, for example students and housewives, are absorbed by whomever they live with. Those who are employed and live with the family share in the food bills and make contributions to rent and the like. If one person in a family does all of the cooking, it is not unusual to dash her something monthly. One is expected to make modest periodic dashes to kin living in the hometown, where participation in the cash economy is often minimal—especially to mother and siblings. This commitment to the reciprocal cycle provides another incentive to earn a few extra cedis.

In general, those who have earning power, no matter how great or small, reinvest their money (for example, a cloth-seller will use some of her profits to buy more cloth), spend it on non-necessities (petty food, clothing extras for oneself and one's children, other personal expenditures), and make dashes or household contributions. Faustina sums it up nicely: she must buy some cloth for herself and her child, sandals, decorations for her room (carpet, curtains), and perhaps bedsheets. If she asked her husband, he would give her some money, but it is not good to buy everything from one's husband's money. "I don't know his mind; maybe he'd smile in my face, but wouldn't like it." All of these disbursements are made possible by small earnings.

For the unmarried women, boyfriends can be an important source of support. Payment can be direct, in the form of a monthly allowance, or indirect, in the form of periodic gifts. The mode and amount of the supplementary income depend upon the women's expectations and the socio-economic level she aims for in her quest for a boyfriend. The Adabraka women with boyfriends receive from them anywhere from N₵ 10 to N₵ 20 per month, bestowed as a matter of course, in recognition of two facts: (1) women have certain needs, which they themselves often cannot meet with the amount of money that they earn; and (2) by contributing to a woman's maintenance on a regular basis the boyfriend can expect certain favors from her. Such an arrangement gives the woman some independence in the sense that it does not tie her to one man, but receiving an allowance perpetuates her psychological dependency.

How Much Autonomy ?

My findings in Adabraka do not support the widely accepted view that African urban centers facilitate a woman's independence by giving her a new economic mobility or earning power as well as freedom from traditional (family, lineage) controls. With the new financial independence a woman gains through her employment, so the argument runs, she can change her relationships. She can live as an individual with a new sense of personal freedom. And she can support herself and her children without being beholden to others.[17]

Few of the Adabraka women whom I came to know can be characterized as economically autonomous or self-supporting. For the most part, they are dependent upon others for continuing guidance in all decision-making areas, for starting capital, for items of material show, and even basic sustenance. In the event of financial crisis (such as the theft of the tools of one's trade), the pattern is to go to kin or consort to be bailed out; the idea of working out the problem independently is not to be considered. This is not meant to suggest that the women of Adabraka are not capable of earning a living; if daughters estranged from their husbands can speak of moving back to mother's house, mother presumably can support them. Supporting themselves is more difficult in the city, because of the added expense, but the fact is that four of the women interviewed are doing so: one a widow, who lives in the family house, another the heir to her husband's house, and two single women. Three of the young singles work and take care of their own expenses (such as rent), but they also have boyfriends to help them out.

Migration itself could be symbolic independence, but I have not found that to be true in the case of the Adabraka women. Three main reasons were given for resettling, all acceptable to parents—marriage, school or job, or the presence in the area of family. For those with specialized training, a city is bound to offer better opportunities for employment than the hometown. Many of the single women coming to Accra do so because they have kin already there upon whom they can rely. Many return to their families when widowed, while others create new family centers— accommodating, for example, married offspring and their families. Without exception, the women said that if they were to divorce, they would gravitate to family, generally mothers. Thus, those who live alone, on their own, are exceptional cases.[18]

It is important to realize that the trappings of financial success (such as patiently sitting in the sun for long hours, selling merchandise) are not necessarily indicative of autonomy *if* we are concerned with the power of decision and the choice of alternatives

---

[17] This is the thesis of Baker and Bird (1959); Little (1959, 1973).

that precedes such success. *Was* there a choice and *who* made the decision ? In her educational, occupational, and financial affairs, a woman is often dependent upon other, generally senior, persons. Very few would oppose their parents if the latter denied them the right to make a choice, and just as they would obey their parents' wishes, so do they expect their children to do the same.

Independence is also associated with the taking of initiative. Men and women alike, with and without education, complain of not being able to find a job if they have training, and of not knowing what occupation to pursue if they do not. They do not know where to look, or what criteria to use, or even what they want for themselves, if there are no patterns to follow.

While it is my impression that the Adabraka women have not been socialized into a sense of initiative, I do not mean to suggest that my informants are dull, lazy, or unimaginative and thus cannot make strides. Rather, I submit that dependencies for men and women exist, that for women especially they switch, and that work cannot be *the* primary goal. A boyfriend or spouse is essential to a woman's well-being. Perhaps this duality of considerations limits the woman's psychological orientations toward work. Harrell-Bond (1975) has found that few female members of the professional class in Sierra Leone are married.

Since the women of Ghana have always worked, perhaps the real show of independence would be to choose *not* to work— particularly since they are still being channeled into traditionally acceptable occupations. There certainly is not much monetary reward in the work most do. While what little they do earn is used positively, its paucity may incur less beneficial effects. Like the Victorian "perfect lady," unmarried Ghanaian women are showpieces for their men. Perhaps if and when women can go into

---

[18] Only two in my group of women live alone. One originally came to live with a sister and work; she took over the rented room when the sister married and moved away. The other originally came to live with her older married sister and attend secondary school. Once established in her employment, she moved off on her own. Just as she had carried our household chores for her elder sister in exchange for payment of the school fees, so a younger sister has joined her in the same way. She insists that she would far prefer living in a family home, if one existed in Accra; then it would not be necessary for her to "waste" her money on rent.

financially rewarding occupations their financial dependence upon men will lessen. This will allow new patterns of relationships, with greater socio-cultural independence from men, to emerge. There *are* those who have been well equipped and have excelled—Auntie Viv, for example, who is a second-generation secondary-school-educated woman. But they, like the others, are still primarily absorbed with the traditional roles of wife and mother, which are examined in the next chapter.

Traditional Female Roles

The women of Adabraka have been socialized into the traditional sexual roles of wife, mother, daughter, and sibling. These are their primary social identities. Each of these roles entails specific responsibilities and expectations that endure largely intact in the urban setting because of the persistent strength of family, lineage, and tribal linkages.

In many, if not most, ways, my informants' daily lives follow the model of their mothers'. Because the rituals of household responsibilities are paramount in the lives of these women, a description of their daily routines is helpful in establishing the context for the discussion that follows of their three primary roles—those of wife, mother, and junior member of an extended family.

The Daily Routine

A woman is no less busy in the city than in the rural areas; indeed, her time is far more precious and it is as carefully reckoned as pocket money. Less time may be needed for walking, since public conveyances are available, but places of business are more scattered. In Accra, there is no business center proper, and not all of the markets carry the same goods. Those who are newly arrived or who wish to maintain special ties with others from the same tribe or hometown may want to budget time for voluntary association meetings. Women with modern skills, such as typing, may have to travel some distance to reach their place of employment. These are not substitutes for, but additions to, their traditional chores such as cooking and cleaning.

The day begins early. At 5:30 a.m., the voice of the GBC (Ghana Broadcasting Corporation) blasts forth from the omnipresent box radio. It is soon answered by the sounds of brooms sweeping public and private compound spaces. The Kumase lorries, which leave from a neighborhood gas station, begin their run. Most of the women get up about two hours before they have to be at work; 5:30 is their average waking hour, though some rise earlier and a few later. The newspaper boy is out hawking by 6:30. Patrons are waiting as the doors of the chop bars open. Since many of the breakfasters drive cars, and traffic taking a shortcut to the ministries also passes through Adabraka, hooting fills the air. Children leave for school at 7:00. Most office hours start at 7:30 or 8:00 and market stalls open at about 7:30. The women have much to do before departing for office or market. Housewives, like hawkers, have a more flexible schedule; yet even they are up by 6:00, carrying out the same household work as the others.

Early morning tasks include sweeping out rooms, making beds, straightening out rooms, drawing (and heating) water for bathing, bathing self and children, preparing tea and a light repast for husband and children, and washing clothes (a daily chore when there is an infant in the family)—all before 7:30 ! Certain tasks, such as washing and ironing clothes, may be put off until later in the morning if one's schedule is flexible.

Most women do not eat breakfast *en famille*. After sending off other family members, the non-office working women, some of the market women, and others, go to the market to buy perishables for cooking. Alternatively, depending upon their place of business, they may go at midday or during the late afternoon. Most say that they prefer to do their own marketing, because they are afraid that anyone else sent would either get bad produce or pay a bad price. Thus the individual who does the cooking usually does the shopping; exceptions may arise when there is a hired housemaid or a dependent sibling who is not too young: the former probably having a hand in the cooking and also having been trained by the mistress of the house, the latter being expected to help out in this way as a form of reciprocation. Since most households lack refrigeration, the frequency of marketing usually depends on the frequency of cooking. Those who cook daily market daily. Even those who do own refrigerators tend to market frequently—partly out of habit and also because the refrigerator is used mainly to keep a stock of cold liquids.

When women go to the market, they have their purchases in mind. Should they run into friends, they go through the rituals of greeting and exchanging gossip, but most are pressed for time. The gossipping and socializing characteristic of rural markets (which meet periodically) is minimal in Accra. Women do not hang around the market; their domestic duties are more than enough to keep them occupied during the daylight hours. If anyone loiters there, it is the men.[1] The marketplace is a commercial arena, and the traders are businesswomen. Just as women maintain that they do not patronize one trader regularly, so they insist that friendships do not necessarily eventuate in a trading relationship.[2] What socializing does take place occurs mainly among the traders themselves, but even here business has priority.

Frequency of meal preparation seems to be associated with the presence of an adult male. If a woman does not have a husband, she will cook every two or three days; if she is polygynously married, she will cook on the days that the husband comes to stay with her (or that she stays with him). Ellen, unmarried though affianced and living on her own, felt this to be an obstacle to her freedom:

> If you get married, you are not going to be free, because of many
> things. Like as now, cooking is not compulsory. I can buy something
> and eat. But as soon as you get married you should cook for your

---

[1] The only men who regularly shop at the market are either exceedingly Westernized or house stewards, the latter mostly working for Europeans. A Ghanaian woman would do her own marketing even if she had a steward, on the assumption that a man would be cheated or overcharged.

[2] Just because a woman has a girlfriend who sells tomatoes, she does not need to feel under obligation to buy from her. Most women buy from strangers and get to know them through a trading relationship.

husband and children every day. If you are not going to eat, your
husband will eat.

If the women is by herself, enough stew or soup can be prepared to
provide meals for several days; even without refrigeration, the food
will not spoil if it is heated periodically. In addition, all manner of
soups, stews, starches, and snacks are sold on the street.

Those who work at an office job (and those learning a trade) are
away from the house the entire day. They have a lunch break of
one-and-a-half to two hours, which may be spent at a chop bar or at
the place of work after street food is bought. Any remaining
household responsibilities (most likely for a married woman living
with a spouse) must be carried out upon returning home in the
evening. In many families, the main meal is taken at noon; in this
case, a second heavy meal is either prepared for the next day's
midday meal or not prepared at all. When an adult working woman
is a sibling or child in a household, she often takes over the
responsibility for meal preparation only on her days off—Saturday
afternoons and Sundays for office workers.

Market women stay at their stalls the entire day. While there, they
can do their own marketing and cooking, as well as take a nap in the
afternoon when business is slow. Traders who do not sell in a stall in
the market have some choice as to their hours and their location. If
one's compound is on a major thoroughfare or well-travelled road,
a table can easily be set up right out front. In this case, a child or
neighbor can be left to keep an eye on the business while the seller
takes care of household duties; meal preparation can be done on the
spot. Flexible hours also accommodate breaks for such purposes as
marketing, cooking, and napping. At the same time, the work
schedule of many hawkers is constrained by their stock-in-trade.
The porridge, doughnut, and rice sellers are situated by 6:00 a.m.
for the breakfast traffic, the principal source of their trade.
Conversely, bread sellers come out in the early evening and sit
beside a kerosene lamp, catering to those taking the evening repast
of tea and bread. Those who sell prepared foods early in the day
must spend the previous afternoon and/or evening assembling
ingredients, or get up early to do so.

After the long work day comes a new set of chores: putting
together a meal, cleaning up, bathing children and putting them to
bed. Such a schedule leaves little time for extracurricular activities,

If a trader lives on a well-travelled road, a table may be set up in front of the compound as a stall, and a child or neighbor may be left to keep an eye on business while the seller attends to household duties. Here children are seen tending a fruit stall. (Photo: Edward S. Ayensu)

unless they carry a strong commitment (such as church services or church organization meetings). By 9:30 p.m., most residents are inside, behind locked shutters. A woman does not go out, "not regularly, the way a man goes out, but sometimes... No time. As for the man, if he comes home from business and there are meals, and they take their bath, they have nothing to do again. Then they go to the town. But as a woman, she has to bathe her children."

The length of a woman's working day is due in part to the amount of time required to carry out the most basic of tasks. To bathe, which everyone does twice daily, requires the drawing of water, either from the compound's water pipe or a public tap, often some distance away. If it is chilly, the water must be heated on the little coalpot before the bath, more like a cross between a sponge bath and a shower, can proceed. Children bathe out of the bucket next to the gutter out front, but adults must wait their turn to use the shared shower room. Marketing also takes time; one must walk to the market and at times to more than one if a speciality such as fresh fish is on the menu, haggling for every item, and then walk home. If the Adabraka woman patronizes Salaga or Makola Market, both in the center of Accra, she usually takes the "tro-tro," and that means a wait and an uncomfortable ride.

A good example of the time and tedium involved in a common duty is provided by cooking. Light soup, a broth with meat and vegetables, is regular fare. From start to finish, when it is time to pound *fufu*, preparation takes about two hours. First, pepper and eggplant is parboiled. Once soft, the fresh red pepper is ground to pulp, either with a pestle in a ridged bowl, or on a grinding stone. Meat (or chicken or fish) is cleaned, shallots chopped, and both are cooked over a fire. Whole tomatoes and the pepper are added. The eggplant is cleaned and ground up. If smoked fish is to be added, it is done at this point. The tomatoes are removed. (Some women, in removing whole vegetables from the boiling soup, dip their fingers in cold water and pick the vegetables out, without using a spoon.) The tomatoes are then peeled, ground, and put back in. Then the starch must be prepared. *Fufu* takes about ten minutes to pound; *banku* (a starch made from fermented corn) must be continuously stirred. (There is a special pot for cooking *banku*: an iron loop on either side making it possible to hook two iron poles to the pot. The cook can then hold the pot steady by keeping her feet on the poles as she stirs the increasingly stickier *banku*.) Some women take modest shortcuts, such as buying *banku* or *kenkey* on the street to eat with the soup; others, particularly those with a helper, will go so far as to make their own groundnut (peanut) paste (used as the base for groundnut stew) rather than buy it in the market.

Sunday afternoon is the one time during the week that the pressure eases. Even then there are children around to supervise and house-chores to take care of that do not fit into weekday schedules. All of the interviewed women profess religious observance. The Christians attend church, some more regularly than others; the Catholics and assorted Fundamentalists may attend services on the weekdays in addition to Sundays. The three Muslims pray at home the required five times daily and sometimes attend the Friday service at the mosque. But even religion does not preempt household responsibilities; if time is limited, the latter take precedence. Adawkaw, for example, is devoutly religious and attends Apostolic services regularly. Yet when her husband asked for a Sunday dinner of palm nut soup she had to (or felt she had to) stay home, suppress her irritation, and prepare the meal. The fact that the two were not living together (as a Ga, she lived with her matrilineage) did not change the responsibility to accede to her husband's wishes.

This superficial account gives some idea of the activities and priorities of a typical Adabraka woman's day. Let us now turn to the traditional roles of a woman as they manifest themselves in the context of the urban compound.

The Wife

As we have seen, marriage in Ghana does not always lead to a break with extended household living. Suppose that a newly-married couple migrates to Accra. After a few years of marriage, the man may decide that "he doesn't want to marry me anymore." He leaves and his wife remains, with one or two children that she has brought forth. She may be joined by a younger sister, who is trained in clerical skills and cannot find a job in the rural home town; this sister begins to work and contributes her share to the household. A year or two later, the mother of the two women arrives, her husband having passed away. If she is fortunate, another room may be available in the compound; if not, she can room with others. The household is now composed of three cooperating kinswomen and two children. The cyclical pattern in this example is particularly evident. Variations on this theme are common. Few élite Akan couples, according to Oppong's Accra study (1974), had set up their own households soon after marrying. Accommodations may be hard to find, the husband may be involved in protracted studies at home or abroad, or he may be subject to transfer by his employer. Such couples often reside with kin or in-laws.

> Many house-holders... have either their own relatives... or in-laws staying with them from the initial stages of the marriage onwards. Some of these... are educated relatives, who would have difficulty in finding lodgings elsewhere in town. Many are in search of employment and are either fresh from school or are illiterates. Some have come to attend school, or to get medical attention. Others, especially the wife's kin, come to give domestic help (Oppong 1974: 77).

Nevertheless, the conjugal pair as the domestic unit is the urban

ideal. Of my informants, only Lydia voices preference for extended
family living:

> If I'm living here, I'll get somebody to buy me something, or fetch me
> water. [Or] for instance, I'm washing, the baby is crying. If somebody
> is here, I will take the baby and give it to him. Then I can continue to
> wash. But there, nobody is there. You will stop washing and take care
> of her. After that, you will come and continue your washing.

Lydia lives in her mother's brother's house, sharing a single room
with her four children and her mother. Lydia grew up in this house.
The only time she has been away from it was when she went to
school in Takoradi and lived with an aunt. She has been socialized
into the family-house style of life. When she is neither pregnant nor
nursing an infant, she goes to her husband's place, alternating
visits (and the cooking and cleaning for him) with his other wife.

The other women in my sample who lived with their own or their
husband's kin in a family house or rented quarters were quick to
denounce the situation in favor of separate housing.[3] Martha lives
with her mother in her mother's brother's house. Already married
by custom, she dreams of a "white gown" (church) wedding, after
which she envisions going to live with her husband. But for her, and
many like her, there is no reason to believe that present
circumstances in fact will change. She will not take the initiative in
such a matter, and the current arrangement is less of a financial
drain on the husband. It is also to his advantage in terms of freedom
of movement, although living with a wife would not really restrict
him either. And given the nature of Ghanaian marriage, it is
ultimately to Martha's advantage to have her family round her. All
of those living with their husbands neolocally favor the
arrangement. In the words of Regina:

> Because when you are there like that, I will do something I like. But in

---

[3] In my sample, 18 of the women live in an extended family household; of these,
nine are currently married, and six of these do not live with their husbands.
Another seven women in the sample live in a family house situation and six of
them are married and are living with their husbands. While the extended
household may be coterminous with the family house (or family residence in a
non-kin compound), it need not be; co-residents in a family house may have
separate nuclear households.

our house, plenty people stay there. My aunt's sisters, my aunt's daughters, plenty. And my cousins all in the house. Like that. Everytime I want to do something, I have to tell them; some will go there... I don't like.

There is the requirement to report back to someone else, or ask permission, even if only as a formality, before doing practically anything. There are the questions of custom—"We Akan people can't do that. Can't marry and stay with our mother"—and the rationale of proper child-rearing—"If with husband and child, it's good, it's better. To help train the child to become a good girl or a good boy. So many children living here [in the family house] and different characters." If proper customary marriage has not taken place, it may be preferred that the married couple not live together.

As far as daily household chores are concerned, the two housing arrangements differ very little. Both in a family house and in a tenant compound the whole house is composed of discrete dwelling units, each generally consisting of a room. Living space is organized along lines of relationship. In a family house, for example, one room might house mother, daughter(s), grandchild(ren). Another room might house mother's sister, mother's sister's daughter, and the latter's children; and so on. Marketing, cooking, and eating follow these same lines. Under both systems, a given room is cleaned by those women living in it.

It is the women who are locked into these tasks, and these tasks hold primacy over any other activity. The parcelling out of specific household work is closely tied in to the relationship of seniority, as well as reciprocation for a service rendered. For example, the senior woman (or the women whose room/house it is, alone or with a spouse) has ultimate responsibility for the housekeeping. As children come of age, often as young as eight, they are given small chores, such as sweeping. As they grow, they graduate to different tasks, the younger ones taking over in their stead. Similarly, when a younger family member lives in or partakes of the pot on a regular basis, he/she reciprocates by helping out in the house. There is no sexual division of labor for the young in general housekeeping chores, such as sweeping, washing clothes, washing the floor. Cooking, however, is done by women only.

In the traditional extended family, there was always a young female member to help out; she would be useful especially in the preparation of meals. In the city, family periodically show up, but in general, if a maid-servant is not hired, the burden falls upon the adult woman occupant. Florence is a full-time housewife. She explained that this means she does everything in the house—alone. They cannot hire anyone, so she does her own cooking, washing, ironing. If they had a housemaid, they would have to pay her; but they cannot afford to pay someone, so Florence does it herself.

Nuclear family living is functionally related to the Western idea of monogamy, involving marriage by registry. This marriage type is one of five operative in Accra today; they differ in terms of the authority structure of the union and the ease of dissolution (Pool 1972: 243-44): (1) *customary* marriage emphasizes kin ties, accepts divorce and polygyny, often takes place in the context of an extended family, so that the husband does not necessarily have supreme authority over the wife; (2) *Muslim* marriage emphasizes the conjugal unit, permits divorce on either part (though in practice the wife exercises her right less), favors polygyny, and accords the husband absolute authority; (3) *Christian* marriage stresses the indissolubility of ties and the individuals' joint responsibility and forbids polygyny; (4) *civil registration* (Ordinance) marriage, also monogamous, underlines the binding nature of the relationship and husband/wife joint responsibility; (5) *consensual* marriage is an amalgam of traditional and modern values, as one is free to choose one's partner for what tends to be a monogamous union, but either party can terminate the relationship.

The man's options among these marriage types cover a wide range. He can, for example, combine customary marriage to one woman and Ordinance marriage to another. The forms of monogamy and marriage by registry do not really constrain him. His father maintained wives and/or girlfriends, and so does he. Everyone knows that the wife stays at home, providing children and stability, whereas the girlfriend accompanies a man to his social engagements, providing companionship. The society continues to be polygynous in essence.

A.L. Crabtree reported in 1950 that educated Ghanaian men in government, in missions, or in commercial firms in the southern part of the country, usually married according to African custom, although they might also have a church or civil ceremony This was corroborated more recently by Oppong's 1974 findings on élite Akan civil servants (*See also* Mair 1969: 149).

According to Tetteh (1967), the broader sample of the 1960 Post Enumeration Survey of the Ghana Census also reveals that customary marriage has been the basic and normal method of marrying; 86 percent of persons in the sample who had ever married had done so under customary law only. Those who chose to marry by Ordinance or church did so after carrying out the traditional rites. Next in popularity was Muslim marriage, contracted by 5 percent of the sample population; it was more prevalent in Asante and Brong Ahafo than elsewhere. Third was the combination of customary, church, and Ordinance marriage, undertaken by 2.3 and 1.2 percent of sample males and females respectively. "This type of marriage is associated with urban areas and a high socioeconomic status. Accordingly, the proportions are highest in the large urban centres" (Tetteh 1967: 207). Marriage by customary law followed by a church union carries no greater legal weight than customary marriage alone; it was particularly common in areas where the Presbyterian Church is strong. Marriage by both customary and Ordinance law appeared mainly in large towns; 1 percent of the marriages under consideration were of this type. Finally, common-law (consensual) marriage, although not legally valid, involved 4 percent of the sample males, and 5.6 percent of the sample females.

> The proportions for the Accra City Council were at 2.1 percent males and 4.4 percent females, that is, below the national average. One may conclude that these unions are not necessarily the result of urbanization. The explanation is to be sought in the indigenous social arrangements of the various ethnic groups... the high rate of conjugal separation may be a factor in some of these unions. When a woman has contracted more than one marriage a subsequent husband does not feel obligated to perform the necessary customary rites to validate the marriage. *The women do not insist on these payments for fear of losing the husbands on whom they depend for sexual satisfaction and economic support...* As a woman gets on in years her bargaining position is weaker and she finds it harder to get a man (Tetteh 1967: 209—emphasis added by current writer).

Men and women alike express both positive and negative feelings about registered unions. Such a union assures a woman of Western-style respectability; in the words of one, it means that she may call herself "Mrs." Analogously, men who feel that outer appearance is advantageous for career advancement may marry according to the Ordinance. In 1905, when the British conducted an inquiry into the Marriage Ordinance of 1884, the male populace had four main objections, still prevalent today:

(1) **Expense.** Since Ordinance marriage carries greater weight than customary marriage, the family of the bride expects larger payments; moreover, the groom has to assume other expenses, such as entertaining the bridal party.

(2) **The woman's behavior.** The argument runs that "The wife is apt to become 'wild,' that she 'behaves proudly against her husband,' and 'is not so submissive as a woman married by native law.' It is not surprising that the wife becomes more self-assertive, as her position improves " (Secretary of Native Affairs Case No. 480/1905; ADM 11/1457).

(3) **The difficulty in obtaining a divorce.** This is the chief complaint.

(4) **The law of succession.** Native law opines that the family of the deceased man or woman should receive at least one-third of the private property; the Ordinance, on the other hand, rules that the whole of the private property of a man or woman dying intestate goes to the spouse and the children.

The last objection, the law of succession, is the major factor differentiating customary from Ordinance marriage.

> Reiterations in court that it is the wife's duty to help her husband and that if she helps him, the produce of their joint labour belongs to him alone in his lifetime and to his matrikin at his death, as well as the circulation of harrowing accounts of the dispossession of widows and orphans by the matrikin of the recently deceased, give ample proof...
> [of the maintenance of customary law among the Akan] (Oppong 1974: 44f).

As Crabtree (1950) and Oppong (1974) have both noted, it is particularly educated women and their parents who favor registered marriage—partly for the security provided wives, widows, and orphans.

Of the 28 ever-married women in my sample, only one was consensually wed; the rest had at least gone through the customary procedures.[4] Just one (highly-educated and the daughter of educated parents) had married by Ordinance; she had also gone through the traditional Ga marriage ceremony and Anglican church rites. Only a few express any interest in a church wedding, but its association with high status is clear in its designation as a "white gown ceremony." The fact that a woman does not marry in church has less to do with her attitudes about religion than with her fiancé's social and economic situation.[5]

The power to decide between alternatives necessitates some prior notion or concept of alternatives. Despite the fact that some people are supplementing the traditional rites with church or registry unions, the numbers are still small. To many of my informants, the three types are "all the same": each of the rites signifies that one is a married woman, and that is all that is customarily necessary. Others have no opinions; as Florence said, "I haven't studied this... so will think about it."

But most of the women I spoke with had a definite, though often distorted, understanding of the differences among the three, especially insofar as they affected a woman's freedom of movement. Since ties to traditional family structures are still present, the customary marriage would be a matter of course. Why, then, do through another ceremony? Status and protection are major considerations. The question is which type of marriage provides the greatest degree of protection. My informants had varying opinions on this matter. "If marry church marriage, you

---

[4] For example, among the Akan, "the essential element of the marriage contract is the gift of 'drinks' (*tiri nsa*) by the head of the groom's lineage to the head of the bride's lineage" (Oppong 1974: 30; *see also* Rattray 1929, chapter iv, and Fortes 1967: 278-281). In addition to the *tiri nsa*, there are customary gifts which the bridegroom gives to the bride's father, mother, lineage head, and brothers, but these may be waived. Among the Ga, the first step towards making the marriage public is the *agbosimo* or gate-knocking: the man's kin sending two messengers to the woman's kin with the gate-knocking wine. After the approval of the woman's family, two messengers return to them with 15 pounds: 1 pound for *kplemo da* (agreement wine), 6 pounds for *yi nii* (head money), 4 for *he nɔ to bo* (buying of the waist, i.e. sexual rights, comparable to *tiri nsa*), and 4 for a public party *(bladzu)* (Field 1940; Manoukian 1950 also records a variation on the procedure).

[5] Mary Nyarko, wife of Nana Atakora Amaniampong II (the *Mamponhene*), met her husband at the Anglican church. Both of them were excommunicated when they married, since he already had one wife.

cannot be free, because you are wedded. And if you are wedded, your husband cannot feel to marry another woman." Another felt that customary and church marriage in combination are not "hard, like registered. Because you will be afraid of the law." Still another held that marriage by registry *increases* one's sense of freedom by providing more security: "Some of the men fool the women. Will marry you and won't look after you a-tall. Can take him to court and they will ask him why... If you marry in the church, the man will do something to you, and you can't say anything. You just sit quietly and you can't leave him too.

Only a minority of the women held that customary marriage operates in favor of the wife. Joanna married when she was young, and her husband ran off to America, leaving her with a baby. Her second husband wanted to marry her by Ordinance. She refused, because she says she did not know his intentions:

> I don't know how you are, if you'll beat me... If a man is good, it doesn't matter; if a man is bad, you will suffer. By customary, you don't record it. If he dies, his family will come and collect all and drive you away. By registry, all goes to you. *But* difference is that with registry, you are less free. With customary, if man is bad, you are free to leave him. With registry, get involved with court and fees and so on.

Whether the woman marries monogamously or not, in civil court or in church, she is still faced with the likelihood of having to share her husband with another woman. Does she voice any desire for change, or envision alternatives?

The majority of the women sampled were born to monogamous unions, and so did not experience polygyny firsthand as children. Of those married, only one-third have married polygynously,[6] and

---

[6] Through my Hausa interpreter, I was invited to the wedding of her "brother" (also from Kano, Nigeria), who owns and occupies a two-story house in *Sabon Zongo* (a new strangers' quarter), not far from Adabraka. The interesting thing about this marriage is that he already had two wives of differing ethnicity, the first Ga, the second Yoruba; they occupied separate rooms on the first floor. His bride was Ewe, and she was to move in with them! To maintain a modicum of peace, the man dashed each of his first two wives 200 Ghanaian pounds ($400) and many yards of expensive cloth. They were hostesses to the masses of

most of these are quietly acquiescent. Akosua, the only poly-
gynously-married woman to come from a polygynous home, says
that she is worried:

> because maybe I'll suffer with the man at first; we're poor but
> slowly make something, have a child and look after him, and then he
> goes and takes another wife who shares in the money and none of the
> suffering (*Translated from the Twi*).

Those monogamously wed are almost unanimously opposed to
polygyny, no matter what their background, although a certain
amount of ambivalence is sometimes apparent.

> Some rivals [sic] good, some too are not. Even my husband doesn't
> want because says spend too much money. It can be good; she can
> converse with you and even you can work like sisters...

But others are too quarrelsome. So speaks Faith, whose father
married four. Hope's response, translated from the Ewe, reflects
the predicament of most of those who voice any disfavor about
polygyny: "Ghanaian men, that's the way they are. Whether you
like it or not, they can marry. If you say you won't like him to
marry another..." Her husband has no other wife; if he took
another, she would not like it, but what can she do about it? "It's
good to marry more than one; Ghanaian men, that's how they are.
Whether or not it troubles the wife. But it will not trouble me."
Thus she ends on a positive note. Many of the other monogamously
wed women qualify their responses similarly. Some add that as long
as the man takes care of her, or as long as there is harmony, what
does she care?

My impression is that most of these women have probably never
confronted their feelings about this before. One does not consider
alternatives that one cannot conceptualize. Expressed feelings are
tied to concrete realities, situations seen or experienced, but
Western patterns are encountered only in newsprint and the

---

women who arrived throughout the day for the traditional fete; every few hours,
each of the two would change into a new outfit, complete with scarf, shoes, and
purse! Their husband paid well for his third marriage; both his and his wives'
status went up in the community.

recollections of "been-tos." Hence the wavering note in the opinions expressed.[7]

In general, among married and unmarried alike, the major reasons for opposing polygynous marriage are finances, jealousy, and possible disharmony among the co-wives. Its proponents, as well as those who are simply accepting, cite possibilities of harmony, more help in the house, and the husband's increased satisfaction. And Ruby points out the obvious: her husband "jollies" (has girlfriends) anyway.

This brings us to the issue of "friendship," the functional equivalent of polygyny. The women are split in their sentiments. Significantly, an informant would often react in the same way to the prospect of her husband (or future husband) taking a second wife or having a girlfriend; this was true for more than half the sample. Lydia, for example, who has a co-wife, does not mind her marital situation, because she never has to come into contact with the other woman. By the same token, she does not care if her husband has a girlfriend, as long as she need not deal with her. Ellen, an articulate young woman who is affianced and living alone, puts it this way:

> If the other woman will give you due respect; if he'll go and take another woman and hide it, then it's all right. It won't be anything. But anybody who will bring it here, and say "This is my girlfriend"—some do that... And if you think of how you've been serving the man and somebody too is paying outside—yes, it's very painful. Here they do it. Today is the holidays [opening of Parliament]; go and see the hotels. Men are drinking with the young girls while their wives stay at home.

The wife's jealousy of the social or sexual relationship of her husband with other women is not affectual; rather, she fears being cheated out of material things. Many of those who asserted that they do not care whether their husbands run around said that this

---

[7] Attitudes toward monogamy, like those toward registered marriage, probably become more sharply defined with increased education and sophistication. According to Pool (1972: 251), attitudinal data reveal that "the actions of Ghanaian women mirror their thoughts, for most felt that a man should have only one wife and very few equivocated on this subject." The single women in my sample, who are proportionately younger and better educated than the others, overwhelmingly oppose polygyny.

attitude was conditional upon their being given the things that they "like." Hope's first husband was a womanizer and did not properly provide for her, so, at the age of 20 and after only two years of marriage, she left him.

Finally, there is the matter of male privilege. Men will always philander, the argument goes, so, given the foregoing conditions, nothing can be done—"he must have his fun." At least the wife still has a husband. Those who know that their husbands "jolly" may be annoyed, but the women say resignedly that their opinion is not solicited. On the other hand, for women to carouse or take a "friend" when married is out of the question—"people think bad things." This right is reserved for males alone—"men have authority"; "God made it so." Of course, it is possible that some of these women do carry on affairs, with those living in the family house away from husbands the most likely candidates. Yet each of the few times that such an affair came to light while I was in Ghana, it created a stir. In any case, the women interviewed are expressing the social rule as they know it.

When it comes to such things as polygyny and girlfriends, the woman already married to the man involved really has no way of changing her situation. She could, perhaps, try to divorce her husband, but this is impossible without due cause, and in a polygynous society a husband taking a second wife or "jollying" is not necessarily due cause. And the never-married woman is not free to remain single;[8] that alternative is envisioned in neither the indigenous nor the imported culture. In the past, she also was not free to choose her mate; her family did so for her. Among the Adabraka women interviewed, this tradition is barely alive; only a handful were married off in this way, all of them illiterate. Many

---

[8] Many women do not go through the formal marriage ceremony; traditionally among Akan, "we are told that permanent cohabitation or procreation with a minimum of formalities or public rites may be practised with relatively little prejudice to the social status of the wives and children concerned." (Oppong 1974: 31). A major reason for marrying or remarrying is to have children, but a child born to parents who do not marry receives full legitimacy (as does the mother) when the father publicly acknowledges paternity. Mair (1969: 120) notes that the followers of Islam, exemplified by Hausa, consider marriage as the necessary prelude to legitimate conception. Their traditional rigidity has broken down in Accra, as seen in the passing of *purdah*.

meet their prospective husbands in the course of daily perambulations. For example, a young man comes by while the woman is selling in the market and they chat, or a neighbor's cousin comes to visit in the compound and is introduced. In *African Women in Towns*, Little (1973) states that urban African women insist upon choosing their mates, and that this is a true sign of independence. While this may seem to be true on a superficial level, the crucial question is how much of a choice "everywoman" perceives that she has. The tale of the first encounter is often told as if she were peripheral—the man saw her, liked her, asked her guardian's permission, went through the formal introductions, made engagement payments, etc.

Much of the literature on West African urbanization takes the view that ethnic restraints weaken with escape from the city, and that it is much easier for two strangers to come together on the neutral turf of urban life. The whole extended family and lineage organization is not necessarily present. Learning English is officially encouraged and nationalism is promoted over ethnicity. Indeed, my informants expressed positive views about ethnic intermarriage, some maintaining that they would marry a man from a different ethnic group should they fall in love. It is a large step, however, from mouthing idealistic platitudes to putting them into action. For example, I find that 20 of the 28 ever-married Adabraka interviewees assert that intermarriage is good "because we are all human beings," or does not matter as long as "he can look after her"; yet 12 of them have married fellow-ethnics. The balance of married women are split between having married outside the group and approving of exogamy and marrying endogamously because they disapprove of the other. Among the 11 single women, seven have boyfriends. The only ethnic differences in their matches lie on the sub-group level (e.g. Kwahu with Asante). All, however, aver that they will marry anyone. It appears that even in the city, marriage to a fellow ethnic is still significant, possibly even preferred and expected.[9] As one modern young woman says,

---

[9] Evidence exists that the percentage of marriages that are inter-ethnic increases at the higher levels of social class. For example, among the professional class in Sierra Leone, "...with the shortage of professional qualified men, Creole women, given the choice, may find it preferable to marry a Provincial professional man than not to marry a professional at all" (Harrell-Bond 1975:

"Mostly our family wants us to marry customary."

Those wary of ethnic intermarriage speak of a dislike for outsiders, the simple desire to be among one's own (at least if one has to live in a compound of strangers, one should share one's room with a countryman), and child-related problems. This last concern, in fact, probably has a great deal to do with the infrequency of intermarriage, as is indicated by the responses of three of the women. Ellen is literate in Ga, Twi, and English, is educated, and lives alone. Of the single women, she is the sole one to express a preference for endogamy; in fact, she is engaged to a fellow ethnic, an Asante man.

> I don't want my children going to the other side. Maybe they will be living with their father, who is not Asante and who speaks a different language. And they will repeat that language. When they come to my mother, my mother can't speak with them.

Auntie Rose is an illiterate Ga, who lives with her children in the house of her matrilineage. Having married a Ga, she says that if she had not done so, "one day, if I leave the child in the house, I go to some place, maybe by the time I will come, the man will take the child away. And I will not see him." And Lydia, also a Ga, living in the family house, literate in Ga and in English, says:

> I like to marry Ga. I don't like to marry Fante or any other. As for me, I don't like that, because if you have children with a stranger, and you divorce with him, some of them take the children away. If the Ga man takes the children away, you will meet him. Maybe you are staying here, the man is staying at Jamestown. If you want to see your children, you can join a bus or taxi then you go there. If the one is a stranger and he is staying at for instance Nigeria, if you haven't got money to pay your transport, you can't go. That is why.

The women's fears have a basis in fact. In general, a very young child remains with the mother, while an older one lives with the parent of the same sex. For example, among the Akan, the divorced woman either leaves weaned children with their father, or is

---

171). On the other hand, Little (1973) reports that among the Ijebu-Ode of Western Nigeria, there is great parity in higher education for both men and women and as a consequence they tend to marry endogamously.

provided with money to carry out the normal paternal obligations of feeding, clothing, and maintaining them (Manoukian 1950). As this society is matrilineal, the children ultimately belong to the mother's clan (Kaye 1962). Children of Ewe, a patrilineal society, are exclusively the divorced mother's concern until they reach the age of two or three. When old enough, they traditionally go to their father, although a daughter may opt to remain with her mother (Manoukian 1952). The patrilineal Ga award full possession to the man if he has paid the bride price to his ex-wife's family; if not, they may claim the child. It is unclear what occurs when the bride price is refunded (Field 1937).

Childbearing, in fact, is a reason for marrying. And it intermeshes with other equally-persuasive motives. For one thing, as we have seen, marriage is an accepted custom. Indeed, the woman's status as an adult, *even in the city*, depends on her tie to a male and the production of offspring. If she is a successful businesswoman, or wields power in her voluntary association, she is accorded all appropriate respect. But if she is unattached, the respect accorded her is diminished. She need not live with the man or be totally supported by him (although rent and chop money are sacrosanct). The mere fact of a man "making her a respectable woman" fulfills the minimum requirement. Perhaps this is why women put up with polygyny and "jollying."[10] It is an embarrassment *not* to be married, in part because any man feels free to approach a woman not accorded proper respect with unbecoming comments.

> As a woman, you must have somebody...If you say you are not going to marry, you are going around and having boyfriends and the rest. This man, he may not want to pay for the pregnancy, or anything like that. But if you are well-married, you will know that by all means, this man is your husband and the man too that this is his wife. He has to do everything for you (*Aba, 26, unmarried with a child*).

> Because if stay and don't have a husband... it's bad... when stay and

---

[10] In a personal communication, Professor Rémi Clignet questioned my uncritical acceptance of the generally negative view of polygyny voiced by my informants. He reasons that so many would not put up with it if it were not to their benefit, in the sense that it enables them to comply with social and cultural norms.

don't have a husband, everyone can feel to talk with you... When he sees you don't have a husband, he can come to your place anytime *(Jeanette, 39, and married).*

In addition to childbearing and the respect factor, women speak of support as a reason for marrying. The last is often thrown in as an afterthought, but its extreme importance becomes apparent when the women discuss reciprocal marital responsibilities and what they want in a husband. Many combine all three concerns in their responses. An as yet unmarried girl put it this way:

A woman wants to bring forth, and you want to get a man who works so he can look after you... And you marry for respect. If you don't marry in Ghana here, people won't respect you...

Akosua, twice-married and illiterate, reasons as follows:

A woman married because (1) if she's sick, the man will send her to hospital because her parents are no more now. And again, if the man is also sick, she also will help him and send him to the hospital. (2) A man cannot go to market and chop [eat], so he must marry a woman to cook for him. (3) A man needs a woman to wash for him and the money that he would give to a washman goes for chop for them. (4) If a woman has no money, the man will give her money. And if they have children, the man will look after them and send them to school.

She went on to explain why, male carousing notwithstanding, some women do not want to remain single if widowed or divorced:

Marriage here is not like European marriage. After marrying you, he will marry again and not mind you. So you too go and find another man... To marry is difficult: if I had work, I wouldn't marry. Having to wash his clothes, clean the room. Even I don't have time to eat. I have no money and no work. If I had money, I would have a store of my own and wouldn't have to marry.

Similarly, Auntie Atta, widowed in her twenties, wants to marry again, because the man will look after her.[11]

This brings us to the content of marital relationships. According to the women questioned, this adult relationship primarily revolves around finances. Both men and women are practical-minded.

Traditionally, any emotional content that might exist was incidental to the marriage, and it is my finding that things have not changed much in this regard. As individuals, husband and wife are both detached from their roles; a special personality is not required to perform them. While players are needed for the roles, the players are interchangeable. What women mainly expect from their husbands is material support[12]: household and chop money, money for the basic needs of the children and their schooling, and "anything I want, he will give me." In fact, customary law recognizes the wife's right to maintenance by the husband; as she is " 'under his control,' " he owes her the " 'necessaries of health and life' " (Daniels 1974: 286). Lydia pinpoints her husband's obligations to her as his wife:

> He is responsible for everything you need: your eating, going out, coming, your clothing, everything. He is responsible for it. Monthly money, pocket money, money for the children. Pocket money for you. If you see something, maybe a scarf, you can't be going to him "I want to buy a scarf, I want to buy sandals." But if he is giving you pocket money, you will use some of it.

Clearly the man's financial (and social) position and his wife's degree of sophistication have a lot to do with her expectations. Auntie Elizabeth explains:

> Only to assist you, he can do it. If he has the means. But if not, he might say, wait small. But some people are evil. Like looking after the

---

[11] Oppong (1974) found that Akan women in Accra will stay with an élite marriage, even if they find it disagreeable, because they become dependent upon the material advantages it makes possible. Social distance (in life-style) between them and their rural kin has become vast, and remarriage to a man of the same status as the first is unlikely. Thus, neither a return to kin nor remarriage is an acceptable alternative.

[12] Only four of my informants did not couch their desires in explicit economic terms; the wishes expressed in these cases were that the man would look after her and be with her, as she would be with him; that they would make demands on each other, smile, and go out once a week; and that he "provides for me, advises me, is a companion to me." All four are in their twenties, three of them are informed about Western ways and values, and only one is married.

children, clothing, helping with household expenses. They expect you
to feed him three times a day and he just gives small and goes away.

On the other hand, the woman sees her wifely responsibilities in
an equally traditional and non-affective light: "to cook, wash, do
everything for him." Her obligations are all domestic; she is
expected to maintain order in her husbands home life, and to bear
and raise his children. Lydia says of her responsibilities:

In the morning fetch water for his bath, prepare tea for him, clean his
shoes; he will go to work and you will prepare food and he will come
and eat; go again. In the evening he will come again, you will fetch
water for his bath, prepare food for him again.

One woman will do as well as the next. Faustina, for example, has
a sister, Auntie Akuye, who "squeezes her face" all the time and
gets along with no one in the family house. One afternoon, she kept
wandering back and forth and in and out, crying. First it was
because one of her nephews spilled her cooking water, then
something else happened on the same order of magnitude. When I
asked about it, everyone just shrugged, indicating that she cries all
the time. Yet she is married, has four children, and carries out all
normal housewifely duties. Her mental imbalance does not become
a central issue because her husband and she do not live together and
she need carry out only the most basic functions for him—bearing
his children and cooking. Since she lives in the family house, sisters
and cousins aid in child-rearing. Companionship he can get
elsewhere.

The wife has her own life, but it is acted out according to the
desires of others, especially her extended family and her husband.
She has no control over her spouse's comings and goings. The wife
acknowledges her husband's seniority through deference to his will.
In many homes the use of the title "Mr." is symbolic of the type of
relationship they maintain.

The subordinate role of the wife affects sexual relations. If a man
and a woman are married, it is accepted that they must sleep
together. But it is my impression[13] that the women regard sex as a
duty of the relationship rather than as a source of enjoyment. It is a
means of conceiving children and pleasing the man. The idea that
lovemaking should be a source of reciprocal pleasure seems to be
absent. A sophisticated woman of my acquaintance, who lives in

the suburbs of Accra and has spent several years abroad, complains of how unfulfilling sex with Ghanaian men is. All they are interested in is "taking their pleasure." In nonmarital liaisons, such as hers, women barter sex for other desirables. In marital relationships, this is less so.

Women not expecting much in the way of a sexual return do not yet see this as an issue. One "been-to" woman journalist, Stella Addo, feels otherwise. In a 1970 article entitled "Woman, Do you lie about 'it'?", Ms. Addo alludes to the past, when "the woman's role on a marital bed was a simple one. She was expected to be submissive and unresponsive. Her place was not to receive pleasure but to provide it" (*The Daily Graphic*, 19 October). Now, she writes, there is a more liberal attitude towards the woman's role in general and sex in particular, yet many women still find the sex act a disappointment. Should they confide this to their partner or lie? According to Ms. Addo, it is dangerous to be open and truthful: *"Apart from becoming aware that he had been deceived for years, it could undermine his masculinity and challenge his virility."* Instead, one should adjust oneself to the circumstances and not strive for perfection.

Wives of polygynists alternate in their conjugal duties, including sex. The more co-wives, the less each sees the man. Since fidelity is expected of the wives, they do not have much opportunity to flex their sensuality. The same is often true for the monogamously wed: men have girlfriends. Furthermore, the wife frequently fears pregnancy, and, given the choice between conception and abstinence, she may opt for the latter. This is especially likely if she knows that her husband has another outlet. In any case, it is the man who is the initiator. As one Adabraka woman pointed out to me, it is not the woman's place to approach the man (even her husband) directly. If she feels interested in sex, she might do something "like go and bathe and then come and stand in front of him naked, or in bodice, and put on oil and powder and then the man was crazy!"

---

13 On a few occasions, I tried to enquire about conjugal sex life. This is a sensitive question; such information was never volunteered when women spoke of their marital duties. With a few of them, however, I achieved enough trust to be able to discuss the subject.

When would a woman leave her husband? As long as he provided for her material needs, no matter how lacking the relationship might be in companionship, she would probably stay. Wife-beating, as such, is almost non-existent. Men do, however, box their women on the ears if they feel that they have not behaved properly. One woman said that a husband only beats his wife if she has a boyfriend. Most would accept such bursts of temper—"So if he beats me, I abuse him." Indeed, several of the women cannot imagine what circumstances could be so bad as to warrant their leaving the marriage.[14] Others, such as Vivian, simply insist that splitting up is not possible. Single at the age of 26 because she is looking for a love relationship, rather than just financial security, she believes that marital problems must be talked out. Perhaps this is because she has few illusions about the content of the average marital union. "They can say anything that comes into their mind. They figure that because they give their wives money, that they can push them around; don't realize that a woman also takes part in the house and should be given a chance to say what is on her mind. Most men are so."

Sometimes, of course, it is not the woman who seeks to terminate a marriage. Akosua was involved in an interesting dilemma which led to divorce. At the age of 14 she married "Paapa," an older man who had been married several times before. She is Nzima (a small Akan group whose members speak Nzima rather than Twi and live in the Western Region) and he is Kwahu (Twi-speaking Akan). His family was unhappy with the union, because of the ethnic difference; however, they wed by Nzima custom, since the marriage took place in Akosua's hometown. A few years later, they moved to Accra, and the man went into the provisions business. Six years after the marriage, "Paapa's" family was still antagonistic toward Akosua and pressed him to take a second wife. She came and left, as did a third and then a fourth wife. As the senior wife, Akosua doled out household chores to the other, while she herself worked alongside her husband in his store. She thus weathered out the

---

[14] In such cases, coaxing was necessary to elicit a response; the reaction was similar to the blank-look response I received from unattached women when I asked what kind of a man they wished to marry. I had to provide multiple-answer lists in each case—examples of *why* a woman might leave her husband, and of what a girl might find appealing in a man.

"rival" problem. During the Nkrumah regime, she and her
husband lived at Flagstaff House (government headquarters),
where they had a provisions store. During the 1966 coup:

> ...soldiers came and I ran away to my hometown and stayed there. My
> husband's family said that because I ran away and left my husband
> alone, he should not marry me again [i.e. remain married].
> *(Translated from Twi).*

Despite the extenuating circumstances, her in-laws finally managed
to "sack her."
The actual mechanics of divorce depend on the type of marriage
being dissolved.

> Divorce is easily obtained, even from more formal marriages, with the
> single exception of marriage under the ordinance which can be
> dissolved only judicially. Other divorces require little more than
> agreement, or even desertion... (Caldwell 1967: 70).

Crabtree (1950) has pointed out the sexual discrimination built into
the general rule for divorce in southern Ghana—reminiscent of
Victorian law in this regard. A man may sue for divorce on grounds
of adultery, barrenness, witchcraft, *juju*, neglect of household
duties, disrespect of him or his parents, or desertion, while a woman
may sue only for neglect, cruelty, or impotence. (The latter would
have a disproportionate effect on her sexual activity, for she must
restrict such relations to her spouse; in the reverse situation, the
man need not leave the woman, since he can marry another or
father a child out of wedlock). The financial technicalities are fairly
involved: if the husband has proof of good reasons for a divorce,
the wife's family must refund the bride price and money spent on
her to date. If his reasons are judged trivial, he forgoes the money,
and if the woman has proof of good reasons, the money her
husband has spent on her need not be refunded.
The Matrimonial Causes Act, 1971, represents an attempt to
reconcile civil and customary law, with respect to marriage and
divorce, permitting the judicial unification of monogamous and
customary (including Islamic) unions (Adesanya 1976). Thus its
provisions for those petitioning the court for a divorce reflect
customary law. Adesanya (1976: 93) cites subsection (3):

The court shall have regard to any facts recognised by the personal law of the parties as sufficient to justify a divorce, including in the case of a customary marriage (but without prejudice to the foregoing) the following:-

(a)   wilful neglect to maintain a wife or child;

(b)   impotence;

(c)   barrenness of sterility;

(d)   intercourse prohibited under that personal law on account of consanguinity, affinity, or other relationship;

(e)   persistent false allegations of infidelity by one spouse against the other.

Like the Nigerian Matrimonial Causes Decree of 1970, the Ghanaian Act stipulates that a petition for divorce be granted only once the court is satisfied that the marriage has irreconcilably broken down. One proof of such a condition is adulterous behavior by the respondent which makes it intolerable for the petitioner to continue to live with the respondent; the Nigerian Decree, however, points out that an allegation of adultery is not sufficient basis for intolerability: "Human beings, or at least many of us are of a forgiving nature and it is well-known that the woman or wife is in this respect of adultery of a more forgiving nature than the husband' " (*Eyo* v. *Eyo* Taylor C.J. 1972, quoted in Adesanya 1976: 98).

While this may in fact be so, the Ghanaian Act accords the right of petition in the wake of adultery to either party. Whether women will readily take advantage of this right remains to be seen. As already mentioned, both partners to an Islamic marriage have equal rights to initiate divorce, yet women exercise this right less often than do men.

Not one of the women interviewed professed knowledge of her rights concerning divorce, or of its financial complications. All (but one) who "married" had at least gone through the traditional engagement and could describe the ritual of exchanges. Most, however, did not know the exact goods or amount of goods that changed hands. In this case, as in so many others, they feel no need to know, since others are around to evaluate situations and provide guidance. About half of the sample women maintain that they would be financially self-supporting in the event of a divorce; others say that they would opt for the role of a family dependent, with the mother as the main agency of help, for, as one woman phrases it, "my mother is there to support me."

Perhaps most intriguing is the fact that only one woman spoke of remarriage as a natural way of resolving the problems that a divorce would create, and even she did so with hesitation: "Anyway, I don't know that I would leave him; anyway, maybe I would have another husband." Those who were widowed also exhibited no burning eagerness to remarry, although some did speak of remarriage as a way out of the financial hole, or complained that life had become more difficult since the husband's death because money was short. Despite the financial jitteriness of the typical Ghanaian wife, it seems that the real incentive for marriage is social and cultural in nature, rather than financial, and that, having been married once, the divorced or widowed woman does not feel the same push to be so again.

The Mother

A major prerequisite for being considered as an "adult woman" or an "adult man" is evidence of children. Procreation is preferably undertaken within the bounds of marriage, and it is also a good reason for marrying—"You must marry to bring forth; and if you don't marry, people won't respect you." Just as the state of marriage confers respect, bearing children enhances it. If it is not the definitive characteristic of the woman's persona, childbearing is certainly an important part (cf. Paulme 1963).

Caldwell (1966) notes that the 1960 fertility rates were lower in the larger towns. In Ghana as a whole it was most common for a woman to have five to nine children. Thirty-three percent of those with less than five live in urban areas, 23 percent live in the southern rural areas, and 15 percent live in the northern rural areas.

The average size of "everywoman's" brood is two, below the national average. This may be largely a matter of age; the childless are in their twenties, and, with one exception, all of those who have borne four or more children are over 30. On the average, "everywoman" *hopes* to be the mother of four. Getting this information required persistence on my part: their outlook seemingly reflected the fatalistic belief that such things are fore-ordained. Some of the more traditional women would reply, "It is all up to God," or "I can't answer because God provides." Of all those interviewed, only two (both single) wanted less than three children.[15]

Offspring carry great value for economic as well as cultural reasons; in general, the greater the number borne, the more contributions to parents in the latter's old age. The amount of such support is not *directly* proportional to the family size; rather, children are markedly less likely to contribute at all if there are only one to four of them. As Caldwell reports, sons are likely to be more valuable than daughters in this regard:

It is interesting to note that, even in Ghanaian society, where females enjoy a great deal of independence [sic] and often regard themselves as breadwinners in much the same way as males do, 72 percent of all respondents, who received assistance from children, received most from sons. Only 17 percent received most from daughters, and in 11 percent of cases the two sources were of roughly equal importance. In the extreme cases, 37 percent received assistance entirely or almost entirely from sons and 5 percent entirely or almost entirely from daughters. Those receiving assistance almost entirely from daughters almost approximate to the number of families where one could expect daughters to be the sole survivors, and those receiving most from

---

15 The following chart matches up the number of children wanted with those actually brought forth.

Number Brought Forth	Number Wanted							
	0	1	2	3	4	5	6	7
0a			1	2	5			
1b			1	2	7			
2					2		2	
3c								
4					6			
5d						1	1	1
6							2	
10						1e		

---

a. In addition, one childless respondent gave no answer.
b. In addition, one respondent with one child gave no answer.
c. In addition, one respondent answered: "I can't answer because God provides."
d. In addition, one respondent answered: "All if God gives."
e. "[Only four or six] but God didn't allow it."

daughters to families where the great majority of survivors would be
daughters (Caldwell 1966: 18).

In the urban areas, perhaps because of the greater possibilities for
gainful employment, 23 percent are aided by daughters, as
opposed to 15 percent in rural areas (Caldwell 1966).

At the same time, once four have been born and the mother still
has several good childbearing years left, further pregnancies are
look upon with some ambivalence. The notion that she has a choice
as to how many children she will bear is only beginning to filter in,
while the idea that she can choose whether or not to have children at
all is foreign to her ken. And while *having* many children is
different from *wanting* many children, the cultural expectation may
result in a blurring of distinctions between the two. On the one
hand, there is no alternative to motherhood; it is the adult woman's
role to reproduce. On the other hand, she feels little power to exert a
negative control over her own body. That is to say, contraception is
contraindicated by the traditional cultures which make up
Ghanaian society today.[16] She holds little control over her own
body in a social, psychological, or physiological sense. Joanna, 23
years old and pregnant with her third child, had only recently
discovered her condition. It was something of an inconvenience: her
husband, their two children, a cousin (an unannounced arrival from
the hometown), and she shared one room. Joanna said that to
conceive is unpleasant, for she cannot eat and "grows lean." This is
due to the baby "taking all of my blood"; in fact, she refers to her
pregnancy as her "sickness."

Unmarried and married women alike are unsophisticated in
modes of contraception. Only one of my sample informants said
that she uses oral contraceptives. To avoid impregnation, women
sometimes turn to the age-old alternative of "not going to the man"
and of coitus interruptus. Many will advise that the woman should
abstain from intercourse for at least one year after a baby's birth,
"so that the vagina will dry up." Whether one waits or not, nursing
is still held to ward off menstruation and thus the possibility of

---

[16] The only account I heard of native abortificants was confused. This was from
Gloria, an Ewe: "Peel leaves from the tree...If use, can prevent. I don't know
what it is. If you have no children and want, take. If you don't want, do the same
thing."

conceiving.

Most of these methods involve avoidance, whereas modern methods of contraception imply involvement and decision-making. Are they known and used? In 1969, the government adopted a family planning policy, eventuating in a program one year later. In the ethnographic present (1970-71), Accra houses one Planned Parenthood clinic, as well as the offices of the parent organization, the Family Planning Association. ("By 1972, the government had established 140 clinics [in the country] and licensed over 600 chemical retailers selling subsidized contraceptives" (Smock 1977: 209). At that point, 25 percent of the women between 20 and 34 years of age were participating in the family planning program in Ghana.)

Any Accra woman who reads English, and many who do not, knows the phrase "family planning" and recognizes the triangular symbol. A number of my respondents spoke of family planning in reference to birth planning. But they used the phrase as a generic label. It is a seemingly modern variant of the "as God wills" sentiment. Somehow it represents an external agency which will determine how many children the women will have, thus removing the whole process from their hands. Only one of those who used the phrase had ever visited the clinic—the nurse's wife mentioned above. Regina, for example, is 28, has three children, and wants only one more. "We have Family Planning." ["So you use it?"] "No, I can't [haven't] use it, but will go. They came here and talked about it."

Access to contraceptive devices and information is problematic. A leisurely conversation with Hope, a 30-year-old woman with five children, the youngest an infant, turned to the topic of men and sexuality. Suddenly she asked if I could tell her how to prevent more children. I suggested either oral contraceptives or an IUD, explaining how each works. In the end, she said that she would just avoid intercourse for a year or so, that is until after she had stopped nursing

Those who do know something about the modern appliances are often misinformed. On one occasion, I stopped by a neighbor's compound to say hello. Juliana, in her late twenties, was grinding up vegetables for soup. I asked how many children she had (three), and whether she wanted more. "Three is enough, is good. Maybe you can help?" I agreed to take her to the Planned Parenthood clinic. "But I don't like those rubber things that you put in your privates." Moreover, "they" say that pills are very dear, that each costs two shillings (20 cents). I assured her that two shillings would purchase a whole month's supply, and the following week took her to the clinic. She was given a supply of birth control pills and took them for one month, but later she told me that she had "passed menses" for the first time since conceiving one year, nine months earlier; she did not take the pills again.

One interpretation of Juliana's behavior is that she did not want to be bothered. But there is a deeper interpretation: she was not prepared to assume the responsibility of also determining for herself whether she would bear children. This attitude is reflected in the society at large. Doctors generally give their patients injections, rather than prescribing a liquid or pill. They know that the patient only expects to be acted upon, and will not take the initiative to the extent of swallowing medicine at regular intervals.

Furthermore, some men do not encourage their wives to seek out contraceptive information because they fear that an explosion of extramarital affairs would result. A former Minister of Health—one of the individuals responsible for legitimating dissemination of such information—personally communicated precisely this view. He was not concerned about the time-consuming and exhausting nature of child care, infant mortality, the difficulties of childbearing, insupportable costs, and so on. Rather, he railed about immorality, saying that it is a woman's duty to bear many children and to stay at home and mind them; if a woman has access to birth control, she might stint on her domestic responsibilities, or worse yet run off with another man.

In his discussion of population control among the urban élite, Caldwell notes two important influences:

> One is the increasing pressures resulting from high fertility in a situation where nearly all children survive to demand extended education, high standards of dress, opportunities for entering high status occupations, and so on. The other is resistance to innovations and particularly such radical innovations as the use of modern contraceptives (1968: 169).

More than two-thirds of those in his élite sample favor establishment of clinics, and two-thirds expect to use them. "These statistics have to be placed against the equally attested facts, that love of children and pride in large families are deeply entrenched characteristics of African society'' (Caldwell 1968: 169). Amongst my non-élite sample of women, there is little attempt to take precaution—even when the birth of additional children poses a threat to economic security, no real attempt is made to take precautionary measures. "When I give up with four, I'll go and see a doctor"; "if the time comes, I'll find my way out"; "maybe use medicines, so my stomach will spoil." Much is left to chance or fate.

In societies where tradition is still strong, the mass media may provide factual information and create new desires; however, personal influence—especially that of an in-group authority figure—remains the most effective way of changing individual decisions and actions involving moral judgements (de Sola Pool 1963). The basic reason so few inroads have been made in limiting the size of the Ghanaian family is that almost all of the information on family planning is communicated through the mass media, and too little attention has been given to personal campaigning through channels of authority at grass-roots level.

The campaign of the Family Planning Association, in particular, is too intellectual; the pamphlets and posters shown at their exhibit at the Trade Fair in 1971 were written by expatriate employees. They emphasized the importance of "protein" in children's diets and the difficulties of meeting these nutritional needs when a family gets too big and has too little money. People came from all over Ghana to see the Fair exhibits, and the Association had a rare opportunity to present their case; the approach they took and the wording they used meant nothing to the majority of the booth's visitors.

The lone Planned Parenthood clinic in Accra has short pamphlets, written in the major Ghanaian languages, about oral contraceptives and Intra-Uterine Devices. The midwives and other clinic personnel speak with clients and give them literature. The women who have made their way to the clinic presumably do not have to be convinced. Yet, the effect of the visit is often short-lived.

Many of the misinformed antagonists to contraception have misconstrued the items printed in the news media. Newspaper readers can learn about the different methods and devices and their respective cost. Ironically, these efforts are often counterproductive, for I found that many of the women who oppose contraception have read or seen this material. The problem is that neither the content nor the process of communication follows lines with which they are comfortable.

In fact, the most significant role of the papers in the birth-planning program has been as a forum for moralizing about the pros and cons of contraception. During the summer of 1971, the Ministry of Education and Sports issued a communique stating that as of September 1971 female students in secondary schools and training colleges who became pregnant would be dismissed. This stimulated a torrent of letters-to-the-editor, and informal conversation on the subject of contraception. The major focus of concern was the possibility that the non-selective dissemination of birth-control literature and contraceptive devices would weaken the moral fiber of the female population. The following extract from a February 1971 article shows that such fears were present even before the controversy generated by the communique:

> Should unmarried girls be allowed to get help from family planning clinics? This was the topic of conversation I overheard at the Trade Fair Site the other day.
>
> ....I very soon concluded that they were against the issuing of contraceptives to unmarried young women because of the low moral standards it would breed, the irresponsibility, too much freedom, and the dangers in some forms of contraception.
>
> To my surprise, no mention was made of the most important aspect of the whole family planning affair: birth control. As far as I know, the immediate aim of the campaign is to give people a choice in the number of children they can afford and want, but in the final analysis, it's to control the population of each country and in the long run, that of the world so as to enable everybody to have his fair share of the worldly kenkey.
>
> Now I would say that the bulk of our population comes from unmarried mothers—working girls and school girls who have to drop out of school. Therefore, if birth control devices are made available only to married women, only part of the problem is solved because we'll still have unmarried mothers and a rising population.
>
> ....Of course some old fogeys will come out and say that it'll lower the morality of the young girls. Don't they know the old proverb which translates "the yam which will burn when roasted will still burn even

when boiled?'' (''Yaa Yaa's World,'' *The Mirror*, 13 February, 1971: 6).

Yaa Yaa's point is well taken. In my own sample, five unmarried women have each had one child.[17] The youngest was 15 when she gave birth; two were 18, one was 19; and the eldest was 23. Only two of them did not finish Middle Form Four, dropping out after the pregnancy began to show; the others had already finished. In earlier times, in rural areas, they would have been married by this age, or responding to the custom which promoted premarital conception. For example:

> Among the Krobos, a patrilineal people, the first child born by a girl belongs to the girl's family. The rights *in genetricem* which a husband has over his wife are therefore transferred only after the girl has had one child. This being the case, the girls are not so anxious to contract valid marriages before the birth of their first child (Tetteh 1967: 208).

None of those unmarried pregnant girls in my sample could marry at the time because they felt that they were too young, because the pregnancy was a mistake and they did not want to marry the boy responsible, or because the ''friend'' would not marry her. The following newspaper exchange took place after the Ministry's communique. Writing in response to a diatribe by *Daily Graphic* columnist John C. Hagan against the provision of contraceptive devices to teenage girls, another columnist, Gladys Kotey, was quick to point out in the pages of the same newspaper that:

> *The mere use of contraceptives does not turn a woman or girl into a prostitute. I know a number of women in this profession who never heard of contraceptives through a research I carried out sometime ago.*
>
> ....A good knowledge of birth control methods can abolish illegal abortions that cause a lot of deaths among teen-age girls.
>
> ....Educate the young ones in family planning, and half the battle is won (13 September 1971).

---

[17] Adawkaw had an abortion in her late teens, and Viv a miscarriage. It is also quite probable that others among my sample had children before marrying. I only know for sure of one, who is now married with two additional children. There was generally no diplomatic way for me to investigate this in depth.

As I have already suggested, the potential impact of Ms. Kotey's atraditional views is diminished by what the readers want to believe, at least until some significant other redirects their beliefs. It is doubtful that the press can play that role. Dissemination of birth control information in a form and through channels more appropriate to Ghana would help to reduce the number of deaths due to abortion. Backroom abortionists are patronized by unmarried girls who do not always survive the experience. Joanna had been to one several years earlier, and the operation left a profound impression, judging from her uneasiness in discussing it and her graphic description. "They do it with an instrument that looks like scissors. They stick it in and cut the fetus off from the cord. And it pains horribly for about a week, and you bleed a lot."

There is an extensive mythology associated with abortion, only some of which has a basis in fact. Leafing through *The Daily Graphic*, the *Mamponhene* (paramount chief of Mampon, one of the states of the Asante Union) seriously repeated to me the commonly held belief that every young girl listed in the obituary section has died of abortion. Patience, a young neighborhood friend of 14, insisted that:

> If you have a baby in your stomach and you go to hospital to get rid of it, they will give you an injection and kill you... We read it in the *Graphic*... Otherwise, you can buy medicine for an abortion from the dispensary. If the man likes you, he'll give it to you. But you must take your boyfriend along. If he refuses, take another fellow. If you get pregnant and he doesn't care, he will not want to see your face. If he likes you, he will either marry you or give you money to "spoil" it... Surely if you want to die, just go to Korle Bu [the hospital] and tell them you want to spoil your baby.

What Patience maintains she read in the *Graphic* is probably an extrapolation based upon the local lore.

Much of the birth control problem is tied to the men's beliefs about the proclivities of their women. Hagan urged that contraceptives be distributed only on a selective basis and stressed that:

> ....the whole idea of birth control and its planned campaign is an indivisible part of that inviolable reality called MORALITY on which

the life of every nation depends. Destroy it and you destroy the very
life-blood of society. That is why some would urge caution,
discernment and discrimination in this rush for the propagation of
birth control devices (*The Daily Graphic*, 28 September 1971).

What he and those who share his view are in effect suggesting is that
an adult woman is a married woman and that only adults should
have the right to assert themselves. Many men would not even go
this far, and instead would share the perspective of the former
Minister of Health. This leaves even the married women with fewer
options, since she is still beholden to her husband for advice, for
permission, for respectability.

Since premarital sex is not categorically discouraged, it is not
unusual for girls to get involved. Most leave it to their boyfriends to
provide the means of contraception.

> If only you don't want children, you will take the medicine or
> something else. And now in Ghana, they say they are asking Family
> Planning. So if you go, I think they will give you anything. [For now?]
> I used to [am accustomed to] take medicine, Alophen 21. I get it
> myself.

Georgina has heard of Alophen through others, who got it from
boyfriends. In fact, like Apoenstill, it is a purgative and has no
contraceptive usefulness.

Whatever their thoughts about childbirth in the abstract, most
women who conceive accept the pregnancy and the bearing of the
child with good grace, as a fact of life. Once the child is born, he is
easily absorbed into the family and is loved as much as those who
came before him, without further thought as to whether he was
"wanted" or not.

The children of Adabraka are allowed their fun, but basic
discipline is not neglected; this generally falls to the supervising
woman, who is more often than not the mother of the children. She
has the closest physical contact with her children; for the first years
of their lives, she carries them on her back, enfolded in her cloth.
While they are still small, she cleans up after them and accepts their
trespasses. As they mature, she tries to imbue them with moral
fiber. She assigns them household tasks and oversees their
completion. Often her closeness to the children mitigates the

effectiveness of her guidance: indulging their whim one day, blowing up at them the next. Hence, fostering is a popular alternative. Those looked after by a female other than the mother—grandmother, aunt, elder sister, foster parent—are of course socialized, at least in part, by that same person. Auntie Atta has two children, a girl and a boy. Her husband died when both were young. She turned over the younger, the boy, to her mother, who lives quite far away. For one thing, she could not afford a maid, but more than that, she felt that the child would be better off if sent "home" for care and discipline.

Unmarried mothers, who tend to live with the family, do not have sole responsibility for the child's upbringing. Many, in fact, spend little time with the child, leaving him in the hands of mother or senior kinswoman. The relationship of unmarried mother and child in such situations approaches that of older and younger siblings, or aunt and niece / nephew.

In general, children do pay heed to both parents, as well as to other familiar adults who chastise or correct them. Fathers tend to bask in the glory of having produced offspring and to handle them gently. According to Joanna, her baby cries more often when his father is around, because he knows that the man does not allow Joanna to spank him. "As for the child, must be patient... Africans beat [spank] children badly." When mother is occupied, older women, especially kinswomen, often caress and soothe the child; a menopausal woman may even put her breast into a baby's mouth in order to calm the infant.

Among the unmarried and the young marrieds who do not yet have children, some interest is expressed in sharing the responsibilities of caring for a prospective child with their husbands and/or hiring someone to care for the child during the day. Although I question the realism of such expectations on the part of these women (they remind me of the young married woman's dream of having a "white gown" wedding), they are not just fantasies dreamed up by the women themselves. The newspapers are full of articles portraying the image of the "modern" woman and her lifestyle. Moreover, these women are exposed to Europeans (even if only through visual contact) who hire Ghanaians as nursemaids, and to Ghanaians of the upper class who can afford to hire help and do so.

Even among élite civil servants, child-raising is the woman's role.

"Few couples can be classified as *joint,* as far as this assumption of responsibility for housework and child-care is concerned" (Oppong 1974: 110). Although most have full-time help of some kind, including kin, the resolution of domestic problems is still the wife's responsibility. For the minority without household help, the wife may have to quit her job in order to manage the home.

The Member of an Extended Family

The married urban woman-with-child is still the child of her family network. Her ties are not severed when she leaves home, and the influence that family and parents wield over grown offspring is not to be underestimated. This influence manifests itself through ingrained obedience and respect for senior family members on the part of the individual. The family may also intervene to protect the younger member and uphold her rights.

One lever for family influence is provided by the institution of fostering, already touched upon in an earlier chapter. Although the woman who has moved to the city might like to lead a life independent of family interference, she is likely to be saddled with a child or two, and if she is to work full-time she cannot take time off to raise them. Given her earning capacity, she cannot afford to hire a housemaid either; moreover, if she is married, her husband may well resist the idea of his wife's relinquishing the role of mother and bringing in a stranger. In such a situation, the woman must willy-nilly turn to her family for assistance.

Most of the Adabraka women interviewed were raised by their own mothers. In the case of those living in family houses, however, other female relatives living on the premises have also taken a hand, and the youngsters readily relate to them. Lizzie makes the relationship explicit when she refers to her mother and maternal aunts as "my mothers." Children raised with cousins in this way often refer to them as brothers and sisters.

About one-third of the sample had experienced fostering, although those sent away during prepubescent and teenage years to attend school would not regard their experience as such. The women associate fostering more with rearing during the earliest years of life. As children they were variously "lent out" for financial reasons, upon the request of the fostering woman (often because she was barren), for better instruction with less pampering, or simply because it seemed appropriate. All went to women—to

the patrikin if from a patrilineal ethnic group, to the matrikin if
from a matrilineal group.

None of them regarded fostering as a particularly negative
experience, although some might have preferred not to go through
it. Lydia lived from the age of 9 until 19 with an aunt who had
moved to Takoradi. The aunt lived with her husband and wanted
Lydia to stay with them. Lydia's preference would have been to
remain in her mother's house "because I am a stranger there
[Takoradi]; I don't know anybody there. If [when] I went to school,
I have friends. When we close, no friends." Yet she continues to
sense with considerable discomfort the pull of kinship obligations
with regard to her own children:

> If my aunt is there and she says she wants to look after one of my
> children, I would give her. But now my aunt has grown up; she can't
> look after them properly. Maybe if you go there, you will see the
> children dirty and so forth, and you are dress up. It's not nice. But
> once you are all right and you can look after them, you can look after
> your children.

It was generally agreed that kin could be trusted to look after
children, whereas fostering by others would be chancy. Only a
minority of the women are unequivocally opposed to fostering their
own children. Reasons given in support of the institution are
identical to those of their parents' generation—to teach the child
respect (since he/she would be more apt to listen to someone other
than the mother) to give a child to a barren woman, to provide a
better environment if there were financial problems at home.

Unless one's mother is incompetent, the chances are good that
she will take over responsibility for her daughter's child, and the
daughter in turn believes that it is her right to expect it of the older
woman. Indeed, this is doubtless another reason that unmarried
girls are not more circumspect in their sexual encounters—although
the future grandmother may grumble about the pregnancy, the
child will always have a good home. Benedicta moved to Accra to
live with her older sister and find a job. She had a boyfriend for a
short time, albeit long enough to become pregnant. She has given
over to her sister most of the ensuing child-care responsibilities.
Nevertheless, she finds the few hours spent with the toddler trying:
"How she worries my mind. I will send her to my mother soon."

This is quite possible. Thirty of the Adabraka women are mothers; 10 of them are currently participants in fostering. All but two have lent out one or more children, primarily to female kin; the two are recipients. Akosua, who bore only one child, is taking care of the daughter's children; Auntie Viv is reciprocating a past favor. "Crisis" fostering followed divorce or the husband's death in a few cases. For others with many children, fostering relieved the mothers of some of the burdens of child-rearing. A few report that their mothers complained of being alone. Fostering, in the strict sense of the word, is especially popular among those whose family (potential foster parents) continues to live in the hometown. Moreover, better than one half of the mothers in the sample live either with immediate family or in an extended-family household. Thus, when they work, they can (and do) leave small children in the care of mother or other close female kin.

The two major objections expressed by interviewed mothers about fostering are interconnected: fear of maltreatment, while she, the mother, would not be there to intervene, and concern that the fostering parent might be a "stranger." When the fostering woman is a family member, it is assumed that "she will look after her well. But if not, sometimes she don't look after her well."

Hiring a nursemaid from outside the family, on the other hand, is not considered objectionable. She is supervised and only sits in for the mother, whereas a foster parent, in contrast, takes over completely. Still, most mothers prefer leaving children with kin.[18] The traditional household provides an analogue to the modern maid in the person of a member of the extended family who is given room and board (indirect payment) in exchange for the performance of household duties. According to custom, such a girl would be given the dirty work rather than child care, however, and thus her presence would not obviate a fostering arrangement.

---

[18] To explore feelings about the importance a woman attaches to raising her own child (as compared with fostering or allowing the child to be cared for by day help), I asked each woman what she would do if she were offered a good job that required she make provisions for the care of her child or children. Two-thirds of the women replied that family care was preferable to a hired nursemaid, and two-thirds of those opting for family care specified that the child would be better off with the mother's mother.

The bearing of children has another dimension as well. A woman's actions continue to affect her family, even if they are hundreds of miles away. The act of childbearing—like marriage—reaffirms one's responsibility to others, sustains the balance of indebtedness, and shows tangible respect for custom and for those who represent it—both the hometown folk and one's husband. A particularly strong bond ties together the woman and her mother. The returns on the birth of a child are great for both. When a woman produces offspring, she changes her mother's status and helps to perpetuate the family line. In return, her mother offers to take a hand in the child's upbringing, or is receptive to her daughter's request for help. Just as the young girl in her mother's house helps with the daily chores, so the mother helps her adult daughter in those areas where "mother knows best."

A good example is the mother's assistance during the daughter's postpartum period. Even after the birth of several children, women will still go to mother, unless the two women are resident in the same house or town, or the distance between them is too great. In the first instance, the mother may just come over on a day-to-day basis; in the second, the seasoned child-bearer may decide that the trip is too long or, more probably, she has other small children in the house who cannot all go with her for an extended stay with her mother.

After delivering, either in the hospital or with the aid of a midwife, every mother interviewed was ministered to by her mother or a mother substitute if her biological mother had already died. Some gave birth in the hometown, others went there after the baby's birth. In either case, they spent an average of four months in their mother's homes, leaving husband behind. If the distance involved is not too great, he will visit periodically. For those whose mother comes to them, the visitation period is shorter; but if at all possible she comes. For, as Ellen said (in the context of a working mother's child-care problem): "a housemaid may be someone who has not brought forth, she doesn't know anything about a child. But my mother knows everything." When Ellen gives birth, she will follow the pattern of her elder sisters who have also left the hometown. She will deliver in Accra and be cared for by her visiting mother. After two weeks, she will return to Asante with her mother for the duration of her maternity leave.

The exchange of favors between mother and daughter becomes especially pronounced if the latter is unmarried, has a child, and is living with the mother. The case of one 19-year-old, Dora, exemplifies this; to an outsider, her life seems to run according to parental manipulation. She gets up between 4:30 and 5:00 a.m. to sweep the compound and then, while everyone else sleeps, she prepares the porridge that she will sell for her mother. Then she cleans the kitchen and carries the paraphernalia for selling porridge and *togbeh* (doughnuts) out in front of the compound. Between 6:00 and 7:00 a.m. she moves out front to sell; this involves cooking dough in hot fat while dashing out porridge to breakfast customers on their way to work. Dora's mother is a baker, and Dora helps her on baking days by firing up the oven and putting in the bread; on those days, she comes out to sell at 7:00 a.m.

She sits in the morning sun till almost nine o'clock when she customarily cleans up her selling area, takes all of the utensils inside to wash them, bathes, and then prepares for her part-time employment as a housegirl. But one morning she was still sitting and selling at nine—"Please, the porridge is not finished, people aren't buying." She could not go inside because her mother would harrass her, even though she was late for her outside work. Her mother's occupational and household chores took precedence.

In the late afternoon, Dora helps with the bread, going with her sister to have the flour ground, bringing it back and mixing the ingredients, and helping her mother to make and bake the loaves. At some point, she must also find time to buy corn dough, sieve it, and get it ready for the morning porridge. When the bread is baked, she takes it to the bus stop to sell. There she stays until 11:30, when she comes home, puts away the remaining bread, takes in the laundry, and goes to sleep.

While Dora is at her mother's disposal, the other side of the coin is that her mother has taken Dora's 14-month-old child as her own. It is the mother who disciplines him, watches over him, and has accepted complete responsibility for his upbringing. This is the older woman's trump card; in absolving her daughter of most motherly duties, she keeps Dora beholden to her. Moreover, the father (a man concerned with appearances) has done all in his power to keep the "mistake" a secret, and Dora must reciprocate his protection and help.

Although all of the women agree that their earnings are theirs to

Children inspect a newly-completed bread oven, shaped like
a beehive.   *(Photo: Deborah Pellow)*

do with as they please, disposal of income to kin outside of the
conjugal unit can be a source of tension. Lucy Mair (1969)
comments that among the matrilineal Akan both husband and wife
have financial obligations to their respective kin as compelling as
those they have to each other, and often more so. Oppong (1974)
suggests that "closure" in the conjugal relationships of Akan senior
civil servants is manifested in part by the cutting of financial
contributions to kin. She argues that this strengthening of the
conjugal bond is a natural outgrowth of living in the city, where one
is away from the traditional networks and subject to Euro-
American influences.[19] Those for whom this transition is not yet

---

[19] Unfortunately, I obtained no data from married couples on the actualities of
financial decision-making. Discretionary spending may not be much of an issue
for low-income Adabraka couples, given the recurring fixed expenses that must
be met.

complete may suffer conflict, with the man caught between the competing demands of his matrikin and his wife.

The woman herself may become a pawn in contest between her own family and her spouse. This is vividly illustrated by the following extract from a letter written by a secondary school tutor to the Secretary of the Committee on the Status of Women:

> Many men complain that failure of marriage is mainly caused by the wife's mother. I support it....
>
> I married a woman from Anum since July 1953. I performed all marriage customary rites. We have five children. We never quarrelled, but in April, 1964, her mother refused to allow her to continue the marriage because I was not giving money (the mother was asking from me) to my mother-in-law. As a result, my wife has left her five children with me, and now has become a prostitute.
>
> My wife.... has declared in writing that I had not performed any customary rites to make her my wife. She added that she was not interested in either the marriage or the children....
>
> I have no interest to pursue the marriage, but all I know very well is that my wife has been influenced by the parents to leave the marriage contrary to her will....
>
> That her parents do not wish her to continue the marriage because I was not paying the unnecessary monies demanded from me. Whether I shall take any legal steps or not, I wish your committee to investigate thoroughly into this, as an example to all married women and see to put an end to such practices... (Letter to Janet Tay, Secretary, Committee on the Status of Women, Ministry of Social Welfare, Accra, from "G. Agyekum," 6 August 1967.)

It is possible, of course, that the woman involved decided that she wanted to be rid of her husband and had her mother and father stand up for her and perhaps even invent a story. As Dora says, "If he does you something and you don't like it and you tell your mother and they see it isn't good, you can't marry him again." The family may not always agree that the woman's reasons are justified, however, and so may insist that she stay married. Most abide by mother's and father's decision. Hope (an Ewe), for example, left her husband because he was reneging upon his financial responsibilities to her. She went to her mother who "sacked her to go back." When the man continued to do badly by her, she again approached her parents, and this time they upheld her.

Should a divorce occur, all but one of the married women would move back in with family—two-thirds specifying mother. The odd woman out envisions setting up house on her own.[20] In the last chapter, we saw that women came to Accra because of family (or marital) attachments, *not* to get away from it. Now we find that even after they are married and oriented to life in Accra, they do not see divorce as an opportunity to try out autonomous living; rather, they would run right back to the refuge of the family. Can they conceive of living in a situation other than with family or with spouse? They do not appear to.

In the context of the hometown, one's family are one's friends, the people who can be depended upon if need be. Adabraka women tend to be more comfortable in relying upon family than non-family friends. This dependency is never a one-way street, however, and kin expect some return for solace or for money. When money is dashed, the future reciprocation may be in cash or kind.

> The fact that incomes are on the average higher in the towns does not mean that economic pressures are felt less there. Just the opposite is the case. For most Ghanaians, the town is still something of an 'unnatural' existence. Its delights can be enjoyed more easily if one is aware that welcome and security is waiting in the village as soon as things begin to go wrong in the town. Failure to help relatives in the village or to visit them occasionally could well destroy that welcome, and this is a state of affairs that comparatively few urban Ghanaians would be prepared to court. Life in town without a job can be very difficult, especially if one's family lives hundreds of miles away (Caldwell 1967a: 143).

Lending money is a somewhat different story. Most people who

---

[20] This does not contradict two earlier points: that women like to be free of family interference and that upon divorce, a woman could become self-supporting. The women are obviously tied to their kin, even though they may sometimes express the opposite, more "modern" view. Furthermore, the women do distinguish between living with the family and being a financial dependent. In both cases, they want their family ties *when they want them* and are ambivalent when the dependency comes from the other side.

lend money would prefer to be repaid in cash, but the protocol of Ghanaian family relationships is such that this cannot be assured in all cases. A number of those with whom I talked about this subject quoted local lore to the effect that lending money to family is the same as giving it away. Even so, the majority of the women concluded that they would be inclined, on balance, to lend to family in preference to a friend—assuming that they had any money to spare. Those who took this majority view and the minority who said that they would prefer to lend to a friend because of the greater likelihood of repayment seemed to be equally aware of the risk factor in lending to kin. But, for most, keeping intact the web of family support has higher priority than assurance of repayment.

Travel is almost always undertaken for the sake of family. If "everywoman" has kin outside of Accra, she visits them. When distances are great, travel is undertaken less frequently and then only for good cause (a parent's illness, funeral, etc.). Only one woman in my sample does not make the customary trips to visit her mother: Vivian's mother fears that kin and townspeople envious of her daughter's good fortune will use *juju* against the girl. Boyfriends are also known to take their women on junkets, and church groups sometimes sponsor trips. Regina exemplifies the general thinking about travel: "I haven't got anybody there, but when I have got anybody there, I will travel."

New Female Roles

This chapter looks beyond those roles and relationships that are traditional in context and content, and examines the development of new roles and behaviors in the urban milieu. As we shall see, the new identity relationships are generally similar in basic content to the old. Male-female interactions continue to be sexual in essence. Interactions with other women outside the immediate family are limited. This is due in part to the highly structured work week, but also to traditional distrust of non-kin women based on a perception of them as potentially threatening to one's marriage or other relationships.

Relationships with Women: Neighbor

I have portrayed Adabraka as an urban village, where Western lifeways and values are overshadowed by common folk traditions. The urban compound is an adaptation of the traditional family house. Outside of her place of work, this is where "everywoman" spends most of her time. Its heterogeneity, the feature that distinguishes it from its traditional predecessor, encourages the development of new forms of interaction and the identities that go with them. Although the content is still domestic, the woman is eased into the transition to city life as she learns how to deal with strangers in the role of urban neighbor:

186

> If as in some simple villages, neighbors are also clan and blood
> relations, then the concept of neighbor cannot arise. It arises precisely
> because the neighbor is the proximate stranger, defending interests
> that are partly his alone and partly those he shares with other
> neighbors... In most tribal and peasant villages this presents no real
> problem, for though the neighbor may be considered a stranger in the
> sense of not being a blood or affinal relative, he is, nonetheless, a
> familial figure whose antecedents are as well known as his current
> habits. In cities, however, the neighbor may actually be a total
> stranger, one whose ancestors and habits are unknown and whose true
> personality must be pieced together from fragments revealed only in
> the course of time (Keller 1968: 22).

Neighboring has latent functions, which provide clues to the newcomer on how to behave and what to acquire (Keller 1969; Perry 1939). These are: (1) reciprocal social control to help sustain common standards and shared communications; (2) gossip chains, to spread information; and (3) the creation and maintenance of social standards of correct belief and conduct.

Neighboring is affected by social change. Since compound life is no longer congruent with the extended family, dependencies are different. One must remember that in the city, a neighbor need not be a friend or a relative. The first is a chosen role, the second one prescribed. They also differ because "physical distance does not destroy these relationships whereas a neighbor, by definition, ceases to exist as a neighbor once spatial distance intervenes" (Keller 1968: 24). If two neighbors become good friends, the friendship usurps the neighbor relation.

Perry (1939), among others, has suggested that most urban dwellers are not acquainted with the people living next door. In the case of Adabraka, I found this to be true when the neighbors did not share common kinship or ethnicity. In those compounds where kin reside together, behavior is more solidary than in those where compound residents are "strangers" to one another. In one compound, for example, there was a neat social and physical split between Kwahu (an Akan group) and Ewe. Illiterate Ewe tend to be clannish and suspicious of outsiders generally, in addition to being the target of pejorative ethnic labelling. Solidarity is one way of dealing with diversity. It need not be xenophobic only. The Kwahu, among all the ethnic groups with which I dealt, were outstanding in terms of their high regard for each other; they seem to stick together out of mutual esteem. In the Kwahu-Ewe compound, the Kwahu are on one side, the Ewe on the other, and their interaction is fairly limited. "Oh, I know them, but I don't know their hometown. But we come together and if anyone needs anything..." The younger members of each group know everyone's names irrespective of ethnicity, but the adults do not. Both groupings are self-contained and have perpetuated their respective hometown scenes; they appear to have little interest in or need of each other. Yet, inter-ethnic (and inter-linguistic) encounters are becoming common for those heretofore accustomed to homogeneous situations.

In compounds inhabited by one family with a few stray tenants, the latter are usually known by name (family name). In compounds that begin as a family establishment and are then expanded into family and tenant housing, and in those inhabited exclusively by tenants, on the other hand, it is not unusual for neighbors merely to recognize each other by sight and possibly to know each other's ethnic backgrounds. Often as not, compound-mates come into contact with each other only if there is a definite reason for it.

Social intercourse among women in the compound is limited not only by mutual apathy but by work schedules. All of the women, outside work notwithstanding, have their domestic duties. This does not leave a great deal of time for socializing, especially with others not regarded as anything more than people who happen to live next door. As one young woman said, "If I am cooking and you are in the kitchen, I will just chat with you. As soon as I am finished, I will come to my room."

Nevertheless, some interaction even among "strangers" does occur. One component of compound interaction is voluntary; this involves the depth of residents' interrelations, the type and extent of social intercourse, and the locale of the interaction. Most of the women claim to know everyone in the compound, at least for purposes of greeting. The formulas used by neighbors in addressing each other depend on the statuses (seniority, sex, ethnicity, marital status) of the interacting parties. Each of the non-Muslim women has her own Christian name, as well as a Ghanaian day-name; the latter is more commonly used when conversing parties are on a first-name basis. This would be the case between peers; "sister" is a common alternative. If the woman being addressed is considered an adult (for example, if she lives on her own) but is childless, she is usually called "auntie" by those junior to her. When she has a child, she may still be called "auntie" or the teknonymous term "mother of X" (e.g. Maame Kofi).[1] Mothers call their daughters by their daynames, while daughters address their mothers and other women whom they place in the same category as *maame* (mother). The Muslim women are known by their ethnic names, often consisting of first and family (or husband's) name (e.g. Adisa Harona).

The distance between men and women is mirrored by the terms of reference and address used for each. Just as traditional leaders are addressed by their title (*Nana* for an Akan chief, *Nii* for a Ga chief), so ordinary non-kin men are often called "Mr." by non-Muslim women. On the other hand, men may address women by their day-name or sometimes as "auntie." Women are rarely called "Mrs." Such a title accrues only to those married by the Marriage Ordinance. Young boys may be called by their day-names, though it is far more common for them to be known by a Christian first name.

Although there may be an occasional outing to the cinema, social interaction tends to be confined to the compound yard. It usually takes place for short periods of time before bed or on Sunday when no one works, and in passing during the day. Generally people are not in the habit of sitting around and socializing in the room of a neighbor (compound mate) who is not kin or from the same hometown. The major exception is when there is a television on the premises. Ownership of a set confers additional status on an individual or family, and it benefits one's reputation to allow neighbors to watch. In a sense, television is a gimmick which allows for altered behavior.

Interaction among non-kin in a compound runs the gamut of "If I see, I will greet" through informal conversation and Sunday afternoon games of Ludo. In every compound, someone owns a Ludo board. Ludo is a game, somewhat on the order of Parcheesi, which is played primarily in the British Isles and in West Africa. In Accra, it is played with great zest, particularly on Sunday afternoons, when people have free time. The board is brought outside and taken back in when the game is over. Playing and watching promote interaction among compound-mates. The other

---

[1] This is a clear instance of a woman becoming a personality (or, in a sense, losing her personality) through the birth of children.

major leisure-time activities around the house are chatting in the yard and retiring to bed, perhaps to read the paper or a "storybook."

Women's casual interactions with others in the yard are usually limited to other women or to male kin. I found only one case of a woman spending time with any of the men in the house who were not her kin; her husband is a nurse, which probably accounts for his less traditional attitude toward social interaction between the sexes. The two of them entertain friends together and go out drinking or dancing with compound-mates as well as outside friends. Perhaps equally atypical to the other extreme was the attitude of Ruby's husband. An illiterate Kwahu woman, Ruby had become best friends with her immediate female neighbor. The two women, who lived together with their respective spouses and children in chamber/hall arrangements, cooked together, shared cloths and kerchiefs, and enjoyed sitting and chatting together in the afternoon. For reasons not explained to her, Ruby's husband separated the two women friends. Perhaps the autonomy implicit in this relationship violated her husband's rule of role.

Contact among women living in a compound is often promoted by similarities in tasks, such as cooking and marketing. Since most women cook outdoors, and eating schedules generally coincide, they often converse during these activities. As a woman learns to develop neighborly relations with one or two others, they may market together or, on occasion, one woman may buy a few items for another. To allow another to shop on one's behalf is an exception rather than the rule, however, and requires a greater than usual sense of trust. As reported in earlier chapters, Ghanaian women enjoy a good bargain and for that reason are rarely willing to trust the negotiations to another; in a society where children are trained in adult tasks from an early age, few are sent to the market because "they are children and they will be cheated."

The layout of the compound may also promote or inhibit interaction. Ruby, who owns a kiosk at the front of her compound, knows all of the people in the double house, mainly because they buy their petty goods and provisions from her. She never sees the women, however, when they are "at the upstairs." "Upstairs" is the main building, and is "up" in the sense that it has six steps leading up to it.

Age also affects interactions. "In the house... I work alone.

They are older than me. They are married, have got husband. How can a small girl like me make friends with them?'' This was the query of a young woman in her early twenties, who has a two-year-old child and lives with her sister. Her relative youth may be exaggerated by her marital status; as an unmarried woman, she is still free of compulsory daily household tasks, which puts her into a different social category than her married neighbors.

The population of a compound usually includes numerous children. Just as a neighbor is "not really a friend, only we are living together," and free time is not spent playing together, so a neighbor is not family and is not to be depended upon as such. This is the attitude expressed by the more traditional women who will not leave their small children in the care of compound people—"no, if [unless] one of them is my parent [kin]..." On the other hand, women whose children are older and who have working relationships with neighbors—marketing together, talking together—also help out in caring for one another's children. If a woman's baby eliminates in someone else's yard, a female resident (even if only a peripheral acquaintance of the mother) will immediately come to the child's aid. Children are fed on demand, and a hungry child can always find something to eat from someone if his own mother is not available. Unlike adults, children seem to feel no restrictions—social, psychological, or territorial. They often disregard boundaries and trespass where adults would not dare.

Since the residents share the use of compound facilities, they must also share the responsibility for the care of these facilities. Thus, the second measure of neighborliness examines basic working relationships, necessary to the operation of the house. The division of labor for this caretaker function involves all of the *female* inhabitants, whether stranger or kin. Male residents are exempt, as they are from all domestic tasks. Men learn to deal with strangers in the public domain, beyond the compound walls. Women learn to deal with strangers through their domestic roles, thus perpetuating a traditional theme.

Whether a house is newly built or a vintage product, maintenance problems are complicated by the heat and humidity, which combine to eat away at any paint that is applied. Floors, public and private, are always carefully swept, but walls, doors, and baseboards are grimy and spotted.

Early in the morning, one of the women living in a room or set of rooms will sweep out these quarters and her corner of the compound; or, if there is a child available who has reached the age of seven or eight, the task may be assigned to the child. If the occupants are husband and wife, the wife always sweeps; if a mother and daughter, the "child" defers to age and takes responsibility for the cleaning even if she is as old as 20. If the occupants are housing an extra family member on sufferance, or if they have been lent someone else's child, the guest will take over the job.[2] It is of interest that prepubescent family members participate without regard to sex in general housekeeping chores such as sweeping, washing clothes, and washing the floor; cooking, however is done by females only. If the room is upstairs in a two-story building, no yard-cleaning duties are involved, but most storied buildings have some kind of balcony arrangement or a connecting hallway which must be cleaned regularly. When a room is off a hallway, each occupant's area of the hallway is individually swept.

These individually maintained public spots, outside or on balconies, are swept as many times a day as meals are prepared. A woman drops refuse on the ground as she cooks, afterwards sweeping up the parings as well as the trail of ashes and dead charcoal left by the coalpot.

The middle of the yard may, or may not, be swept regularly, depending upon the women living there. If there is a common kitchen, it is not cleaned in rotation, rather, each woman cooks individually and takes care of her own area. Conflicts do not seem to crop up over refusals by one person to clean a spot that she has not used, probably because there is always a child around who can be given the task. Nor do the women appear to be particularly concerned about distributing the tasks equally. According to Aggie, one may sweep:

> in any spot...If I like I can sweep all the house...and clean the toilets and the bath. And if there is something bad, and that thing is going to spoil us, I can take it...Like a milk tin or a rag or anything.

---

[2] This is by no means unusual. There seems to be an understanding that a girl who moves into a household, for whatever reason, will offer her services in exchange for lodging. Thus, without anything having been said, I awakened at 5:30 a.m. the first morning after my second interpreter had moved in with me to the sounds of her sweeping out the house.

Toilet and shower facilities are shared in every compound. There is at least one of each, and most compounds that are not family houses have one set per housing structure in the compound. (Three sets are shown in Figure 5 on page 88). If the compound does have several sets, the use of toilets and showers may be assigned according to house, ethnicity, or, less frequently, sex.

Cleaning the showers and latrines follows sexual lines; in one compound where one of the rooms is inhabited by a man and his child but no woman, and where the job of sanitation goes according to room, the man is skipped entirely. The decision-making involved in who cleans what and when varies, but a few generalizations can be made. In most cases a system of rotation is followed: the job may pass from room to room in a weekly cycle—"it just came about when one day the lady from the first room did it and the next the next room and so on"—or the women might sit down and discuss the matter and decide whose turn is when. Regina, whose mother-in-law owns the house where she lives, says that it is her husband's decision, "and they have shared it, my husband with those in the house." What actually happens is that the women in the house get together in the morning, afternoon, or evening on a daily basis and discuss "about the house." The children wash the latrine and shower daily and then the women back them up monthly. Regina's husband gets into the act when something goes wrong—as when he goes to the toilet and it is not clean. But he calls *only* the women together to straighten things out.

The women in another compound may divide sanitation chores among themselves, meeting to discuss this only at intervals of a month or more. Some women insist that no system whatsoever exists at their compounds; where Ekua lives, "If you look and see the toilet is dirty, you can wash. If you see the bath is dirty, you can wash." In cases where the men share one set and the women another, it still falls upon the women to clean both. Even if there is only one woman in a compound, and the other occupants are men, it is her ascribed task.

Sometimes the system in a mixed compound follows the lines of that in a family house, where seniority and ownership are most important. The eldest woman in the compound may dictate who cleans when. In an Adabraka family house, the senior woman is invariably the head of the house—either the head of the matrilineage, the house-owner, or the eldest sister of the house-owner. If no one takes the initiative to do the cleaning, she will allot the jobs. More often than not, the women of the house carry out this work themselves, rather than passing it on to the children, who do the simpler sweeping. If it is a question, however, of a young adult woman versus her mother or aunt, the former will accede to the latter's seniority and do it.

Aunt Viv, the successful contractor whose story was partially recounted in an earlier chapter, continues to live with her mother and sisters in her mother's house, despite the fact that she is in her early forties and married. Her husband is not in evidence, having been transferred to Ho (in the Volta Region), but her brothers live in the compound. The mother has two rooms. Each daughter has her own room, and also shares the front room with the others; they also share their own bath and toilet. The brothers are housed on the other side of a separating wall, because they complain of noise. The sisters cook in a temporary shelter, whereas the mother has a proper kitchen, bath, and pantry all at the rear of the house. She thus has no duties in the front of the house. Housework is done by housegirls, one for the two brothers and two for the main house; one is a relative and another is fictive kin. (The father of the latter had been looking after one of Auntie Viv's children, a student at Achimota. His wife became mentally ill after giving birth to the girl in question, so the father brought the child to Auntie Viv when she was eight months old; she now is sent to school and taken care of in return for household work.) Despite the presence of the maids, every woman has her set tasks: Auntie Viv must see that the table is laid and breakfast ready; someone else must see to the garbage being cleared.

From the foregoing description of neighboring, we get a sense of how the compound provides a starting point for the development of new roles, and yet how the context and content of the roles continue to emphasize traditional female responsibilites. Inasmuch as female roles continue to have a strong traditional content even in the city, compound life teaches the women something of the ways of the city right outside their doors.

Relationships with Women: Friend

In traditional areas, women friends are usually kin. A distinction is made between family (the "in" group) and others (the "out" group), though members of the latter may be incorporated through fictive kinship. Some urban women make an attempt to befriend outsiders. They meet first at work, at church, in the neighborhood, the compound, and often through some significant other. Yet women in Adabraka impressed me as being somewhat afraid of each other. As noted earlier, in the city, unlike the hometown, a significant distinction exists between friend and relative. Is friendship beginning to replace kinship as a relationship of trust? To answer this question, we must first find out how the women define friendship.

The concept of friend is not unknown and in fact most of the women say that they have at least one friend.[3] The women's description of "a friend" tends, however, to be vague. In general, it is safe to say that two friends are usually peers. Joanna phrases this nicely: friends are referred to as "equals" because when two women are friends, "you are the same size." Furthermore, titles denoting differences in status (e.g. auntie) are de-emphasized; Faith says that she and her three friends all call each other by their first names "anyway [because] we are friends."

Friendship with others may also be described in negative terms—someone is a friend because she does not abuse or talk roughly to the informant. "Because she is good for me," is a common explanation, sometimes associated with a difference in age; an older friend can show one the right path.

Ethnicity is often a factor in choice of friends. The preference often expressed for those of the same ethnicity—"because of language"; "we are all the same"; "the people I know the best"— is remarkably coincident with actual practice. The same agreement of words and behavior holds for the minority involved in mixed friendships—"we are all one"; "depends upon the person." It is not clear whether a trend toward increased interaction across ethnic lines exists. The individual's knowledge of English is probably not a factor here, since most of the women are polylingual in African languages.[4]

---

[3] So say 27 of the 34 women interviewed.

[4] Two of the 10 women who are inclined toward engaging in friendships with "strangers" do not speak English and belong to language groups (Buzanga and Ewe) dissimilar from the others, while two-thirds of those who prefer the company of members of their own ethnic group *do* speak English.

What do women who are friends do together or expect of each others? Material obligations are often mentioned—"if I need something, ask for it," "we buy things for each other." It follows that shopping together for cloth or other articles of clothing is a common activity. In general, meetings among friends consist of visits at home or brief encounters, which are accidental and end when the activity that brought them together ends. "If I meet them, we can converse, cracking jokes, then pass away, bye bye." Those places where their husbands and boyfriends, fathers and brothers, go and engage in heady discussion—bars, in particular—are off limits to women unaccompanied by men, unless the women do not mind being marked as loose—"Accra boys are bad and will try to follow you and boss you."

"Visiting together" has a variety of connotations. Those who speak of going to visit a girlfriend at her home might mean stopping by for a brief greeting, or a meal and a game of Ludo, or sitting and conversing, or "speaking my mind." How often they see each other is partly a function of the need (dependence) each has for the other. Amina, for example, is from Yendi, which is several hundred miles from Accra. She speaks of having close friends, but they live in Yendi. She never sees them because of the distance. Auntie Viv said that she has two close friends; one of them moved to the United States in 1965, and Viv has not seen her since. It seems that the intimacy and deep feeling that we associate with close friendships is absent. Those friends who work together or live together have some contact daily. In general, however, most see each other on an average of once every 10 days to two weeks, although some see friends on holidays only—friends that they refer to as "the" friends. One reason friends get together so seldom is that they do not have the time (or the need, and thus do not make time). Another is that few forms of diversion are available to women not accompanied by men. If they belong to the same church, they go there alone, sit together, and return home alone. Membership in associations is based upon work (as in the market women's association), church, or ethnicity. If they hail from the same hometown, they may travel together to visit kin or attend festivals. They can plait each other's hair. They can take an early evening walk to the Circle[5] and on Sunday afternoon go to the cinema.

A major reason for the lack of intimacy among women is a fear of each other that they themselves verbalize. Lydia speaks for many of my informants:

> Going to friends' house, I don't like it. Some of the friends are not
> good. If you go there, they will gossip or something else. I don't like
> going to friends. If I'm lazy then I'm in the house, reading my
> Bible or any story book...If you meet at the Ambassador [Hotel] you
> can joke and do everything from there, it's okay. Because you alone
> aren't going there.

For some, such as Hope, the issue of secrets is pivotal:

> As for other girls, when you tell your secret things to them, they will
> reveal your secrets; but as for this girl, she doesn't do that. And
> whenever we want to go out, to buy the cloth, we share it together; we
> do everything together.

Although Amina's mother and father are still living in Yendi, she
continues to describe them as her only intimates. Because of her
parents' distance from her side, she has no one to tell if something
happens. Indeed, of all the women in the group, only three say that
they tell secrets to "friends." Others, like Georgina, either keep to
themselves or tell family (especially mother):

> I don't tell my secrets to friends, I used to [usually] converse with my
> friend [boyfriend] or my mother. Though I can tell something to my
> friend [boyfriend] but not so deep. In Ghana, friends they are not this
> thing. If you think you'll give all your mind to her, or to him
> [boyfriend], what they will do you might not like it.

A sizeable minority of the women do not purport to have close
friends. Lizzie, for instance, says that she is "free with everyone"
and close with no one. Much of her time is spent with family, as is
no less true of many of those who do have non-kin friends. Others
explicitly deny friendship apart from kinship; their close
relationships (in which secrets are freely told) are with sisters.
Indeed, living with immediate family—in the family house or rented
rooms—seems to discourage the formation of attachments to
extrafamilial females. Faustina's only friend is her sister with whom

---

5 Liberation Circle. The Circle is a block from the cinema and the Lido dance
hall. These attractions, along with the nightly sellers of prepared-food, bring
many people to the area.

she lives, and Ellen, who lives alone, has no friends.

> I don't know why...It's the nature of my business. Each time I come
> home, I can't go out and I don't think somebody can come to visit,
> because by the time I will finish it will be getting to seven o'clock. And
> I have to come to my room. Unless on the weekend...

And on the weekend she prefers to go to her sisters, her "closest
friends."

Many of the women who avoid friendship are concerned about
malicious gossip. Since a woman never knows when and by whom
she will be victimized in this way, she often chooses to avoid such
risks altogether by not striking up any friendships with non-kin
women. Akosua is a case in point. Maybe, she says, if they are
sitting down conversing, she will say something and the friend will
also say something. And when the friend leaves, she will say
something to others that Akosua did not say in order to bring
trouble to her. That is why, she says, she has no friends. The theme
of conversational inadequacy sometimes comes up; women fear
that their words will be distorted because they do not speak well. "I
don't know how to converse and maybe if I have a friend and I'm
conversing with her, what I don't say, she will go and say that I said
so. So because of that I have no friends" (Fatima, translated from
Ga). But women must beware, even if they say nothing, particularly
if family are not at hand. Says Auntie Elizabeth, "Even I don't like
to go out. People are bad. They're not good in this country. They
talk about you. And I don't have parents. So if anything
happens..." Interestingly enough, the women believe that only
women gossip like this. "As for the men, they don't gossip. And
whatever you tell them, they won't tell anybody." But women
cannot have male friends, "because some people will say that he is
your boyfriend."

Several of those who do socialize to some extent also express fear
of bad-mouthing and/or give this risk as a reason for keeping to
oneself, though in practice they may very well be just as sociable as
any of the others who maintain that they have friends.[6]

---

[6] Amina, the young woman from Yendi, discussed earlier in this section, did not
mention being afraid of gossip, yet she has no friends in a functional sense. It is
only with respect to her mother and father that she sees possibilities for intimacy,
yet they live far away. Since she belongs to an ethnic association, she does have
some social contact with members of her own ethnic group.

Relationships with Women: Rival

The defining role of the adult woman traditionally is as wife to a man and mother to his children. Such a situation cannot help but pit women against each other. In the rural milieu, female kin are one's friends and all other women potential rivals for one's husband. As was noted in an earlier chapter, one word for co-wife is "rival." This sense of rivalry is more intense and takes on new forms in the urban setting. Under these circumstances, the hesitation expressed by the women about friendship as a relationship of trust is hardly surprising.

Ramatu's tale of her troubled marriage with Suli is illustrative. After being married to his first wife Abu for three years, Suli, a Muslim, took Ramatu as his second wife. Each wife had her own quarters in a different compound; since Suli could not afford a third room for himself, he kept his belongings with Ramatu and spent much of his time there.

From the outset of the new arrangement, Abu disliked Ramatu and used any excuse to behave badly toward her. Ramatu complained to Suli; she had entered into the marriage with an intention to respect Abu, and had even cared for Abu's three children, bathing and loving them as her own. Even though Ramatu was older, Abu did not accord her proper respect. When Suli called the rivals together to discuss the problem, Abu turned on Ramatu and told her not to touch the children again—to go and have her own. Although Ramatu had alread borne two boys to her first husband, Abu taunted her with the accusation that she was not able to conceive. And even when Ramatu announced that she had become pregnant by Suli, Abu continued to spread the gossip that it was a lie and that she was barren. After the baby was born, Abu, joined by her mother and father, persisted in the harassment, insisting that the baby was not Suli's at all, but that of another man.

Whenever Abu visited Suli's family, she would interogate his sisters about Ramatu—how many pieces of cloth she had, whether Suli and she ever argued, and so on. One day, Abu's mother and father went to a *juju* man to get him to use his magic powers to cause trouble for Ramatu. They were accompanied on this mission by a woman who—unbeknownst to them—had been married to Ramatu's uncle. She subsequently told Ramatu of the secret incident, and sent her off to get the bad *juju* neutralized.

Five days after this episode, Suli began to "act crazy." He told

Ramatu, who was now seven months pregnant, that she should leave for her mother's to prepare for the birth. Ramatu asked her father-in-law to intervene to delay the journey. Suli came into the bedroom while Ramatu was in bed and broke her wardrobe and six of the porcelain pots given by her mother on the occasion of the marriage. Other residents of the compound tried to reason with him. Suli left the following morning, taking his radio, bed, and chairs with him. Within a short time, however, he though better of his hasty departure and returned, continuing to support Ramatu as well as Abu.

A month later, the story took another turn when Ramatu told Suli that she was going to her mother's and that he should come there and name the child and then leave her. She said that she had no interest in remaining married to him. Suli solemnly asked her forgiveness, asked that she ignore the kind of behavior he had demonstrated should it recur, and dashed her money and gifts. After she had stayed at her mother's for three months, Suli's brother came to urge that she move back to her husband; however, he warned her to stay away from Abu, whom he characterized as a bad woman who liked *juju* and had no respect for the institution of the family.

Ramatu's return upset Suli, who was clearly afraid of his first wife and her family. When Abu resumed her harassment of Ramatu, Suli finally resolved the problem by finding new accommodations for Abu away from her parents,[7] and arranged to divide his time equally between the two wives. A semblance of peace was achieved by keeping the two rivals apart.

This tale illustrates some important facts. Rivalry over men continues in the urban setting, and so does distrust of other women. A woman may invoke magic and exploit her parents' sympathies—acting always against the other woman, not the man. And women keep each other in line through the sanction of gossip.

Another example of conflict among women over a man is provided by the events following the death of Mr. Disu, a veteran of the Foreign Service. He was a Krobo, and the funeral was held in his hometown. Mr. Disu's widow, an Adabraka businesswoman, is a Fante, from a family of considerable wealth and fame. After Mr.

---

[7] Abu had lived in a variety of houses; in each case, she did not get along with the other occupants and moved back to her parents' house.

Disu's death, his family literally would not speak to the widow or children, so jealous were they of her inheritance. They insisted that not a drop of water be spilled on the corpse until every possibility be ruled out that he had died of unnatural causes.

The wake and the viewing of the body took place at his father's house. Because Mr. Disu had been a "big man," there was an overflow crowd at the chapel where the funeral service took place; a number of the mourners went off to the cemetery to await the burial. The voice of one woman, a member of the deceased's family, kept rising in pitch. Her litany, which took no note of the fact that the widow was a person of means in her own right, went something like this: Mr. Disu has made his wife a rich woman, and she will live out her days in wealth. Look, she hasn't even shed a tear; that shows you how bereaved she is! If he had not married her, she would be nothing, nobody. Why did she keep the body so long? In order to find out exactly what his assets were and how much he was worth and what she can expect from his estate, that's why. And when he died, how she held and kissed him—as if she were eating his flesh![8]

In the city, where multiple marriages are on the ebb, a woman's rival may be the girlfriend of a man they share. If the woman herself is also a girlfriend rather than a wife, the need to protect her position may be specially acute: lest the material support received from the man be ended at his whim. She has no leverage against the philandering man himself except to leave him for another. Here again, as in the more traditional forms of rivalry, she goes after the woman who has caught his favor, not the man himself.

The same basic principles apply if the women in question are prostitutes. Evelyn, a resident of Adabraka whose nighttime activities are often professional, is a case in point. One Saturday night, she was barred from entering the Ambassador Hotel's dance pavilion—a popular and "nice" spot. She was with another

---

[8] Insult-throwing is a traditional way of letting off steam in Ghana, but there was a special ethnic dimension to this tirade. Krobo women are reputed to have loose ways, and fear of infidelity is one of the reasons that Krobo men are said to think twice about marrying them. A Ghanaian friend, who was translating for me at the grave site, insists that the majority of prostitutes in Accra and Abidjan are Krobo. In any case, there is much resentment among Krobo women, especially kinswomen, when a man reinforces the stereotype by marrying an "outsider."

woman, and the doorman kept insisting that she could not enter
without a man to accompany her. Evelyn sputtered in protest, but
to no avail. It seems that the decree was aimed specifically at her,
the result of an incident that had taken place three weeks earlier.
She had come to the Ambassador and had seen a rival (prostitute)
sitting there with Evelyn's "boyfriend," so Evelyn had beaten up
the other woman (*not* the man) and was then thrown out.

The replacement of polygyny by "befriending" is exacerbating
female rivalry. If a man is to marry more than one woman, it is to
his advantage that the co-wives get along if and when they come
into contact. Sororal polygyny could be one solution, since sisters
grow up together and learn to work together. Or the polygynist
might house his wives separately. No matter what the arrangement,
the women receive equal treatment. A gift to one necessitates a gift
to the other(s).

In the case of a "friend," no such attempts are made. A wife
perceives herself to be the object of harassment by the other
woman. Indeed, many girlfriends feel that they have special rights
and often choose to "bluff" the wife, reminding her of the
existence of a threatening rival. Not only does the man fail to
prevent disharmony, he often provokes it. According to Patience,
still in her teens, it is a fact of life that a husband will bring a
girlfriend into the room where his wife is sleeping, wake her up and
tell her to go away, and then take his pleasure with the girl. When
they are finished, he comes out, tells the wife to lie down again, and
leaves with the girlfriend. No matter how exaggerated this
description may be, it is indicative of what even very young women
conceive their lot to be.

Relationships with Men: "Friend" and Wife

In speaking of male-female relationships, one informant indicated distaste while at the same time shrugging. Not only is there
nothing that one can do, but there is also no point in discussing the
particulars of such relationships much with other women. "It is not
good to talk about such things. When you are married, not good to
talk, because you don't know what this other person will do with
that man." But you *do* know that there is a good chance that if
something transpires, it will not be to your interest. Women know
that husbands and boyfriends alike always have their eyes open
should an eligible young lady happen by.

The only complaints ever volunteered to me came from women who have spent time in Europe or the United States; when they return to Ghana, they too feel that their hands are tied. One such person asked if I were not becoming bored with the conversations I was having with women, since all they talk about is sex and men. And for good reason: across the board, their lives are bound up with men, defined by men, and controlled by men. Identity relationships with men (other than blood relatives) are primarily sexual. Any woman who reads the newspaper is reminded of this, as in articles like "The Sensuous Woman: You too Can Be a Goddess."

Show me a woman who is sexy, desirable and exciting and I will show you a woman who has worked hard in becoming so.

How many times have you been in a man's company only to have "his" interest diverted to the stunning woman who has just made her entrance?

Moreover, it is "she" that he thinks of while you are making love?

...But before you can hope to start driving him crazy with desire you have to awaken your own sexuality and so become aware of your own prowess.

...If, when you slide between the sheets you are covered in sticky creams or lotions, with your hair uncombed or not plaited, and wearing a faded cloth or an old night dress, note that this might excite only a gorilla.

...A favorite with men is the see-through, short nightie in light pestal [sic] shades...

...Wigs, whether Afro or conventional, can be very attractive in or out of bed.

...It is likely that while he is making love to you, he imagines you are the good-looking girl next door, the current DRUM [monthly magazine] *cover girl, his girl friend or whoever else excites him sexually.*

Sometimes his sexual day dreams may appear in more bizarre forms. Man in his superego believes that any woman finds his charm irresistible.

Unfortunately not many wives happen to be psychologists...

But with a little coaxing, some tempting and a few bottles of beer, try and make him reveal his secret sexual longings.

...Be honest in your flattery...Comment on his fine physique, his handsome face, his big eyes, his sexy voice...

Some foods are supposed to have certain qualities that act as sexual stimulants...

Also, you may know or have heard the local man who sells aphrodisiacs: Why not give some of his wares a try.

The marriage vows are not enough to stop your man from straying. What you have to do is act out the parts of many different women. You can change the style of your clothes and makeup. And even your sexual personality can be altered occasionally.

Wives should also be lovers too! (Stella Addo, *The Daily Graphic*, 23 November 1970).

In Ghana, the identity relationships possible between a man and a woman fall into two main categories—"friendship" and marriage.[9] The consumerism which is characteristic of relationships in general dominates male-female negotiations in particular. This produces a kind of bargaining. As mentioned earlier, the assumption that male-female relationships are not platonic is implicit in polygynistic mores. No matter where they meet, a woman is perceived by a man as primarily a sexual being. Any other status notwithstanding, that is how he relates to her. Knowing this the Ghanaian woman exacts an exchange: sex and sociability (*see* Collins 1971: 13) in return for material recompense.[10] This is true for both marriage and "friendship." The greater the sought-after status which accrues to the relationship, the greater its worth to the contracting party. And the less advantageious to one in the face of long-term norms, the more the other party must pay in order to make it worthwhile. In Ghana, the woman who resists marrying in favor of befriending must note the advantages and disadvantages, immediate versus long-run, of each type of relationship; then she may strike the bargain. Since we have dealt with marriage in the previous chapter, let us now look more closely at the relationship of "friendship."[11]

[9] Little (1959a) includes prostitution in his classification of major male-female relationships. I do not, because prostitution is more explicitly a business operation. It is not a viable alternative for the respectability conferred by friendship or marriage. Despite its obligatory fee, prostitution may be a less expensive outlet for men in search of sexual relationships.

[10] Greater worth or heightened reputation do not necessarily accrue to the chaste woman in modern-day Accra (including Adabraka), particularly since sexual permissiveness brings positive results in the form of material goods.

The girlfriend may be a potential wife or a social companion. One difference between the two roles is that the married man's companion often receives greater exposure in social situations and possesses greater mobility. The adult woman's status and mobility is tied to men in two ways: the fact of attachment, and the specific attributes of the consort. Both men and women are cognizant of how association with the other is reflexive, especially when the two gain exposure as a couple.

The "typical" girl's upbringing is strict and emphasizes family ties at the expense of those with outsiders. Being women themselves, mothers are aware of the sexual content of "friendship," and of the fact that the most innocent-seeming encounter may eventuate in conception. And since legitimized offspring are preferred, they try to prevent "friendship" altogether. "What I have seen is...some of the people don't allow men to come to their house when they are having girls. Or when they see the girl talking to boys, you see it is a very bad intention." Such a parental approach has helped to breed sneakiness on the part of the girls. All but one of my informants with boyfriends express hesitancy if not outright opposition to the man visiting them at the parental home. On a work day, a "friend" may pick the woman up at work, take her out for a drink, and then drop her near the compound. His practice of never coming in has nothing to do with his marital status, but the fact that sex can somehow be managed and parents are fearful.

> That is the thing. Our parents, when they see you moving with a certain boy, they used to [usually] quarrel with you or say something which is not good. So, whenever you take a friend, you used to [usually] hide it. Even when you...say about 16 or 17 going, they don't want you to take any boyfriend till someone come your age to marry you. That is their mind. If they see you they will talk, talk, talk, talk, which you'll be sorry. You are not grown up, you are not grown up. They think you will conceive, and maybe you have not finished your schooling. That is the whole problem.

All of the women with boyfriends originally met their "friends" either on their own (e.g. at work, school, or in the neighborhood) or

---

[11] Eleven of the sampled women have not yet married and eight of them have boyfriends. The responses of all but one are the basis for most of the ensuing discussions.

through mutual acquaintances. The latter, according to one, is the style nowadays. Not one was introduced by the family.

> The comparative freedom with which young persons now enter sexual unions means that parents are no longer able to exercise much control in the selection of mates...The role of the parents and the extended families in the choice of mates is limited to advising the young persons to avoid certain categories of mates. When two young persons intend to marry they inform their respective parents and/or heads of their extended families (Tetteh 1967: 205).

The word "mate" is the key. Friendships are not necessarily set up with permanency in mind. Thus, whether she lives at home (with mother) or elsewhere, family may have no inkling of her involvement. Her behavior could be interpreted as a step by the woman toward extricating herself from the control of those who traditionally wield power over her actions, and toward the consideration and implementation of alternatives. I say *could*, not *is* , for two reasons: (1) marriage still looms large as a future given, and families must still be consulted, eventually; (2) until a relationship is to be formalized, it is kept secret from kin because of the continuing influence that they (and especially the mother) *can* bring to bear.

Only two of the young women do not exhibit the attitude described by Tetteh above. They usually confine their leisure activities to the compound, where the "friend" may come by, and to occasional walks. They, too, express disapproval of visits that will give away the secret. But they have little leeway in their movements. Each is young, lives with her mother, and has a child who is being raised by its grandmother. Supervision is strict because of their past indiscretions. Indeed, when Dora was staying with her aunt in Saltpond, only that woman knew of the boyfriend's existence; the pregnancy was already six months along before Dora's mother was told by the aunt:"In Ghana, don't like the mother to know[about a "friend"], because she will tell you to wait small." The man was ready to marry her, but it was decided Dora was too young so her mother should raise the child.

Ellen expects to marry as soon as her fiancé is transferred from Takoradi to Accra. Her mother does not even know yet of their intentions.

I don't know why we don't do it, but don't...I just want her to meet the man when he's ready to come forward. I don't want to show him to my mother and in the long run maybe he's not going to marry me. I don't know quite what will be her reaction.

The fear of being "disappointed" by the man is not only common but justified. It is also the rationale used by the one woman in the sample who has not hidden her relationship from her mother:

I think if your mother knows, it is good...Because Ghanaian boys are not good and they used to [usually] disappoint girls. They disappoint girls always. So if your mother knows this is the boy you are walking with and if something comes [she becomes pregnant] and he wants to refuse, the mother will come. Some boys seem to refuse...

Of course, the mother will come to her daughter's aid, whether she knows ahead of time or not.

To what extent is the furtiveness described here inconsistent with the importance accorded the mother-daughter tie in the context of female friendship? One explanation lies in the very concern that mothers have for their daughters, and the difficulty they have in conveying the perils that arise from the easy contact between girls and boys in the city. On the other hand, interaction with men may always have been a bone of contention between mothers and daughters, even in traditional society. A third possible explanation is that the young women involved in clandestine sexual liaisons are among those who are in fact breaking away from family and who have struck up friendships with other women that diminish the mother-daughter tie. Indeed, most speak of sharing time and certain confidences with female friends not from their families.[12]

What do a Ghanaian man and his "friend" expect of each other? In Accra, a woman has no more power of possession over her boyfriend than over any other man; neither, however, does he hold such powers over her, at least not until he formally betroths her.

---

[12] Six of the eight singles with boyfriends claim to have non-kin girlfriends. None of the eight speaks of her mother in terms of intimate friendship. Two say that their closest relationships are with their sisters; one of these two also speaks of having female friends.

"As he has not married me," says one woman, "he has no authority over me." He brings her gifts and he gives her a monthly allowance. Just as she knows that she has every right to expect begifting and support, so he knows that he can expect sexual favors. In fact, for men, sex is a primary reason for a friendship. Benedicta is 20, unmarried, and the mother of an 18-month-old girl. She sells oranges near a taxi stand. Consequently, on any given day several drivers and their friends are likely to be hanging around. One afternoon, one of the fellows began to tease Benedicta about having a boyfriend, which she then denied.

Man:	She doesn't fuck, so she doesn't have a boyfriend.
D.P.:	Is that the only reason to have a boyfriend?
Man:	Yes. She has one baby who doesn't have a father, so she doesn't want a boyfriend.

Courting behavior in Ghana employs much prestation. In Accra, women have come to enjoy the good things that the city offers and which they themselves cannot afford to purchase. Their boyfriends accommodate their material desires. Their dalliance is extremely honest. And no self-respecting woman would remain in a "friendship" without material recompense. The actual form and extent of the material support a woman receives from her boyfriend may depend on her social class and economic expectations. At the upper extreme, there are women who at the very least expect interested males to keep them supplied with liquor, so they can entertain others (men and women) in style. One such woman even allowed a man who proclaimed his love for her to furnish her house—and then she terminated the association.

The Adabraka women fall into a less exalted category. Everyone with a boyfriend receives a nominal sum of money each month;[13] this "chop money" is for her use and does not obligate her to cook for the man. Most also receive periodic gifts, such as cloth and extra dashes of cash. Almost all equate such assistance with good treatment and respect.

---

[13] All but two of those with boyfriends receive money regularly. Vivian, one of the exceptions, tries to be self-sufficient and only asks for money when she is broke.

Yes, he [boyfriend] is good to me, because he give me anything I want...As I'm not working and I'm grown up too, my parents can't give me money too, because they know that I have a friend. So, he was responsible to do all these things.

The mere fact that she is receiving gifts does not insure the girlfriend's fidelity. For this again a bargain must be struck. If she feels that the "friend" is reneging (stinting on his material "due"), she may search for a more lucrative "friendship." Instead of being remorseful over such a move, she is likely to feel only annoyance with her former boyfriend for what she considers to be his stingy treatment of her.

Some don't treat them well. Some boys, if they are sitting with you, all those things in talking, they don't care about it. If you ask him, he will refuse. That is why the girls are used to usually take two friends or three friends, because if you are asking him and he wouldn't give it to you, so you will try this boy. I want to go, if only he will give me.

The line between courting behavior and whoring behavior is thin. Once a woman has a few boyfriends, the distinction may be spurious, except for the context of their meeting.[14]

Premarital and inter-marital sexuality for the women is the mirror image of extra-marital sexuality for the man. More than one young man from the neighborhood complains about the expense involved in having a girlfriend and the fickleness of women.[15] Jimmy insists that he has no girlfriend because he does not have any money and girls are only interested in what they can get. And Agnes' estranged boyfriend decries the amorality and infidelity of her behavior. To his mind, Ghanaian women are impossible to deal with until they are married. If they approach you for something like

---

[14] Prostitutes do not operate out of houses. They hang around dance halls, such as the Lido, the Ambassador, and the Star Hotel. As they rise on the ladder of occupational success, they change their mode of dress and the places they frequent. They may be paid on a nightly basis; most, however, opt for a longer term arrangement as concubine or mistress.

[15] In many cultures, men fear that women are weak and easily seduced. The institution of *purdah* among Muslims is a means of impeding unchaste behavior.

money, and you cannot or will not give it to them, they will not wait. They will sleep with someone else who will. So it is difficult to hold onto a woman without giving her many favors.

Amawkaw responded to this male description, defending her peers. Her boyfriend, to whom she is affianced, does well by her. He takes her out to movies and clubs, tries to give her some money at the end of the month, and helps her out of financial difficulties. *Most* men, however, do not, "because they have to go about with many girls." My young friend Patience says that since boys like to have several girlfriends, a girl learns not to depend upon any one boy—"because he will abuse you." An unmarried girl still has her freedom and her bargaining card; she can take off if she so desires.

The role of girlfriend also has some intangible advantages over that of a wife. A man's girlfriend gets more attention, and does not have to clean up after him (for instance, do his laundry). The women with boyfriends have far more of a social life than do those who are married. They have a good time—"If I want to enjoy, then I went to my boyfriend; maybe we go to town, roaming about, come back, that's all." The fact that she has a husband protects the married woman's image; the visibility of the boyfriend is similarly supportive for the unmarried. Most of a woman's outings with her boyfriend involve activities that she prefers not to do alone or in the company of females only—especially nighttime activities. Lizzie, who likes to go dancing, expresses the sentiments of many:

> Anyway, I don't like going out in the night with my girlfriends. In Accra here, in Ghana here, when you used to go out in the evening with some girls, they suspect that you are this thing—a Lido girl. They used to (usually) stand behind you and make rough comment.

Throughout the city, the major outlet for "friends" is visiting night clubs where they can drink or dance. Married couples are in the minority, except on special occasions such as Christmas.[16] When the men go, they take their girlfriends instead of their wives. The clientele includes all classes, although regular patrons tend to be those whose incomes can absorb the cost. Saturday is a big night for women to go out with their boyfriends. If the man is not

---

[16] Only 3 out of 22 married women report going to such places with spouses for a regular evening out.

interested in going to a night spot to dance or drink, his girlfriend either does not go out or gets another man to accompany her. Both Lizzie and Vivian have male friends who escort them around when their boyfriends are unavailable. Lizzie's companion, however, terminated the relationship when she refused to become his "friend." When Vivian and her male friend, a co-worker, go out, it is usually in the company of a group of people.

In recent times, public clubs have been supplemented by quasi-private clubs. The clientele is predominantly élite; only a few of the Adabraka women have been to such places. They are stomping grounds for men and their girlfriends, and often facilitate extramarital trysts. Although some of the male members are single, most are not. They drink and dance, often meeting with friends or acquaintances. To some, going to clubs like Keteke is valuable because they gain visibility by doing so. The Accra Club is typical of the new spots. The Club is primarily for drinking and socializing; the membership consists of professional men and two female lawyers. Although attendance is not open to the general public, members are welcome to bring any women, with the notable exception of their wives. The explicit nature of the restriction is underlined by the institution of an annual "wives' night." Many wives refuse to attend on the one night they are invited, because some non-wives come and the married women justifiably fear unpleasantries from "bluffing" girlfriends. Peer group pressure among the men and the double standard maintain the system. One member, a prominent doctor, expressed his belief that women should be strictly limited in their autonomy. His married male friends and he may have affairs, but as for married women doing the same—"Good God, no!"[17]

Besides the clubs, outings may include the cinema and an occasional concert or football (soccer) game. Only if the woman has no weekend domestic duties is such an excursion possible. Most young women who work and live with the family take their turn at cooking on off days. As a result of nationwide economic distress, parties have become a thing of the past for those who are not of the

---

[17] As Little (1959a: 75) has pointed out, "men and society generally still tend to regard a man's relationships with other women as acceptable polygyny" and deny women the equivalent right.

élite—"Not like during the old regime," when Nkrumah was in power.

While a "friend" generally enjoys more of a social life than does a wife, the man and woman tend to see less of each other as time goes by. When a man first meets someone he likes, he will try to see her daily, to ensure that she has no time for anyone else. Once he has staked his claim and has some assurance of her loyalty, he will ease off in his attentions. The visits and outings will drop to once or twice a week.

> What to do about a boyfriend who you never see, who abuses you, keeps you waiting for days on end. That's the way Ghanaian men are. The men here are dreadful. They hold all of the cards and too bad for you. If they come, they come. If they don't, they don't (Vivian).

As noted earlier, the woman has no more control over her boyfriend than he has over her. After all, even a woman who is married cannot control her husband's movements, and in that relationship she has at least some sort of formal contract. Unless the boyfriend is misbehaving, and she wants to make a point, she tends to avoid creating jealousy on his part,[18] since this just makes for trouble in the long run. Married women give this as a reason for not indulging in adulterous affairs, or even in interactions that could possibly be construed as such:

> Men are different. Men are so jealous, he will prefer to go with you. Maybe you have some society, like *Zumunchi,* all women. But if some young men, husband will be jealous.

At the same time, a husband who severely mistreats his wife has cause for worry; if another man comes along, the outcome may not be to his benefit.

> ...if he's treating you bad, you're in financial difficulties and he don't give you something... maybe want to leave the man and get somebody to hold onto before you leave the man. Depends upon the man... Some women like to. Women too are sometimes jealous, hear

---

[18] Vivian was having friends over for lunch—four women and one man. She had not invited her boyfriend and was afraid that he might arrive during the meal, become jealous, and make trouble. To prevent such an incident, she prepared a complete meal for him the day before and took it to his house that morning.

something, whereas may be no sex involved.

And yet there is an undercurrent of female acquiesence and reticence. Whether literate or illiterate, living in Adabraka or an affluent suburb, women in mixed company rarely talk. Even the "bluffing" girlfriend holds her tongue when around men. If she feels threatened or displaced by a rival, it is the other woman who suffers the brunt of her ire. At parties, women are primarily dancing partners for their escorts, or ornaments to be worn on the arm. Conversing men do little to draw the women into a discussion. On the contrary, men often speak for their women,[19] viewed by both sexes as the male role.

While men are the means to women's consumerism, men too are consumers—especially of single women. Unmarried women feel that they are most likely to suffer neglect and abuse at the hands of eligible bachelors over the age of 30. Male attachments are valued, and available single men with appeal are few once the woman has reached her middle twenties; the eligibles who are around know that they are in demand. It is not that there are so many single (unmarried, divorced, widowed) women; the shortage of companions arises from the preference by most for men older than themselves:

> Oh, the perversity of today's young women! They are turning up their noses at their male contemporaries who try to attract them by wearing the trendiest fashions, shoulder-length hair, perfume lotions and sprays. The fact is that the mad dash by the young Romeos towards being "with it" is helping drive their girlfriends into the arms of older and more mature men (MacGregor, *The Ghanaian Times,* 14 September 1971).

This is partly due to the material wants and needs of the women; older men are likely to be better established and more solvent than their juniors. Married men appeal to the unattached woman because they tend to be less conceited, pleased to have a regular diversion from married life, and more apt to stick with one girlfriend. The fact that more of them may be around, however,

---

[19] When a male acquaintance or the husband of an informant happened along in the course of an interview, more often than not he would take over while the woman sat mute. My only recourse in such a situation was to cut the interview short and return at another time, or beg the man to give us some privacy.

does nothing to lessen the competition among women to make a good match or catch. Rivalry for male attentions and attachment, be the man single or married, fans the fires of distrust and jealousy and sets up barriers between potential female friends.

Georgina and Lizzie are seeing married men, yet both say that they would resent their own (future) husbands having girlfriends. It is bad, says Lizzie, and going out with a married man is "dangerous," but nothing can stop them from taking girlfriends. Georgina conducts her current relationship on terms that take account, at least to some degree, of her avowed disapproval of the way most Ghanaian men treat their wives:

> ...maybe some men, when they close, they won't come home a-tall as they have girlfriends. Say maybe till 10:30 or 11. If you want to tell him something, you won't get time to do it. That's why every night my boyfriend has to leave at eight o'clock. If he wants to come back, that's all right. I know that he has gone to see his wife. You should force him to go and see the wife, else he won't go. As he has got a new friend, he won't go...

If boyfriends give adequate material support yet become neglectful in other ways once the shine has worn off, how does a relationship with them differ in substance from one of marriage? To those who expect to marry the "friend," it is an interim phase. But for Lizzie, who does not expect to marry the "friend," there is a difference. To her, marriage means living together; by extension, it is a union recognized both by society as a whole and by family. It accords her adult status, while at the same time she is fulfilling traditional obligations to her kin. As both Lizzie and Georgina attest, marriage also means the fulfillment of bearing legitimate children. Furthermore, a husband must "do everything" for the woman. "Whenever I'm in need of something, he has to give me and provide me everything."

Thus the differences between being a girlfriend and a wife lie mostly in the area of the woman's status. For the man, the major difference is that he fathers legitimate children and is beholden to support them. Therefore, I take issue with the argument that polygyny in urban areas is easing up due to expense. Admittedly, surveys indicate that migrants to the town maintain that supporting a family is far more difficult there than in the village. Caldwell reports:

The answer was clearer still in the case of polygyny. Only one in sixteen said that more than one wife could most easily be supported in the town, while over four-fifths voted for the village. There are, then, economic pressures of which the urban poor are also becoming aware, and which militate against both polygyny and large families in the Ghanaian town (1967a: 143).

The fact is that maintaining an outside woman carries financial obligations similar to those of taking a second wife. To say that the city woman seeks to improve her situation through the premarital or intermarital exploitation of men is not to impugn her. She lives in a society that worships material gain and rewards dependency; it is only natural that she would operate in accordance with the system. The more astute the bargain she drives, the more she can adjust her appearances and her circumstances, and the higher up the scale she can rise in terms of the men she attracts, the places she is seen, and so forth. Thus, her mobility increases and the scope of her activities and associations widens. What is not open to negotiation is that sooner or later the woman must marry if she is to be considered a respectable adult. The role of girlfriend does not substitute for that of wife, and, once married, the woman's options are circumscribed by the propriety of that state.

Alternate Life-Styles: Ideal and Real

Is "everywoman's" lifestyle changing? There is a "modern" ideal preached by the imported magazines and their Ghanaian imitations and embodied in the externals of élite behavior; yet the actual practices of the majority of the population still follow the lines laid down by tradition so far as women are concerned. Indeed, folk attitudes about women underlie the actions of even the élite types. The newspapers may carry articles about "trendy trends in wigs" and the "NC 175 student glamor girl";[20] they may promote Western gimmickry for maintaining relationships, but they also support the traditional aspects of the female persona. A column in Accra's *Saturday Mirror*, for example, reflects the view that "befriending" can be accepted for what it is, but can never supplant marriage:

[20] This is Kofi Wizeman's characterization of a young urbanite dressed in "sekedelic accoutrements" (*The Ghanaian Times*, 12 August 1971).

If marriage is that horrible and if married women are always left
out of the fun, why do girls still clamour to get married?

One would have thought that girls would prefer to stay single,
knowing that all enjoyment ceases the day you get married.

Why for example did I get married again after my first two attempts
had ended so disastrously?

Could it be that women enjoy being left at home?

Could it be the "old" fashion (sic) idea of a woman not being or
feeling complete unless there is a man around be true? ("Chat With
Grandma," 7 November 1970).

The columnist goes on to describe a friend who is divorced and
has a good job, three children, and a plethora of invitations to go
partying. She wants no more children, and is happy and carefree,
yet she wants to remarry. The prospective mate is neither wealthy
nor handsome, and she is not in love with him. "The last question
is rather interesting, if you consider that she is somebody who has
assured me that she doesn't believe in love any more. She says she
doesn't love him but she just wants to stay with him."

Stella Addo, writing in *The Daily Graphic*, wanted to learn more
about why women are infatuated with, and often marry, "the
charming rogue who loves you one moment and double crosses you
the next." One divorcée told her:

My ex-husband was what you would call a playboy type. But the
brief happiness and few gifts he gave me can never compensate me for
all the hardships and frustrations I experienced during our
marriage.

If I choose to marry again I will certainly look for more lasting
qualities in a man (15 September 1971).

Men would never countenance such "roguish" behavior by a
married woman. Ellis Amenu, also writing in *The Daily Graphic*,
asks whether male society ever realizes what an injustice is done to
the legally married woman:

I do not know why a married woman's extra-marital activities are
looked upon as promiscuous and condemned seriously by her society.
If women have achieved equality in business and education [sic] why
should the stigma of having indulged in extra-marital relationships
brand only the women? Why can't women achieve equality in sex?

Our forefathers were polygamists because they needed the human labour on their large farms...

...Men leave their lawfully married wives at home for "Chicken soup"[young school girls] who could be their daughters...

And these men full of lust breed indiscipline among small girls so they are used as gimmicks and the result of the relationship can only be a gimmick itself, a temporary thing like a new toy. And the man unscathed, unmarked, goes back to his ever faithful wife (29 September 1971).

And yet, after enumerating the wrongs suffered by married women, the columnist concludes that they should *not* be granted sexual freedom. "What I am saying is that MEN SHOULD DIS-CIPLINE THEMSELVES." In another *Graphic* column, Stella Addo discusses the distinction made between wife and girlfriend in terms of the responsibilities of each to the man:

...For those who believe that the quality of the food is more important than the quantity there is still nothing to beat home cooking.

This is why most men demand culinary skill as a number-one quality before choosing a wife. George Meredith might have been a Ghanaian when he said: "Kissing don't last; cookery do!" The girlfriend must be pretty, but the wife must be able to cook (6 October 1971).

It is clear which is the time-honored role.

The influence of the real, the traditional, is apparent throughout a woman's activities. Women, and men as well, are shaped from childhood for roles from which there is little prospect for deviation. For a woman, it all begins at her mother's knee. Every girl, no matter what her ethnicity, generation, or place of residence, receives identical training for her adult role: first in the domestic arts, then in her sexual comportment. Everything is aimed toward making a good marriage and keeping house for a man.

The education girls receive in household work is informal; if the mother is doing something, her daughter helps. The ages may differ in different homes, and the order may be modified, but the pattern of training is generally the same:

Start when about 9 with kitchen—see how things are being

prepared. At about 11, breakfast and laying of table; 13, have her
prepare midday meal. Thus between 14 and 15, she's okay. Then teach
little mending. Washing of clothes go with cooking. She learns to
budget her time. Then, leave younger children with her. By 18, she's
perfect to get married.

No matter what her aspirations, the woman must learn to maintain
a proper household. In a sense, it is another of her obligations to
her mother to learn well:

> You will go to marriage with somebody and if you do wrong, he will
> think your mother didn't teach you, or you mother doesn't know how
> to do that thing. So she should teach you everything... how to cook,
> how to keep yourself neat and your room...

Then there is the point when the girl becomes a woman.
According to my informants, this is marked by menarche (the first
menstrual period) or a later occasion associated with it, such as
marriage or childbirth.[21] (The Twi expression *ye a ne* means
"woman menses" or "become a woman when pass menses"). In
any case, the onset of menstruation does not go unnoticed. Many
still observe the traditional rituals for the occasion. Among the Ga
and Akan, *ɔtaw* is prepared one month after menses; this is made
from yams mashed with palm oil, with a hard-boiled egg on the
side, and is eaten by the young woman alone. All Krobo who
maintain ties with the hometown participate in the *dipo*, a process
of initiation that culminates in a day of secret activities and
communal festivities. It used to be held for groups of girls in their
early teens; now younger girls are also included. Dora went through
dipo at the age of 12; to prove this, she bared her wrist to show the
tiny knife marks.

At this point in life, the concern about pregnancy rears its head.
"If you don't do *dipo* and you conceive, the child doesn't belong to
either your mother or your father; you've brought dirt into the
house." Some of those who did not take part in such a *rite de
passage* (two-thirds of my sample), and some who did, received
advice from mother or surrogate mother. Unlike the training for
housekeeping, this teaching is explicit:

---

[21] Five of my informants say that adulthood begins "when old enough"—mid-
teens to 21—when one has finished school, is working, or is able to go out on
one's own.

Young girls with ceremonially shaved heads, going through *dipo* (the Krobo puberty ceremony). This is done in the hometown, in this case Somanya, and prepubescent migrants to Accra return home to participate in the ritual.

(Photo: Deborah Pellow)

> ...at first when you start your menstruation, she will tell you what you have done—you have been to a woman, so don't play with boys or men. If you do go to them, you will conceive.

In former days, girls in their mid-teens were thought to be too young to be taught such adult matters. In modern times, however, "friendships" begin at an earlier age. Once menstruation begins and until the young woman is safely married, her mother lives with the fear she will become pregnant. Many conceive despite parental forewarnings. "So many girls don't mind their mothers and fathers. They didn't obey their law." Florence is a married woman, with two daughters. She points out that it can even happen to an older person who knows the proprieties but is unhappily married:

You know sometimes we are all weak. Like go to a wedding, meet
many people, don't go with husband. Don't have a car, take a taxi. So
someone offers you a lift; then he says to go take some beer. And the
women are too weak, then he'll get privilege of you, just go and tell
you something...

Mother's advice may also include strictures against "roaming
about," for the girl may fall in with "bad types," who are not
worthy candidates for marriage and who may damage her
reputation.

One reason for mothers to be concerned is that the behavior of
their offspring reflects on them. When Faustina was 20 years old,
her mother told her: (1) when she gets a boyfriend, she must
introduce him to her; (2) he must be a "better," i.e. Ga, boy who
would care for her; (3) he must be without a wife; (4) she must obey
her husband and cook well and serve well; (5) she must not roam
about with other men.

Although adulthood falls some time on one's middle or late
teens, mothers may still have enough influence to forbid their
daughters to go about with men "until they have grown," until
the daughter no longer is her mother's responsibility.[22] In most
cases, this point is reckoned identically for sons and
daughters—when they finish school and/or are working or married.
Those who do distinguish between their male and female offspring believe that responsibility for the boy ends when he has
grown, finished school, and/or is working, and for the daughter
when she marries. Until that time, the older woman wields some
control over her daughter, its extent varying with the amount of
contact the two have.

Beyond basic training and conditioning for marriage, the girls
learn through osmosis that they, as women, have different
capabilities than men, and consequently different (and far more
restricted) roles. Not one of my informants, for example, is
involved or interested in politics. Less than half even exercise their
right to vote. It may be that participation in politics by women has
been overestimated; or perhaps political fervor has ebbed generally
in Ghana with the frequent changes in governments and the

---

[22] The women define this responsibility in terms of the provision of room, board,
and petty necessities.

resurgence of ethnicity in the post-Nkrumah period; or possibly my informants are exceptional cases.

For "everywoman," there are new models on the horizon. And new relationships with both men and women are developing. While all of these are congruent with the urban context, all are also adaptations of the domestic identity. Very few are interested in the housewifely role to the exclusion of all else. Yet "all else" (even income-producing outside work) takes second spot to the roles of wife and mother.

Conclusion

In this study, I have focused upon the content, rather than the form, of the Adabraka woman's participation in the urban system. Adabraka houses a melange of constituencies. Yet despite background differences, these folk exhibit a homogeneity in values and lifestyle. This is due less to an overlay of Westernization than to a commonly-shared set of traditional principles. Imposed Western structures have served to reinforce the indigenous. For women, this has resulted in the perpetuation of traditional social identities and the consequent hindering of new identity relationships.

A woman may move to the city, out from under the direct supervision of the extended family, but she soon comes under the control of her husband. If she goes off to earn money, it must be only within the realm of "acceptable" work. The polygynous ideal, together with Victorian mores, has granted men first right in modern opportunities. While one venue to mobility is education, for a woman it is a necessary but insufficient condition to that end. Her ascribed role is primary. Indeed, her status as an adult is still tied to her relationship with men. In effect, her dependence on men is greater in the city which is rife with consumerism. In the hometown she had fewer expenses, and excesses could be met by kin and neighbors. Furthermore, she lived in the hometown among friends and family, people whom she knew and upon whom she could depend. In the city she is still psychologically dependent upon her kin, but is more physically isolated from them.

She views her roles as sexual and her weapon is ultimately sexual as well. She vies with other women for the favors of men, her avenue to success. Prior to marriage, she readily shifts her attentions from one donor to the next. Few relationships are infused with affect, for persons in roles are thought of as interchangeable. The labile personality does not suffer great disorientation or abandonment when a substitution occurs. The woman does settle into marriage. Her gamesmanship comes to a head in the marital bargaining. She accepts her husband's privilege, his "friendships", and her restricted existence fatalistically. She may only frequent certain places with propriety. Marriage, with or without children, cripples her mobility. She does not assert her right to public participation but accepts things as they have always been. A woman *knows* what the returns are when she fulfills traditional responsibilities and follows traditional models. To take the big step and depart from that for the unknown would mean a return whose value is itself unknown.

As was indicated in the first chapter, I encountered reticence in attempting to probe into a kind of unknown with my informants. Eliciting the individual's understanding of the concept of "independence" or "freedom" and how it related to her life generally required a great deal of cajoling, and even then the answers were often confused and incomplete. This may have been due to the individual's inability to articulate her feelings. On the other hand, the relevant conceptual category itself may have been absent, because the tradition of following established models and/or running one's life according to the dictates of others is so strong. Alternatively, they may have known what the idea meant but lacked concrete information or experiences pertaining to it.

I subsequently asked a series of related questions that were intended to illustrate *my* understanding of "independence," and the answers to which would illustrate the informant's. They included such items as from whom permission must be requested to do a variety of things, whether husband or family limited her activities, whether she could do the same things as a man, and so on. Responses to these were more easily obtained and have been used as documentation in the foregoing chapters. It was generally the case that the women made no connection between the abstract initial query and the more concrete ones that followed. I then posed the hypothetical question: are you more independent if you marry a wealthy man who gives you all you want AND you also have 10 children; OR if you are single and have a good job? The inconsistencies in the responses, that is, in how the women understood the questions, are illuminating.

Some could not only grasp "independence"[1] but also applied the concept to some related matters, in particular that of being married versus being single. These make up less than half the sample (15), but include all ages and levels of literacy, as well as members of all the ethnic groups appearing in the total sample. Adawkaw, for example, is illiterate and in her late twenties; she lives in her family house. She says that if she were to hire a room, do her own work, and look after herself, she would be independent. But, she continues, she is not now, as she is married, and despite today (the day of the interview) being Sunday, she cannot go to church because her husband wants her to cook for him. Her answer to the hypothetical question was to choose the life of a single woman: if you stay on your own, then you can go everywhere you like and you can be happy.

By the same token, Florence, a woman in her mid-thirties, literate and married, says that "you will do everything you think is good for you...don't want anybody to force you to do anything against your wish." She maintains that she possesses this type of freedom. Given the choice between a rich man, and satisfactory employment but no man, she too chooses the latter:

> Wealthy people have hatred and jealousy between their wives... Maybe the man will give you everything, but don't have peace of mind. So prefer to be single. Also these wealthy people have so much money they can spend it on girls and hotels and tell you they have gone to trek [on a trip]. But because of the money, you don't say anything, even if he abuses you.

---

[1] As defined in the first chapter, this is "the right to make decisions and implement them...independence implies *option*— the effective ability to do or not to do a given act."

Money is very important to these women; indeed, many use it as an index of independence. But having children is also important. Many would choose to marry someone with money, if they could have everything they wanted and could hire a maid to care for the children. Alongside those choosing the rich man on purely economic grounds, an equal number made the choice because of the childen. Children provide respectability as well as security in sickness and old age.

> If you haven't any child, it's not good... If you have money and no child, it's not good... If you die, that's all. And if you have child, someone will say "this is Hope's child."

This same individual (who has five children) says "if you have husband, you don't have independence...Because if you go out, he will ask you what you are going to do..." But it is *good* to be married. "Everyday you have owner like your mother or your father." Even some of those who admit to greater freedom when single qualify their answers; they say, for example, that neither being married *nor* being single carries independence, since one must always depend on others, or that "in the long run, single, but what about when old, even if you're in old-age home, you're still dependent. [If] at least you have family [children] to look after you..."

To be under the guidance or control of another is also a significant factor. As Hope implies, it is *good* to be controlled by a senior—first parents, then, naturally enough, spouse. Auntie Atta, hoping to remarry after having been widowed in her twenties, says that it is good that someone will look after her; to her, this is independence. The same thought is expressed in different words by Georgina:

> I think if you are independence [sic], people don't respect you. Because you go here and there...[Independence] means you have nobody to control you. I don't think it's good. I think if you get somebody to control you, that is good. If you are doing bad thing, they will tell you this is not good or this is good.

How does all this relate to the question of free will and

conceptualizing alternatives? As already noted, some women were perfectly consistent in the thoughts and examples they presented; others had no thoughts whatsoever—"anyways, my husband can tell you"—although they could respond articulately to questions about concrete situations. The majority gave answers that were consonant with *their* socio-cultural norms and values, equating "good" with material gain or with an accepted norm. In so doing, they disregarded possibilities that excluded marriage and children, or involved living without others to tell one what to do—or else designating such a hypothetical possibility as bad. Yet, for the most part, the term "independence" has a positive connotation. Since marriage is a cultural given, its compatability with the women's concept of independence is not surprising.

I shall end this study with an individual case history that highlights the stresses and ambiguities that characterize the lives of the women of Adabraka as they attempt to reconcile "new" urban lifeways and traditional obligations.

Vivian came to Accra from a small town in the Volta Region when she was 11 years old. Her reasons for coming were two-fold: to attend school and to help her elder sister, with whom she would live. Despite the fact that she was moving from the protective environment of her hometown to the city, her mother evinced little concern; if a young woman is migrating for a reasonable purpose, and will be staying with kin, parents do not put up obstacles or agonize unduly over her safety. Vivian finished Form Five at Achimota, a prestigious secondary school, and then became a cashier at Barclays Bank in Accra. Once she began working, she moved into quarters of her own.

With her Achimota education, an office job, and unmarried status, Vivian would seem to qualify as a "new" woman. She is exposed to, and interacts with, a variety of situations, and many of the people with whom she comes into contact could be vehicles to new experiences and opportunities. She seems free and "Westernized." She entered a beauty contest at the bank and won. An Afro-American businessman established in Accra was sufficiently struck by her intelligence and capability to begin negotiating a trip for her to the United States for more schooling. She spoke of marriage, but not until she is 30, and then only if she should find a man whom she loved and who loved her. "I wouldn't like to marry a man from my side," she explained, by which she meant that she does not like Ewe men.[2]

To Vivian, to be independent is "to be free to do anything you want, not to have anybody to push you around, say 'do this, do that.' " But Vivian's liberation was more apparent than real. Ruled by practicalities of day-to-day expenses, she said that she would move in with her family without hesitation if the family had a house in Accra. She admitted that while living on her own and supporting herself have allowed her some sense of autonomy, she is not socially independent: "Sometimes I blame myself for being too jealous; that's what prevents me [from experiencing greater freedom]." Her boyfriend came and went as *he* pleased, expecting her to wait on his whims. In a minor declaration of independence, she stated she would go out with others if the boyfriend were unavailable when a particular outing came up that piqued her interest—in part for mere enjoyment, in part to spite her "friend". Because her boyfriend was so undependable, she feared marriage with him, even though they had been seeing each other for several years. Yet, as she made clear, "a woman cannot just be going out with men all her life," and so the tie of friendship becomes binding.

As long as one stays put in the city, family pressures are less obvious than if one were at home, but eventually the skeletons begin to rattle. Vivian's younger sister had joined her in the same way that Vivian had joined her elder sister years before. The younger earned her keep by helping out in the house, but now that she had reached secondary school age, Vivian was expected to take on the financial responsibility of ensuring her an education equal to her own. The employed city relative must provide for any contingencies that may arise in the household left behind; living in the hometown is far less costly than in the city, but there is little ready cash for items such as school fees. Vivian did not question the requirement to see this obligation through, just as her elder sister had done for her, even though helping out would cramp her financially.

A letter I received from Vivian after my return to the United States conveyed between the lines the depth of the dilemma faced by

---

[2] Vivian says she "has no feeling" for Ewes, in part because she subscribes to the pejorative characterization of her fellow ethnics as practitioners of *juju* and other iniquities.

a woman such as Vivian when the two systems within which she must function—the "old"Ghana and the "new"—simultaneously exert their pull:

> Let me tell you something. You know when I went home last year—that was when I was on leave. My mum complained so bitterly about me not having a baby and that all the people whom I was born before had all had children and that what was I waiting for. When I returned, my boyfriend too talked about having a baby this year by all means. So I stopped taking my birth control tablets. You know, I've taken seed and I'm in the fourth month now...it's so horrible at the beginning. I usually feel so sick and lazy. I feel so lazy that sometimes I couldn't do any cooking when I return in the evenings.
>
> I only pray that it stays so that by October my mum will see what she wants, so that I can be free from her mutterings. We Africans are so crazy you know when our daughters delay a bit then we start to complain. I hope one day our ways will change, that we also have the carefree life so that if we [the daughters] don't bring forth early, our parents won't complain.
>
> Our parents don't see that it's very difficult for a young girl these days to find [a] real true lover. Unless you want the hit and miss type —you get a lot of them. And if you are not interested in that then you'll hold on for a long time. Then when you finally bring forth the children, you don't have sufficient time to look after them before death also calls on you. So at times it's better to start life early.
>
> ...My boyfriend is planning to do the engagement after the Easter holidays. I hope he keeps to his words. You know I wouldn't like to have a baby without not being engaged in the least, if I won't have the wedding. I only pray hard that he keeps to his words that I'll be happy when I have my baby.

Vivian subsequently had her baby and was set to care for him for a year or until weaning; then she will send him to her mother. Thus, her mother's role will be ratified, Vivian's adulthood guaranteed, and the father's position established. To fulfill these requirements is still the essence of being a woman in Adabraka.

Appendix I: Methodology

Three major interests prompted the present piece of research. The first was West African urbanization, the second was a growing concern with feminism, and the third was a desire to carry out my research with a minimum of obstacles due to my gender. The last two factors neatly dove-tail: female fieldworkers who have had trouble working in traditional societies are often dependent upon male members of the population for their data. In fact, women have been neatly side-stepped in most ethnographic work. Information regarding the study society's females is generally second-hand or impressionistic. It therefore seemed appropriate for me to pursue a study of the roles of adult women, and to do so in a West African city. Through the process of elimination, I chose Ghana, which has both a good university and a reputation for receptiveness to researchers. The choice of Accra related to my coastal bias and to the nature of my project.

Participant observation, the classic technique of anthropology, was my primary tool of enquiry. In traditional field studies, the anthropologist ensconces him/herself in the midst of a small society; by carefully observing, participating, and asking questions, he/she emerges with information on behavioral patterns, organizational principles, and so on. There are drawbacks to this approach, the primary ones being the danger of generalizing from an unrepresentative group and the high pitch of involvement with the indigenous people, which has a distorting effect on the fieldworker's observations. However, unlike survey research, extremes and exceptions do not get lost in statistical averages. And the product is a view from the ground up, which can surpass a study of externals and penetrate essentials. There are those who argue that this method results in a loss of objectivity, but I think this issue is moot: objectivity is not an attribute of small-scale social research, where human beings must come into contact with one another. It cannot be, because the researcher has little control over his/her subjective involvement with the resident population or their reciprocal response.

In anthropological research, the fieldworker is a tool of the research. The majority of anthropological studies have been done by men, using conventional male analyses; these have produced inadequate interpretations of female participation, behavior, attitudes and perceptions. Like Shirley Ardener (1975), I believe that women must be singled out, not for "reification" (Leeds 1976: 69) but to explore their perspective—one which is generally muted within the dominant male ideology. While an overly-enthusiastic feminist approach will also produce bias, Leith-Ross (1965: 22) has suggested that "even with the highest degree of trained discernment, it is difficult for a male investigator to get an accurate impression of what goes on in a woman's mind when it's revealed to him by another man." In certain situations, the data obtained by an European male from a female informant may be similarly unreliable. As a Northern Nigerian woman said to Professor Ronald Cohen's female interviewer, "All women are against all men!"

While living in the neighborhood of Adabraka, I became part of the scenery. I lost something of my stranger status. Not that I was any less a European; rather I was an eccentric European, who left her door open throughout the day and welcomed anyone who wanted to stop by. At first my visitors were predominantly children; but as the months went by, more and more of my adult neighbors came by to chat. Some of my choice pieces of informal lore came from teen-age girls who stopped in regularly.

My second major technique was formal interviewing, usually carried out in the interviewee's room or compound. On a few occasions, when scheduling with a trader was problematic, I conducted interviews at her market or street-side stall. At first I took down all interviews by hand; this disrupted the flow of conversation, distracted both the informant and me, and resulted in incomplete statements. Switching to a tape recorder proved invaluable. The women exhibited no discomfort with the instrument. Following the interview, or at the earliest convenience, I would transcribe the tape. Two visits usually sufficed to complete the schedule of questions.

To fill out the picture, I took advantage of most opportunities to attend festivals, weddings, funerals, etc. One of my most significant experiences in this regard was a three-day visit at the palace of Nana Atakora Amaniampong II, *Mamponhene*. Staying with Mary Nyarko, the *Mamponhene*'s second wife, provided me with insight into the traditional model of the adult married woman, as still practised by the chief's wife. Descriptions of such events, along with my Adabraka musings, turned into a journal. Fourteen months of entries revealed that there was a pattern to what I was seeing, and this formed the framework of my study analysis.

I made a point of reading many of the popular "story books," magazines, and of course daily newspapers. All of these media conveyed a clearer idea of the popular image of women, especially in the context of the city.

Finally, as a single woman I came into contact with Ghanaian men of all walks of life. Their single-minded approach to me as a female greatly influenced my perspective.

My procedure was as follows: I spent the first several weeks at the University of Ghana, 10 miles north of Accra, while looking for a place to live in the city. I chose Adabraka, because it is ethnically and socio-economically mixed and a renters' neighborhood. Once settled, I first carried out a census, and secondly drew a sample from the census, stratified by occupation and ethnicity. My third step was the formal interviewing of the selected sample. (As noted earlier, much supplementary data was obtained from women who lived nearby, but who were not members of the sample.)

The initial census fulfilled several objectives: it introduced me to members of the community, created a starting point for the project, and provided a generalized profile of the neighborhood women. I followed the suggestions of Nelson Addo, a demographer at the University of Ghana, in constructing my census categories:

1. House number—every compound had a number painted on

one of its walls for the 1970 Population Census. While most residents know neither the number of their compound nor the name of the street they live on, I found both useful in locating sample compounds until I became oriented to the area.

2. Name—invariably the women gave me their Christian names. This caused confusion on my return house call, because most habitually used their Ghanaian day names, the only names by which they were known to their neighbors.

3. Ethnic group—this was narrowed down as much as possible. For example, if a woman identified herself as an Akan or a Twi-speaker, I probed for the sub-group.

4. Birthplace—not necessarily the hometown. The distinction is not just academic, since one might never live in the hometown.

5. Education—in grade or number of years completed.

6. Age—often estimated according to the age of offspring. In a few cases of very old women, I used historical dates, such as pre- or post- the last Asante War of 1900-01.

7. Source of income—employment outside of the home or within the home (housewife).

8. Amount of income—most of those willing to respond gave fairly accurate responses.

The Coordinator of the 1970 Population Census, Mr. K. de Graft-Johnson, allowed me to see the Census Enumeration Visit Books. These contained house numbers (addresses), and the number of households and persons in each. I randomly selected five sub-areas of Adabraka, copying down every seventh house number in each. One of the sub-areas, Official Town, was already occupied by another anthropologist. I cut it out of my study, substituting the more recently built section of Asylum Down. Asylum Down is not proportionately represented, because it is less populated than the rest of Adabraka and because many of the randomly selected houses had foreigners living in them. Given the difficulties of sampling in Accra, and my desire to maintain stringency in my methodology, it seemed wiser not to substitute new house numbers for those where foreigners lived, which I had eliminated.

The census areas included Obuadaban Terrace, Liberation Circle, Adabraka Market, Tuxedo Junction, and Asylum Down. Each of these is named after a local fixture and each comprises approximately two square blocks.

A Ghanaian teacher friend gave me the names of three 18-year-old girls who had recently finished Secondary Form Five and wanted to work before going on to Sixth Form. Two of the girls took several copies of the Census Form to pilot test it in their own neighborhood. With the four of us working, the census took one week. We tried to canvas houses throughout the day. However, most women who "work" or trade are away from early morning until late afternoon or early evening. We found it most effective to visit the compounds between 6:00 and 7:00 a.m. and 5:00 to 8:00 p.m. While both time periods have their drawbacks,[1] we were assured of contact with the majority of residents.

Table 3

Distribution of Census Population in the Five Sample Areas

Neighborhood	Number of Houses	Number of Individuals	Percentage of Individuals
Obuadaban Terrace	15	106	22.7
Liberation Circle	14	78	16.7
Adabraka Market	24	129	27.6
Tuxedo Junction	15	102	21.8
Asylum Down	18	52	11.1
	86	467	99.9

The 467 women are distributed in 86 houses, an average of 5.43 per house. Needless to say, this average does not show that one house contains 16 adults and another only one.

When I began to go through the responses, I realized that there was no independent variable common to all. I returned to the 86 compounds to ask two further questions: length of residence in Accra and literacy in English. A Research Fellow at the University suggested that I cut out everyone except Middle Form Four leavers, which would provide me with a common denominator and fewer language problems. Had I done so, I would have eliminated two-

---

[1] During the morning shift, everyone was in a rush to wash, dress, and eat before leaving for work; in the evening, people were tired and involved in the preparation and eating of dinner. And since many compounds have no yard lights, we had to write by the light of the coal pots.

thirds of the canvassed population. Instead I used length of residence (urban experience) as the basis of eligibility for inclusion in the small sample.

Thus, the first step in grouping the strata was to exclude anyone whose length of residence did not meet my qualification. Only those living in Accra at least since the age of 22 (if born elsewhere) were eligible, resulting in a pool of 353 women. I next set about stratifying the respondents according to occupation and ethnicity. The association of occupation and financial gain, often made by Westerners, provided my rationale for stratifying by occupation. Prior to my field trip to Ghana, I met many returned researchers and read many papers, all attesting to the economic and consequent social emancipation of Ghanaian women. I wanted to know whether "emancipation" is shared by women variously employed. Does a woman's occupation preclude or enlarge her association with different people? Do different kinds of work aid in mobility? These were issues that interested me and that I felt would make occupational stratification worthwhile.

The 1960 Census classification of occupations was either too narrow or too broad for my purposes. I took the list of respondents' employments to five Ghanaians for help—a male neighbor (student), a successful businesswoman, a seamstress, the female owner of a local dance spot, and a market-woman friend. I was especially concerned with the classification of school head-mistress, seamstress, landlady, and the whole commercial group. My indigenous helpers informed me that in Ghana, a head-mistress is a teacher by profession, rather than an administrator; seamstresses similarly have a professional status of their own. Craftspeople and the diamond sorter, came to include all of those previously categorized as technical workers. Ghanaians do not identify a person as a landlord unless he owns a good deal of property. Thus, landlady was classified by whatever else she did.[2] The differentiation of street hawker and shop salesgirl was not settled by the five of us, although the seamstress-advisor pointed out that education notwithstanding, both take specialized training. The final stratification involved more lumping together than I wanted and was based upon empty cells.

---

[2] In former times, houseowner was associated with household head, a position of prestige. Currently the women seem more interested in an active economic role.

The grouped occupations of eligible women are as follows:

Unemployed: 101: housewife (62); pensioner (2); student (9); non-specific (28—including 5 landladies).

Services: 12: ward assistant (1); nursemaid (3); housegirl (1); housekeeper (2); sweeper (2); waitress (1); cook (2).

Crafts: 18: machine operator (1); factory worker (2); diamond sorter (1); furniture maker (1); hairdresser (2); employed seamstress (2); baker (6); book binder (3).

Seamstressing: 34.

Professional: 20: teacher (10); head-mistress (2); midwife (1); nurse (3); TV film editor (1); sand and stone contractor (1); radio studio manager (1); air hostess (1).

Clerical: 34: clerk (12); typist (7); shorthand/typist (3); telephonist (4); receptionist (2); telephonist/receptionist (2); bursar (1); cashier at bank (1); biller for telephone services (1) key puncher (1).

Commerce: 134: salesgirl (5); wholesaler (1); trader (8); storekeeper/kiosk owner (7); provisions (4); beauty goods (3); pot seller (1); firewood seller (1); cloth seller (13); petty trader (26); cigarettes (2); oil seller (3); porridge or *fula* seller (6); rice seller (10); *kenkey* seller (9); *gari* seller (1); doughnuts (1); vegetables (5); herbs (1); fruit (10); drink (3);fried food (3); clothing (6); eggs (1); groundnuts (2); meat, fish (2).

The ethnic stratification was equally difficult, raising problems of representativeness and comparability. If, for example, I was interested in comparing the consciousness of two seamstresses, and of all of the seamstress group only one were a Hausa, her similarity to or difference from the others might be idiosyncratic and have nothing to do with ethnicity. Then it occurred to me simply to take the three predominant ethnic groups in any one occupational stratum and exclude the rest. This might indicate tribe-specific occupations (should that be appropriate), while also providing sufficient representatives to make comparison valid. It is, however, also the case that the lone Hausa semastress is a member of the community, who could add another piece to the map of urban women's perceptions. Furthermore, if it proved true that role differentiation in Accra is based upon sex and not ethnicity, then a cross-section of women would be superior.

For my final sampling procedure, I went to the headquarters of the 1970 Population Census and consulted with one of the

Table 4
Cross-Tabulation of Occupation by Ethnicity

	Non-Employed	Services	Craftsmen	Seamstress	Professional	Clerical	Commerce	Total	Ethnic Percentages
GA	42	4	4	9	11	13	41	124	35
Adangme	4			2	3	1	11	21	6
TWI	29	5	6	11	1	10	34	96	27
Fanti	3		6	3	1	3	7	23	6.5
EWE	14	1	1	8	3	5	18	50	14
HAUSA	3					2	14	19	5.4
MISC.	6	2	1	1	1		9	20	6
Totals	101	12	18	34	20	34	134	353	99.9
Percentages	28.6	3	5	9.6	6	9.6	38		99.8
Original Sample Drawn	13	2	3	5	3	5	19	50	

236

statisticians. He insisted that I change *un*employed to *non*-employed, and that I merge services and crafts, lest the strata be too small and meaningless. With regard to internal (secondary) stratification by ethnicity, he suggested that I order the response sheets according to the proportional size of each ethnic group represented (which meant Ga-Adangme, Akan, Ewe, and the others following), selecting every seventh person for the sample. According to the finalized format, the sample would consist of 50 adult women,[3] drawn from a frame of 353 adult women, either born in Accra and 18 years of age or older, or migrant to Accra by age 22.

While I knew what general areas I wanted to cover, I had to work out exact questions and their wording to ensure maximum response. My first few months of informal study sensitized me to my social surroundings, which was useful when I constructed the interview schedule. No translation difficulties arose during the preliminary census, because the questions were simple and direct, the girls spoke Twi and Ga, and I was able to carry on the short questioning in Twi. Only a handful of non-English speakers—Ewe, Dagbani Dagomba, and Hausa—understood neither Twi nor Ga; however, there was always someone in the compound who was able and willing to interpret for us.

The problem of ambiguity was especially acute when I worked with an interpreter in the formal interviewing. Two-thirds of the sample women spoke English well enough to be interviewed in that language by me alone. The balance were interviewed primarily in Twi or Ga, and a few in Hausa and one in Ewe. Professor Lawrence Boadi, of the Linguistics Department at the University of Ghana, helped me in specifics of language. I had considered back-translating the schedule (from English, to the African language, and then back again). I ultimately chose to bypass this process, because it would have involved at least three languages and was not worth the cost in time and money for the small number of women affected. As a consequence, questioning was at times frustrating, either because my interpreter had difficulty understanding the point I was probing and could not phrase it, or because she simply asked the question incorrectly.

---

[3] For reasons explained in Appendix II, the actual sample consisted of only 39 women.

I did, however, minimize problems of translation in choosing as my interpreter a woman who showed a special affinity for me and my project; her attitude helped smooth the way in interviews. Although "unschooled" in a formal sense, she was fluent in English and five African languages. Her identity as a Hausa had no adverse effects, and in a few cases put Northern women, fearful of the Aliens' Compliance Order, at ease. She introduced me to the (Islamic) women's association *Zumunchi* and took me to events of the Hausa community in Accra. Unfortunately, she became increasingly unreliable in our working relationship, neglecting to appear for interviews. In her place I hired a newly-graduated Fifth Form student who was living in the neighborhood. She, too, was extremely affable and also provided assistance in project-related tasks; for example, she made a listing of all of the local businesses and their owners.

Recognizing how busy the Adabraka women are, I tried at first to make appointments for interviews. Invariably I would meet with disappointment. Life there is spontaneous and few of my informants had access to a telephone; so even if I had had a telephone, it would have been useless for arranging interviews. Often when I arrived at someone's house as scheduled, she would greet me with a mixture of surprise and pleasure, having totally forgotten our meeting. I learned to operate "catch as catch can," carrying around partially-completed schedules and finishing them up as I happened upon their respective respondents.

I waited until my return to the United States to begin my analysis. I had not originally planned to use a computer; however, the census population was large enough and the demographic information sufficient to warrant a statistical analysis. The output provided the profile of "everywoman." The essence of this study, however, is qualitative. I did the bulk of my analysis by hand, sifting my field notes in the same spirit, albeit more removed, as I had collected them.

In retrospect, the hindrances delineated enhanced my experience in Ghana, as well as the quality of my research. They derived from a conflict in values and expectations—Western and Ghanaian, mine and my informants'—and in identifying each of them, I learned a little more about the society. I also gained a greater appreciation of these women who not only tolerated my intrusions but privileged me with their responses.

Appendix II: The Sample

Adabraka's "everywoman" is of course a composite of many unique individuals. Some stand out more so than others, in part due to the individual's loquaciousness, in part to the tenor of her relationship with me. Most of their views are honest, reflecting the individual reality worlds that they choose to present to an outsider. In this Appendix, I shall give first a demographic and then an impressionistic description of the sample women.

As originally drawn, the sample consisted of 50 women. For several reasons, the care in selecting a proportionate representation went askew: some women gave only partial responses to the census questions. For example, a "housewife" neglected to add that she sells fruit full-time. Others had to move away during the months intervening between my initial visit and my return for formal interviewing; finally, I had miscalculated the length of time needed to complete the research. The final sample consisted of 39 women. (*See* Table 5 on page 240).

Interviewing was not completed with five of the 39 who clearly did not wish to be bothered; however, where I have material from any of them, I have included it in my analysis. Cecilia, a young Ga clerk living in her father's house in Liberation Circle, allowed me one truncated session. While she set up further appointments, she absented herself each time. Her excuse, that she was attending

Table 5

Neighborhood	Number of Compounds	Number of Women
Obuadaban Terrace	6	9
Liberation Circle	8	8
Adabraka Market	7	10
Tuxedo Junction	6	8
Asylum Down	4	4
	31	39

choir, guild or communicant class at the Anglican Church, was proffered by her older sister. Maame Afua, an illiterate Kwahu shoe trader living in the Adabraka Market section, was also home to one meeting only. She was cooking soup and not answering in full because, she said, she was distracted. When I returned a second time, she was preparing to go out with her husband. There was no third time, because I left Ghana shortly thereafter.

Amina and Emma, both residents of Tuxedo Junction, were willing respondents at first, but then withdrew. Amina is a Northerner and may have feared that I was connected with the government and implementation of the Aliens' Compliance Order, which had affected many Northerners. She was direct in refusing to continue with the interviewing. With Emma, a Ga oil seller, it was different. After a very successful session by her stall at Adabraka Market, she gave me the run-around. When my interpreter finally made contact with her, Emma berated the girl and said that she was "fed up." Hilda, an elderly houseowner and coal seller in Asylum Down, balked at some of the questioning during the first visit. Her son, who was nearby, persuaded her to let me complete the particular section of the protocol, but she was never at home for subsequent meetings.

I had several interesting near-misses. Adawkaw, Auntie Rose and Faustina are all members of the same matrilineage and live in the same Ga family house. Faustina was one of the first women I interviewed and always welcomed me when I appeared in her doorway. If she had to bathe her little boy, she would do so while I watched. She and Auntie Rose were intimates, and when the older (illiterate) woman refused to see me, Faustina persuaded her to change her mind. Adawkaw was also hesitant, but her bosom pal Akwele (illiterate like Adawkaw) turned out to be another member of the sample who had enjoyed the interviews and convinced her to cooperate. While educated and seemingly sophisticated, Helena momentarily refused to see me, because her husband (a university drop-out) forbade her to answer any more questions! Only after I explained the purpose of my work to *him* did I regain entry.

The sample women fall into the following age-groups: 4 were 18-19, 21 were in their 'twenties, 6 were in their 'thirties, 5 in their 'forties, 2 were 54, and 1 was 64. The "everywoman" is thus 29 years old. She is of the following ethnic groups:

Ga		17
Adangme		2
Ga-Adangme		1
Akan		12
	Kwahu	8
	Akwapim	1
	Asante	2
	Nzima	1
	[Fante/Krobo]	1
Ewe		4
Dagbani		1
Buzanga		1

39

Twenty-one of them were born in Accra. The others came from moderate to small-size towns in southern Ghana, save one who left her family in Yendi, in the north, when she married. Of those born in Accra, only four are not Ga.

More than half of the 71 percent who were English-speakers were between 18 and 30 years of age. Literacy correlates with schooling: 34 percent had at least finished Middle Form Four, and another 23 percent had gone on, either academically or vocationally. Education ties in not only with age but with ethnicity and region of birth as well, but with so small a sample it is hard to make any inferences.

"Everywomen's" religious affiliation is primarily Methodist, Presbyterian, and Anglican, supplemented by Islam, Catholic, and Fundamentalist. And if not currently married, she was in the past or will be in the future. In fact, 24 of the women are married, another four are widows, and of the 11 single women, only two do not have boyfriends. Those not yet married are in their twenties or younger.

I have suggested that women gain mobility through their husbands and boyfriends. Therefore, a further indicator for their positions on the social hierarchy is the educational and occupational backgrounds of their men. Only five of the husbands have had no Western education whatsoever. The balance are almost equally distributed in Middle Form and secondary. The more highly-educated women are married or attached to men of an equivalent background; the better-educated men, however, are not necessarily married or attached to women of the same. In fact, one half of the men are married to women of lower educational background (three secondary school graduates and six Middle Form leavers have illiterate wives). Ekua, the illiterate firewood seller, at the age of 22 is married to her second husband. The first, an Asante like herself, went off to England to obtain a university degree. The geographical and social distance between them was too great and he divorced her. Her second husband is a middle school graduate.

Uneducated husbands include a carpenter, a retired soldier, a butcher, a goat dealer, and a taxi driver; the last three are Muslims. The men working in the modern sector include all of those with secondary school backgrounds (with the exception of one tailor) and middle school education:[1]

Middle School		Secondary School (plus)	
Own business	1	Soldiering	3
Importer	1	Tailor	1
Artist	1	Gas station	1
Photographer	1	Nurse	1
Mechanic	1	White collar	
Driver	1	(supervisory)	4
Secretarial	4	Secretarial	3
Live animal trader	1		

None of the men fall within the bounds of the élite. Some are middle income, but most are what we would consider working class, hence the necessity for working wives. Only ten women are not currently earning any money (for themselves or someone else, such as mother or husband). Of these, one-half are apprentices in a trade (sewing and hairdressing). The women fall into the following occupational groups.

Commerce (trade)	
cloth	1
oil	1
kenkey (for sister 1)	2
oranges	2
rice (for mother)	1
firewood (for father)	1
fried food	1
coal / houseowner	1
shoes	1
nuts, fruit, etc.	1
Kiosk (for husband)	2
/ trade 1	
Services	
sweeper / trader	1
cook	1
Crafts	
baker	2
/ for mother 1	
Seamstress	3
Professional	
nursery teacher	1
TV film editor	1
sand and stone contractor	1
Clerical	5
Non-employed	
secondary school graduate	1
housewife	4
/ seamstress 1	

---

[1] This listing does not include the boyfriends of five of the women and the husbands of four.

Apprenticing
    sewing   4
    hairdressing   1

                                                               39

All of the demographic variables affect and reflect the lifestyles of these women—and in turn the quality of their contacts with someone like myself. A married woman with children, who works outside of the home, has far more constraints placed on her time than an unmarried woman who lives alone. An unmarried woman who is uneducated and lives in the family house will spend her time differently than an educated girl in the same living situation. A woman who is active in a Fundamentalist sect and one whose boyfriend has little spending money are equally unlikely to go night-clubbing.

My rapport with each woman was different. For some of the 15 non-English speakers, my interpreter was an interference; in general, she had no adverse effect. Some of the women employed outside the home found a time to meet with me, despite long and inflexible daily schedules; others made my task less simple. For example, Ekua spoke no English and worked six days a week, from 6:00 a.m. to 6:00 p.m. Yet she made herself accessible on Sundays —the one day of the week when she was free to do her wash and other household chores and attend church services. On the other hand, there were difficulties getting together with Fatima, the *kenkey*-maker. Her schedule was exhausting, and she felt uncomfortable talking and wrapping *kenkey* in corn leaves at the same time. This was true of others as well, due, perhaps, to the subject matter of my visits. As I have indicated, some of my questions related to concepts or actions which are foreign to the women. Auntie Elizabeth, a cake baker, was always at home for me when I stopped by for idle chatter. If I pulled out a list of questions, however, she sometimes had to be cajoled into talking.

Why did Helena feel compelled to tell her husband about our discussions? And after he had voiced his displeasure, how would he have known if she had continued with me during his absence? It was not her style to challenge her husband's control. She has allowed him to set the parameters of her relationships.

Amawkaw has grown up in gracious surroundings at her

grandmother's house. She has finished secondary school, a short commercial course, and was planning a trip to London to continue in secretarial training. Non-employed, she whiled away her time listening to records in between her very minimal household chores. Amawkaw was betrothed to a handsome and successful young man; they partied on Saturday nights, went to football games on Sundays. Yet, she was very unhappy. She felt imprisoned in her grandmother's house. If she wanted to go anywhere, she had to clear it first with "granny." Her grandmother held the purse strings and thus Amawkaw was beholden to her.

Amawkaw resides in the main house, which is equipped with a telephone, a proper bathroom and kitchen, and the material accoutrements of upper class living. Martha and Lydia, in the family compound next door, live in tin-roofed structures, without electricity, adjacent to the main house. Amawkaw's paved yard is filled with flowering vines, flowers, and a large shade tree; her neighbors' yard, of dirt and stones, has no landscaping; the women house their cooking equipment in lean-to shacks. Amawkaw referred to the neighboring family as "quite a character." She elaborated by adding: "Well, only one of the people there has been to secondary school and she's in Britain. All of the rest just *breed*." Her values are quite different from theirs.

Furthermore, the quality of their respective home lives is quite different. Lydia speaks of the supportiveness that is always forthcoming; the cousins all pal around together. Husbands and wives do not live together, but they see each other and carry on traditional duties. Their horizons are far more limited than those of Amawkaw, who has been abroad and yearns for a more Western existence. Her consciousness is different from theirs, as are her primary relationships. When Hope's husband entered the room during our sessions, he would immediately intercept the questions I was asking. In their marriage, she is the passive partner. She addresses him as "Mr." and receives no direct pay for managing his kiosk. Adisa, the mother of four, an orange seller, and a member of *zumunchi*, always had a smile on her face. Her husband disapproved of her work, but she "begged" him because of the children. She had said that when husband and wife show one another "true love", they get along, ignoring any gossip to the contrary. I got the feeling that she and her husband did not get along particularly well: she, my interpreter, and I were sitting hunched up and whispering so that he would not hear from the next room. Gloria and her husband were comparative newly-weds when we met—married for one year. Both were bright; unlike many of my interviewees, Gloria was quite attentive and thought carefully before answering. The first time I stopped by their house, the two of them walked me home. "Tell me," he said, "we hear that Americans are very wealthy and have all that they need; we hear also that Russians are not so wealthy and that they have far less than the Americans. But when Americans come to Ghana, they are always walking in the street, eveywhere they go, whereas the Eastern Europeans are always taking taxis. Isn't that strange?" When Gloria and I were almost finished a session, her husband came in; he was anxious to add to the conversation and one does not easily ask husbands to leave the room, so we all talked and at a subsequent meeting with her, I repeated some of the questions. Florence is a full-time housewife who contributes nothing to the household budget. Unlike most of the other women, she and her husband entertain friends *ensemble*. She has opinions and expresses them freely. Her husband is a professional (a nurse), and a very articulate man. He never interrupted our interviews, though he entertained me at length afterwards with his definite, and rather radical, views on politics in Ghana. They live with their four children in three rooms, in a mixed compound, and he keeps his cages of crabs (which he traps in the lagoon) alongside her cooking gear.

Although Dora was working long hours for her mother, a baker, her father, an unemployed pharmacist with pretensions, persuaded me to hire her as my housegirl so that "she will learn from your ways". Dora took me to her mother's hometown of Somanya, to observe part of the *dipo* ceremony. Our working arrangement came to an unfortunate end, when it became clear that her mother's work always came first. Dora felt beholden to her mother for raising her baby. Aba, a Form Five graduate, was in a similar situation with her mother; yet the two had a comfortable relationship. Aba's mother cared for the child during the day, but unlike Dora, Aba had an outside job; she was also several years Dora's senior. Perhaps most important, her mother was less manipulative and a nicer sort.

Lizzie was still very attached to her family. She took me to Obo-Kwahu to spend a few days at her family house and see her hometown. In Adabraka, she lived in the same compound as her elder sister and mother, yet her mother knew little about her life beyond the compound walls. Georgina lived with both parents and siblings. Like Lizzie, she had a married boyfriend, and like Lizzie, she followed her own life-style; but unlike Lizzie, she hid little from her mother. Both of these young women will marry (if they have not already); neither was so naive as to believe that her "friend" would be the one.

Finally, there is a young woman like Ellen, who had taken over her sister's room and lived there alone. She said that she can pretty much do as she pleases because she is single, yet in fact did not go out much at night. She preferred staying in and reading, and when her fiancé would come in from Takoradi, they would go out to the cinema. While despairing at the change in life-style that marriage would bring, she was resigned to marrying and a life of domestic chores.

Bibliography

Abraham, W.E.

1962   *The Mind of Africa*. Chicago: University of Chicago Press.

Acquah, Ione

1958   *Accra Survey*. London: University of London Press.

Addo, Nelson

1970   Immigration into Ghana: Some Social and Economic Implications of the Aliens Compliance Order of 18 November, 1969. *Ghana Journal of Sociology* VI, 1: 20-42.

Addo, Stella

1970a   Woman Do you lie about 'it'? *The Daily Graphic*, (October 19).

1970b   The Sensuous Woman: You Too Can Be a Goddess. *The Daily Graphic*, (November 23).

1971a   Those Lovable Rogues. *The Daily Graphic*, (September 15).

1971b   Kissing Don't Last, Cookery Do. *The Daily Graphic*, (October 6).

Adesanya, S.A.

1976   Divorce in Ghana and Nigeria—A Comparative Study in Legislative Reform. *Review of Ghana Law* III, 2: 91-115.

Aldous, John

1962   Urbanization, The Extended Family and Kinship Ties in West Africa. *Social Forces* XLI, 1: 6-12.

Amenu, Ellis

1971   Marriage Still a Sacred Union. *The Daily Graphic*, (September 29).

248

Apter, David
  1968   *Ghana in Transition*. (revised). New York: Atheneum. (Second revised
         edition 1972. Princeton: Princeton University Press.)
Ardener, Shirley
  1975   Introduction. In *Perceiving Women*. Shirley Ardener, ed. New York:
         Halsted Press. pp. vii-xxiii.

Ariès, Philippe
  1962   *Centuries of Childhood: A Social History of Family Life*. (Trans-
         lated by Robert Baldick). New York: Alfred A. Knopf, Inc.

Armah, Ayi Kwei
  1971   *Fragments*. New York: P.F. Colliers, Inc.
Bailhe, Pat
  1973   *Window on the River and Other Poems*. Bangkok. Vitayapan
         Press.
Baker, Tanya
  1959   Report on Nigeria. In *Women's Role in the Development of Trop-
         ical and Sub-Tropical Countries*. Brussels: International Institute of
         Differing Civilizations.
Baker, Tanya, and Mary Bird
  1959   Urbanization and the Position of Women. *Sociological Review*.
         New Series, VII: 99-122.

Banks, Joseph Ambrose and Olive
  1972   *Feminism and Family Planning in Victorian England*. (2nd printing).
         (Originally published 1964). New York: Schocken Books Inc.

Banton, Michael
  1965   *Roles: An Introduction to the Study of Social Relations*. New York:
         Basic Books Inc.

Barkow, Jerome H.
  1972   Hausa Women and Islam. *Canadian Journal of African Studies*
         VI, ii: 317-28.

Basch, Françoise
  1974   *Relative Creatures: Victorian Women in Society and the Novel*.
         New York: Schocken Books Inc.

Bascom, William
  1942   The Principle of Seniority in the Social Structure of the Yoruba.
         American Anthropologist. New Series 44: 37-46.

Benedict, Ruth
   1938   Continuities and Discontinuities in Cultural Conditioning. *Psychiatry*
           I: 161-67.
Berry, Jack
   1969   Sociolinguistic Research in Ghana. In *Expanding Horizons in African
           Studies*. G.M. Carter and A. Paden, eds. Evanston: Northwestern
           University Press. pp. 303-13.
Birmingham, Walter Barr, I. Neustadt, and E.N. Omaboe, eds.
   1967   *A Study of Contemporary Ghana. Volume II: Some Aspects of
           Social Structure*. Evanston: Northwestern University Press.
Boateng, E.A.
   1966   *A Geography of Ghana*. (2nd edition). Cambridge: Cambridge
           University Press.
Bock, Philip M.
   1967   Love, Magic, Menstrual Taboos, and the Facts of Geography.
           American Anthropologist 69: 213-17.
Bohannan, Paul
   1963   *Social Anthropology*. New York: Holt, Rinehart and Winston Inc.
Boserup, Ester
   1970   *Woman's Role in Economic Development*. London: George Allen
           and Unwin Ltd.
Bosman, William
   1705   *A New and Accurate Description of the Coast of Guinea*. (Trans-
           lated from the Dutch). (New edition, 1967. London: Frank Cass & Co.
           Ltd.)
Brain, James L.
   1976   Less Than Second-Class. Women in Rural Settlement Schemes in
           Tanzania. In *Women in Africa: Studies in Social and Economic
           Change*. N. Hafkin and E. Bay, eds. Stanford: Stanford University
           Press: pp. 265-84.
Calder, Jenni
   1976   *Women and Marriage in Victorian Fiction*. New York: Oxford
           University Press.
Caldwell, John C.
   1966   The Erosion of the Family: A Study of the Fate of the Family in
           Ghana. *Population Studies* XX, 1 (July): 5-26.
   1967   Population: General Characteristics. In *A Study of Contemporary
           Ghana. Volume II: Some Aspects of Social Structure*. W.B. Birming-
           ham et al, eds. pp. 17-74.

1967a   Migration and Urbanization. In *A Study of Contemporary Ghana. Volume II: Some Aspects of Social Structure.* W.B. Birmingham et al, eds. pp. 111-46.

1968   *Population Growth and Family Change in Africa.* Canberra: Australian National University Press.

Cardinall, A.W.
1932   *A Bibliography of the Gold Coast.* (Reprinted 1972. Westport, Connecticut: Negro Universities Press.)

Chafe, William
1972   *The American Woman, 1920-1970.* New York: Oxford University Press.

"Chat with Grandma"
1970   "Bitter or Not They Like It," *Saturday Mirror* (November 7).

Chodorow, Nancy
1971   Being and Doing: A Cross-Cultural Examination of the Socialization of Males and Females. In *Woman in Sexist Society.* V. Gornick, B.K. Moran, eds. New York: Basic Books Inc. pp. 173-97.

Claridge, W.W.
1915   *A History of the Gold Coast and Ashanti.* Volume I. (New edition, 1964. London: Frank Cass & Co. Ltd.).

Clark, Alice
1920   *The Working Life of Women in the Seventeenth Century.* New York: Harcourt Brace.

Clignet, Rémi
1970   *Many Wives, Many Powers.* Evanston: Northwestern University Press.

Cohen, Abner
1969   *Custom and Politics in Urban Africa.* London: Routledge and Kegan Paul.

1970   The Politics of Marriage in Changing Middle Eastern Stratification Systems. In *Essays in Comparative Social Stratification.* L. Plotnikov and A. Tuden, eds. Pittsburgh: University of Pittsburgh Press. pp. 195-209.

Cohen, Ronald
1972   Altruism: Human, Cultural or What? *Journal of Social Issues* XXVIII, 3: 39-57.

Collins, Randall
1971   A Conflict Theory of Sexual Stratification. *Social Problems* 19: 3-21.

Crabtree, A.L.
  1950   Marriage and Family Life Amongst the Educated Africans of the
          Gold Coast. M.Sc. thesis. University of London.
Crowder, Michael
  1968   *West Africa Under Colonial Rule*. Evanston: Northwestern University
          Press.
Daniels, W.C. Ekow
  1974   Problems in the Law Relating to the Maintenance and Support of
          Wives and Children. In *Domestic Rights and Duties in Southern
          Ghana*. C. Oppong, ed. Legon, Ghana: Institute of African Studies,
          pp. 285-91.
de Sola Pool, Ithiel
  1963   The Mass Media and Politics in the Modernization Process. In
          Communications and Political Development. Lucien M. Pye, ed.
          Princeton: Princeton University Press. pp.234-53.
Douglas, Mary
  1969   Is Matriliny Doomed in Africa? in *Man in Africa*. Mary Douglas and
          Phyllis Kaberry, eds. London, Tavistock Publications. pp.121-35.
  1970   *Natural Symbols: Explorations in Cosmology*. New York: Pantheon
          Books Inc.
Du Sautoy, Peter
  1958   *Community Development in Ghana*. London: Oxford University
          Press.
English, H.B., and English, A.C.
  1958   *A Comprehensive Dictionary of Psychological and Psycho-analytical
          Terms*. New York: Longmans, Green and Co.
Epstein, A.L.
  1958   *Politics in an Urban African Community*. Manchester: Manchester
          University Press.
  1964   Urban Communities in Africa. In *Closed Systems and Open Minds*.
          M. Gluckman, ed. Edinburgh: Oliver & Boyd. pp. 83-102.
Essiah, John Wilberforce
  1971   Letter to the Editor. *The Daily Graphic*. (August 10).
Evans-Pritchard, E.E.
  1940   *The Nuer*. Oxford: Clarendon Press.
  1965   *The Position of Women in Primitive Societies and Other Essays in
          Social Anthropology*. New York: The Free Press.
Fage, John D.
  1969   *A History of West Africa*. (4th edition). Cambridge, England:

BIBLIOGRAPHY

University Press.

Field, M.J.

1937   *Religion and Medicine of the Ga People.* London: Oxford University Press. (Reprinted 1961).

1940   *Social Organization of the Ga People.* London: Crown Agents for the Colonies.

Ford, Clellan Stearns

1945   *A Comparative Study of Human Reproduction.* Publications in Anthropology 32. New Haven: Yale University Press.

Fortes, Meyer

1967   Kinship and Marriage Among the Ashanti. In *African Systems of Kinship and Marriage.* A.R. Radcliffe-Brown and Darylls Ford, eds. London: Oxford University Press. (Originally published 1950). pp. 252-84.

Fortes, Meyer, ed.

1962   *Marriage in Tribal Societies.* London: Cambridge University Press.

Foster, Philip

1965   *Education and Social Change in Ghana.* Chicago: University of Chicago Press.

Friedl, Ernestine

1967   The Position of Women: Appearance and Reality. *Anthropological Quarterly* 40, 3 (July): 97-108.

Gaisie, S.K.

1968   Social Structure and Fertility. *Ghana Journal of Sociology* IV, 2: 88-99.

George, Betty S.

1976   *Education in Ghana.* U.S. Office of Education. Washington: U.S. Government Printing Office.

Ghana Government

1962   *1960 Population Census of Ghana.* Accra: Census Office.

1971   *Educational Statistics 1968-69.* Accra: Ghana Ministry of Education.

1972   *1970 Population Census of Ghana. Vol. II: Statistics of Localities and Enumeration Areas.* Accra: Census Office.

1973   *Statistical Year Book 1969-70.* Accra: Republic of Ghana Central Bureau of Statistics.

Gold Coast Laws

1912   *The General Orders of the Gold Coast Colony.*   (Revised up to 30th June 1912). London: Waterlow.

Goode, William J.

1959   The Theoretical Importance of Love. *American Sociological Review* 24, 1 (February): 38-47.

1960   A Theory of Role Strain. *American Sociological Review* XXV, 4: 483-96.

1963   *World Revolution and Family Patterns*. Glencoe, Illinois: The Free Press.

Goodenough, Ward H.

1965   Rethinking Status and Role: Towards a General Model of the Cultural Organization of Social Relationships. In *The Relevance of Models for Social Anthropology*. (Association of Social Anthropologists of the Commonwealth, Monograph 1). M. Banton, ed. London: Tavistock Publications. pp. 1-22.

Goody, Esther

1969   Kinship Fostering in Gonja. In *Socialization: The Approach from Social Anthropology*. P. Mayer, ed. (Association of Social Anthropologists of the Commonwealth, Monograph 8). London: Tavistock Publications. pp. 51-74.

Gornick, Vivian, and Moran, Barbara K., eds.

1971   *Woman in Sexist Society*. New York: Basic Books Inc.

Gough, Kathleen

1971   Nuer Kinship: A Re-Examination. In *The Translation of Culture: Essays to E.E. Evans-Pritchard*. T.O. Beidelman, ed. London: Tavistock Publications. pp.79-121.

Gough, Kathleen, and Schneider, David, eds.

1961   *Matrilineal Kinship*. Berkeley: University of California Press.

Gouldner, Alvin W.

1960   The Norm of Reciprocity: A Preliminary Statement. *American Sociological Review* XXV 4: 161-78.

Graham, C.K.

1971   *The History of Education in Ghana: From the Earliest Times to the Declaration of Independence*. London: Frank Cass and Co.

Grandmaison, Colette LeCour

1969   Activites economiques des femmes Dakaroises. *Africa* 39: 138-52.

Greenstreet, Miranda

1971   Employment of Women in Ghana. *International Labour Review* 103, 2: 117-129.

1972   Social Change and Ghanaian Women. *Canadian Journal of African Studies* VI, ii: 351-55.

Gugler, Josef
1972   The Second Sex in Town. *Canadian Journal of African Studies* VI, ii: 289-301.

Gutkind, Peter C., and Southall, Aidan
1957   *Townsmen in the Making: Kampala and Its Suburbs.* Kampala: East African Institute of Social Research.

Haase, H.
1972   Plasticity. In *Encyclopedia of Psychology.* H.J. Eysenck, W. Arnold, R. Meili, eds. New York: Herder & Herder Inc. p.17.

Hagan, John C.
1971   Contraceptives and Teenagers. *The Daily Graphic.* (September 28).

Hamilton, Ruth Simms
1971   Urban Social Differentiation and Membership Recruitment Among Selected Voluntary Associations in Accra, Ghana. Ph.D. thesis. Northwestern University.

Harrell-Bond, Barbara
1975   *Modern Marriage in Sierra Leone.* The Hague: Mouton Publishers.

Hayfrom, R.K., compiler
1969   Halakan's Street and Place Guide: Accra, Maps and Indexes. Accra: Akan Printing Press Ltd.

Heggoy, Alf Andrew
1974   On the Evolution of Algerian Women. *African Studies Review* XVII, 2 (September): 449-56.

Hoffer, Carol.
1972   Mende and Sherbro Women in High Office. *Canadian Journal of African Studies* VI, ii: 151-64.

Hoffman, Lois W.
1974   Effects on Child. In *Working Mothers.* Lois W. Hoffman and F. Ivan Nye, eds. San Francisco: Jossey-Bass, Inc. pp. 126-66.

Homans, George C.
1959   Social Behavior as an Exchange. *American Journal of Sociology* LXIII (May): 597-606.

Huber, Hugo
1963   *The Krobo: Traditional Social and Religious Life of a West African People.* Studia Instituti Anthropos. Vol. 16. St Augustin, near Bonn: The Anthropos Institute.

Hurd, G.E.

1967   Education. In *A Study of Contemporary Ghana. Volume II: Some Aspects of Social Structure.* W.B. Birmingham et al, eds. pp. 217-39.

Izzett, Alison

1961   Family Life Among the Yoruba in Lagos, Nigeria. In *Social Change in Modern Africa.* A.W. Southall, ed. London: Oxford University Press. pp. 303-15.

Kaye, Barrington

1962   *Bringing Up Children in Ghana.* London: George Allen and Unwin Ltd.

Keller, Suzanne

1968   *The Urban Neighborhood.* New York: Random House, Inc.

Kilson, Marion

1967   Continuity and Change in the Ga Residential System. *Ghana Journal of Sociology* III, 2: 81-97

1968   The Ga Naming Rite. *Anthropos* LXIII / LXIV: 904-20.

Kotey, Gladys

1971   Contraceptives and Teenagers. *The Daily Graphic,* (September 13).

Kretschmer, W.

1972   Flexibility. In *Encyclopedia of Psychology.* H.J. Eysenck, W. Arnold, R. Meili, eds. Volume I. New York: Herder & Herder, Inc. p.379.

LaBarre, Weston

1951   Family and Symbol. In *Psychoanalysis and Culture: Essays in Honor of Geza Roheim.* W. Munsterburger, ed. New York: International University Press. pp. 156-67.

Lamphere, Louise

1974   Strategies, Cooperation, and Conflict Among Women in Domestic Groups. In *Woman, Culture and Society.* M.Z. Rosaldo and L. Lamphere, eds. pp. 97-112.

Leavitt, Ruby

1971   Woman in Other Cultures. In *Woman in Sexist Society.* V. Gornick and B. Moran, eds. New York: Basic Books Inc. pp. 276-303.

Leeds, Anthony

1976   Women in the Migratory Process: A Reductionist Outlook. *Anthropological Quarterly* 49: 69-76.

Lerner, Daniel

1958   *The Passing of Traditional Society.* Glencoe, Illinois: The Free Press.

Lévi-Strauss, Claude
1969   *The Elementary Structures of Kinship.* (Revised edition, translated by James Harte Bell). John Richard von Sturmer and Rodney Needham, eds. Boston: Beacon Press.

Linton, Ralph
1936   *The Study of Man.* New York: Appleton-Century-Crofts.

Little, Kenneth
1959   Introduction to the Special Number on Urbanization in West Africa, *Sociological Review* VII: 5-13.
1959a   Some Urban Patterns of Marriage and Domesticity in West Africa. *Sociological Review* VII: 65-82.
1965   *West African Urbanization.* Cambridge, England: Cambridge University Press.
1973   *African Women in Towns.* London: Cambridge University Press.

Lloyd, Peter C.
1967   *Africa in Social Change.* Harmondsworth, Middlesex, England: Penguin Books.

McCall, Daniel
1961   Trade and the Role of Wife in a Modern West African Town. In *Social Change in Modern Africa.* A.W. Southall, ed.London, New York: Oxford University Press. pp.286-99.

MacGregor, Fiona
1971   Girls Prefer Mature Men. *The Ghanaian Times.* (September 14).

McNulty, Michael
1966   Urban Centers and the Spatial Pattern of Development in Ghana. Ph.D. dissertation. Northwestern University.

Maher, Vanessa
1974   *Women and Property in Morocco.* London: Cambridge University Press.

Mair, Lucy
1969   *African Marriage and Social Change.* London: Frank Cass and Co. Ltd.

Manoukian, Madeline
1950   *Akan and Ga-Adangme Peoples of the Gold Coast.* Ethnographic Survey of Africa: Western Africa. International African Institute. London: Oxford University Press.
1952   *The Ewe-Speaking People of Togoland and the Gold Coast.* Ethnographic Survey of Africa: Western Africa. London: International African Institute.

Marris, Peter
1962   *Family and Social Change in an African City.* London: Routledge and
        Kegan Paul.
Marx, Emanuel
1967   *Bedouin of the Negev.* New York: Praeger Publishers Inc.
Mauss, Marcel
1966   *The Gift.* (Translated by Ian Cunnison). London: Cohen and West.
Mayer, Philip
1971   *Townsmen or Tribesmen.* (2nd edition). London: Oxford University
        Press.
Mead, Margaret
1949   *Male and Female.* (4th printing, 1971). New York: Dell Publishing Co.
        Publishing Co.
Michaelson, Evelyn J. and Walter Goldschmidt
1971   Female Roles and Male Dominance Among Peasants. *Southwestern
        Journal of Anthropology* 27, 4: 330-52.
Mills-Odoi, Diana
1961   La Family and Social Change. M.A. thesis. University of Ghana,
        Institute of African Studies.
Mintz, Sidney
1971   Men, Women and Trade. *Comparative Studies in Society and History*
        13: 247-69.
Mitchell, J. Clyde

1966   Theoretical Orientations in African Urban Studies. In *The Social
        Anthropology of Complex Societies.* M. Banton, ed. London:
        Tavistock Publications. pp. 37-68.

1974   *Psychoanalysis and Feminism.* New York: Pantheon Books, Inc.
Mohammed
1906   *The Koran, Commonly called the Al-Koran of Mohammed.* (Trans-
        lated by George Sale.) Eighth edition. Philadelphia: Lippincott Co.
Nadel. S.F.
1942   Black Byzantium. (Reprinted 1961). London: Oxford University
        Press.
Nelson, Cynthia
1974   Public and Private Politics: Women in the Middle Eastern World.
        American Ethnologist I, 3: 551-63.

Nkrumah, Kwame
  1957   *The Autobiography of Kwame Nkrumah.* Edinburgh: Thomas Nelson
         Inc. Published in the U.S. as *Ghana: The Autobiography of Kwame
         Nkrumah.* New York: Thomas Nelson, Inc.

Ollennu, Hon. Mr. Justice N.A.
  1962   *Principles of Customary Land Law in Ghana.* London: Sweet &
         Maxwell Ltd.

Omari, T. Peter
  1960   Changing Attitudes of Students in West African Society Toward
         Marriage and Family Relationships. *British Journal of Sociology* XI,
         3: 197-210.

Onwuejeogwu, Michael
  1969   The Cult of the *Bori* Spirits Among the Hausa. In *Man in Africa.*
         M. Douglas and P. Kaberry, eds. London: Tavistock Publications Ltd.
         pp. 279-305.

Oppong, Christine
  1974   *Marriage Among a Matrilineal Elite.* London: Cambridge University
         Press.

Oppong, Christine, Christine Okali and Beverley Houghton
  1975   Woman Power: Retrograde Steps in Ghana. *The African Studies
         Review.* Special issue: Women in Africa. Vol. XVIII, 3: 71-84.

Ortner, Sherry B.
  1974   Is Male to Female as Nature is to Culture? In *Woman, Culture and
         Society.* M.Z. Rosaldo and L. Lamphere, eds. Stanford: Stanford
         University Press. pp. 67-87.

Orwell, George
  1936   *Keep the Aspidistra Flying.* London: Martin Secker and Warburg Ltd.
         (1956 edition. New York: Harcourt and Brace.)

Paulme, Denise.
  1963   Introduction. *Women of Tropical Africa.* Denise Paulme, ed. (Trans-
         lated by H.M. Wright). London: Routledge and Kegan Paul. pp. 1-16.

Pellow, Deborah
  1974   Women of Accra: A Study in Options. Ph.D. thesis. Northwestern
         University.

Peterson, M. Jeanne
  1972   The Victorian Governess: Status Incongruence in Family and Society.
         In *Suffer and Be Still: Women in the Victorian Age.* M. Vicinus, ed.
         Bloomington: Indian University Press. pp.3—19.

Perry, Clarence
1939   *Housing for the Machine Age*. New York: Russell Sage Foundation.

Plotnikov, Leonard
1967   *Strangers to the City*. Pittsburgh: University of Pittsburgh Press.

Pool, Janet E.
1972   A Cross-Comparative Study of Aspects of Conjugal Behavior Among Women of Three West African Countries. *Canadian Journal of African Studies* VI, ii: 233-59.

Porter, Arthur
1963   *Creoledom*. London: Oxford University Press.

Radcliffe-Brown, A.R.
1924   The Mother's Brother in South Africa. *South African Journal of Science* XXI: 542-55.
1967   Introduction. In *African Systems of Kinship and Marriage*. A.R. Radcliffe-Brown and D. Forde, eds. pp.1-85.

Radcliffe-Brown, A.R., and Forde, Daryll, eds.
1967   *African Systems of Kinship and Marriage*. London: Oxford University Press. (Original edition 1950).

Rattray, R.S.
1927   *Religion and Art in Ashanti*. Oxford: Clarendon Press.
1929   *Ashanti Law and Constitution*. London: Oxford University Press. (Reprinted 1956).

Riegelhaupt, Joyce F.
1967   Saloio Women: An Analysis of Informal and Formal Political and Economic Roles of Portuguese Peasant Women. *Anthropological Quarterly* 40, 3 (July): 109-26.

Roberts, Helene E.
1977   The Exquisite Slave: the Role of Clothes in the Making of the Victorian Woman. *Signs* II, 3: 554-69.

Rollin, Betty
1971   Motherhood: Who Needs It? In *Family in Transition*. A.S. and J.H. Skolnick, eds. Boston: Little, Brown & Co. pp. 346-56.

Rosaldo, Michelle Z.
1974   A Theoretical Overview. In *Woman, Culture and Society*. M.Z. Rosaldo and L. Lamphere, eds. pp.17-42.

Rosaldo, Michelle Z., and Lamphere, Louise, eds.
1974   Introduction. *Woman, Culture and Society*. M.Z. Rosaldo and L.

Lamphere, eds. Stanford: Stanford University Press.

Sai, Florence
1971 The Market Woman in the Economy of Ghana. M.S. thesis. Cornell University.

Sampson, Ronald V.
1965 *The Psychology of Power.* New York: Pantheon Books, Inc.

Sanday, Peggy R.
1974 Female Status in the Public Domain. In *Woman Culture and Society.* M.Z. Rosaldo and L. Lamphere, eds. pp.189-206.

Sartre, Jean Paul
1943 *L'être et le néant: essai d'ontologie phénomenologique.* Paris. (Translated by Hazel E. Barnes as *Being and Nothingness.* 1956. New York: Philosophical Library.)

Schlegel, Alice
1972 *Male Dominance and Female Autonomy.* New Haven: HRAF Press.

Sewall, S.A.
1869 *Woman and the Times We Live In.* (2nd edition). Manchester, England.

Simmel, Georg
1955 *Conflict and the Web of Group Affiliations.* (Translated Kurt H. Wolff and Reinhard Bendix). Glencoe, Illinois: The Free Press.

Smock, Audrey Chapman
1977 Ghana: From Autonomy to Subordination. In *Women: Roles and Status in Eight Countries.* J.Z. Giele and A.C. Smock, eds. New York: John Wiley & Sons, Inc. pp.175-216.

Southall, Aidan W., ed.
1961 Introductory Summary. In *Social Change in Modern Africa.* London, New York: Oxford University Press. pp. 1-66.

Stephens, William N.
1961 A Cross-Cultural Study of Menstrual Taboos. Genetic Psychology Monographs 64: 385-416. (Reprinted in *Cross Cultural Approaches.* Clellan S. Ford, ed. New Haven: HRAF Press. pp. 67-94.)

Stevens, Evelyn P.
1973 The Prospects for a Women's Liberation Movement in Latin America. *Journal of Marriage and the Family.* 35, 2 (May): 313-21.

Tanner, Nancy
   1974   Matrofocality in Indonesia and Africa and Among Black Americans.
           In *Woman, Culture and Society.* M.Z. Rosaldo and L. Lamphere, eds.
           pp.129-56.

Taylor, Richard
   1974   *Metaphysics.* (2nd edition). Englewood Cliffs. New Jersey: Prentice-
           Hall, Inc.

Tetteh, P.A.
   1967   Marriage, Family and Household. In *A Study of Contemporary
           Ghana. Volume II: Some Aspects of Social Structure.* Evanston:
           Northwestern University Press. pp.201-16.

Tillion, Germaine
   1966   *Le harem et les cousins.* Paris: Editions du Seuil.

Trutenau, H.M.N.
   1968   Some Moral Paradoxes Concerning Alliances Between Europeans and
           Ghanaian Women. *Ghana Journal of Sociology* IV, 2: 119-21.

Tuden, Arthur, and Leonard Plotnikov, eds.
   1970   Introduction. *Social Stratification in Africa.* New York: The Free
           Press. pp. 1-29.

Tufuo, J.W. and C.E. Donkor
   1969   *Ashantis of Ghana: People with a Soul.* Accra: Educational
           Publications.

Vallenga, D.D.
   1971   *Attempts to Change the Marriage Laws in Ghana and the Ivory Coast:
           Ghana and the Ivory Coast: Perspectives on Modernisation.* Chicago:
           University of Chicago Press. pp.125-50.

Van Allen, Judith
   1972   Sitting on a Man: Colonialism and the Lost Political Institutions of
           Igbo Women. *Canadian Journal of African Studies.* VI, ii: 165-81.

Veblen, Thorstein
   1899   *The Theory of the Leisure Class.* (New edition, 1972. New York:
           Houghton Mifflin Co.).

Walker, Alexander
   1840   *Woman Physiologically Considered as to Mind, Morals, Marriage,
           Matrimonial Slavery, Infidelity and Divorce.* (2nd edition). London.

Ward, W.E.F.
   1958   *A History of Ghana.* (2nd revised edition). London: George Allen
           & Unwin Ltd.

Weber, Max
  1946   *From Max Weber: Essays in Sociology.* (Translated H.H. Gerth and C.W. Mills). New York: Oxford University Press,

Wittner, Judith
  n.d.   Changing Sex-Roles in America. Unpublished manuscript.

Wizeman, Kofi
  1971   The NC 175 Student Glamour Girl. *The Ghanaian Times.* (August 12).

Wollstonecraft, Mary
  1972   *Posthumous Work of the Author of A Vindication of the Rights of Women, with Strictures in Political and Moral Subjects.* Charles Hagelman Jr., ed. Clifton, New Jersey: Augustus M. Kelley, Publishers.

"Women at Work"
  1963   *West Africa.* February 2: 115.

"Yaa Yaa's World"
  1971   *The Mirror.* (February 13).

Young, Frank, and Albert A. Bacdayan
  1965   Menstrual Taboos and Social Rigidity. *Ethnology* 4: 225-40. (Reprinted in *Cross-Cultural Approaches.* Clellan S. Ford, ed. New Haven: HRAF Press. pp. 95-110.)

Archival Sources

Documents from SNA (Secretary of Native Affairs). Also referred to as ADM 11. Accra: National Archives of Ghana.

Index